MALBOROUGH
CHURCH
LIBRARY

Called to Serve

A History of the Dominican Sisters
in Trinidad & Tobago

1868-1988

Congregation of
Saint Catherine of Siena O.P.
Etrépagny, France.

With best wishes

Sr. Marie Thérèse Retout OP.

March 12, 1988

Other books
by Marie Thérèse Rétout O.P.

Historical Brochures:

Centenary of St. Dominic's Children's Home (1871-1971)
out of print

150th Anniversary of the Cathedral of the Immaculate Conception, Port of Spain (1832-1982) out of print

Books

Parish Beat (1976). Inprint Caribbean Limited, Trinidad and Tobago — out of print

A Light Rising from the West (1984). Inprint Caribbean Limited
Second Edition (1985)

Called to Serve

A History of the Dominican Sisters
in Trinidad & Tobago
1868 – 1988

Congregation of
Saint Catherine of Siena O.P.
Etrépagny, France.

by

Marie Thérèse Rétout O.P.

Produced and designed by Paria Publishing Company Limited.
66 Woodford Street, Newtown, Port-of-Spain, Trinidad, W.I.

ISBN 976-8054-12-3

Cover Picture: "Sunset over the Caribbean Sea, Trinidad, West Indies" courtesy Noel Norton

Printed in the Republic of Trinidad & Tobago by:
Superservice Printing Company Limited
187b Tragarete Road, Port-of-Spain, Trinidad.

This book is dedicated to the humble Virgin Mary of Nazareth who, in consenting to be the Mother of the Son of God, has been given the unique honour of being the Queen of Heaven where she reigns as Queen and Mother of us all.

Contents

CONTENTS

Plates

Foreword

The indefatigable pen of Sister Marie-Thérèse Rétout O.P. is at work once again! This time she has given us "CALLED TO SERVE" — A History of the Dominican Sisters in Trinidad and Tobago.

No one except an author (or authoress) knows the tremendous and painstaking labour that goes into the compilation of historical data. Sister Marie-Thérèse is no stranger to hard and unremitting work.

The history of the Dominican Sisters in Trinidad and Tobago is full of drama. It is a real life story of truly heroic women who, whatever their human limitations might have been, came to give their lives in the service of the people of Trinidad in the first place and whose successors continue to serve the independent country of Trinidad and Tobago.

Who will not admire the extraordinary patience and long-suffering of those early French Sisters who looked after the lepers at a time when the modern treatments now available were not even thought of?

I am reminded of the good nun in a certain hospital who was observed by a rich visitor calmly cleaning the putrefying matter from a horribly stricken patient. "Gee!" said the visitor, "I wouldn't do that for a million dollars!" The nun looked up and smiled sweetly: "Sir, neither would I!"

The Dominican Sisters did what they did and accomplished what they accomplished not for a million dollars but for the love of Jesus Christ.

As Archbishop, I am more than happy that the spirit of service is still being displayed in so many different ways by the Dominican Sisters.

While we salute the stalwarts of the past, we pay, ungrudgingly, homage to the workers of the present. They have inherited a rich tradition of untold sacrifice, devotion, dedication and love. May they continue to walk in that magnificent tradition while making creative adjustments to suit the needs of the time.

I heartily congratulate Sister Marie-Thérèse on her production which, I am sure, will be read with great interest and edification by all.

+ ANTHONY PANTIN
ARCHBISHOP OF PORT OF SPAIN

November 16th 1987

Preface

On November 21, 1936, Fr. Leo Mc Ardle, O.P. delivered
a lecture to the members of the Historical Society of Trinidad
and Tobago on the topic "The Dominicans in the West Indies".
Towards the end of his address he made reference to the
Dominican Sisters who came from France to Trinidad in
March 1868 to take charge of the Leper Asylum in Cocorite.

About the work these valiant women had done in Trinidad, the Irish Dominican remarked:

"The grand apostolate of the Dominican Sisters in
Trinidad is so unobstrusive that it is scarcely noticed or
recognised. Yet the mission of those who so wonderfully take
care of our thousands of orphaned and neglected children, and
whose heroic charity brings consolation and hope to the
otherwise dismal lives of the unhappy victims of leprosy in
Chacachacare, is a work that ought to make us pause and
ponder.

"Perhaps, some day, a student of this Higher Philanthropy
will confer the benefit on Trinidad and Tobago of revealing
the complete nature and magnificence of this all important
national work in our midst."

In 1987, 50 years later, Fr. Mc Ardle's wish is fulfilled by this publication entitled "CALLED TO SERVE". The work retraces 120 years of history of the Dominican Sisters in Trinidad and Tobago.

It has been an arduous task of research to uncover the facts and translate numerous documents from French into English. Not only were the utter dedication of the Sisters and their works hidden from the public but they were also concealed in the foreign language in which their history is recorded in diaries, chronicles and circular letters.

The Dominican Sisters who came from France in 1868 brought with them their strong faith in God, their indomitable courage and endurance, as well as the richness of their culture. This is the heritage they have passed on to the Trinidadian women whom God has called to be trained in the Dominican way of life.

From 1946 onwards, after the opening of the Novitiate House for the formation of candidates into the religious life, the Dominican Sisters of Trinidad and Tobago, building on the legacy passed on to them, have gradually blended their own culture and their natural endowments with what has been handed down to them by their predecessors. Some of their activities have changed but the spirit is the same — a spirit of love and dedication to God and to others, a spirit of loyal service to the Church.

My aim has been to situate the various works of the Sisters in the historical context of the times, an approach which should make the reading of this book all the more interesting.

In these pages one can hear the voices of old telling us today their own stories — stories of gladness and stories of sorrows but stories which all tell the noble and generous dedication of those whom God "CALLED TO SERVE".

Marie Thérèse Rétout, O.P.
Chaplaincy of the University of the West Indies
St. Augustine
August 31, 1987
on the 25th anniversary of the
Independence of Trinidad and Tobago

Acknowledgements

It was sometime in the early 1980's that Sr. Moyra Ann Roach O.P. who was then Regional Prioress, asked me to write about our history — the Dominican Sisters in Trinidad and Tobago. At that time I was writing about the St. Augustine Campus of the University of the West Indies and I simply told her, "Please, hold on; not now. We shall see later."

However, my conscience was not fully at rest because I was well aware of the lack of written information on the origin and growth of our Congregation on Trinidad soil. So far, what we have relied upon has been oral tradition but even this is destined to disappear with the passing of our elderly Sisters.

The moment came when I had to surrender and so I accepted the challenge to write our history for the sake of present and future generations, as well as to pay homage to those of our Sisters who have, to use a comparison, passed on the torch to us. Only God can give them the reward they deserve for the good they have done for the people of this country of ours.

The first person I want to mention in my acknowledgements is Sr. Moyra Ann Roach for the confidence she has placed in me and for her steadfast support throughout my research and writing.

Next comes Sr. Bernadette de la Bastide, the present Regional Prioress, for helping me to cross the formidable barrier of the launching of this book. Her understanding and encouragement have been a constant source of inspiration to me.

I also appreciated the support of Sr. Helen Gomes, Counsellor of the Congregation, who read the larger part of the manuscript.

I am most grateful to Sr. Marie Yolande Skrzydlewska, the only survivor in Trinidad of the Sisters who lovingly cared for patients affected by Hansen's disease, and who passed on to me valuable information.

Sr. Bernadette Robert in Paris, who facilitated my access to the archives of our Congregation in the Mother-house at Etrépagny for the purpose of research.

His Grace The Archbishop of Port-of-Spain, the Most Reverend Anthony Pantin C.S.Sp. for writing the foreword of the book and Miss Maureen de Verteuil for making available to me the files concerning our Congregation in the Archives of the Archdiocese.

Miss Yvette Guelon who provided me with information from the Municipal Library of Chalon-sur-Saône, France, on the early Dominican Sisters.

My dear relatives in Paris, Claude and Suzanne Gillmann who refreshed my memory about French history.

My dear friend Olga J. Mavrogordato who affectionately supported and encouraged me throughout the arduous work of writing this book and who greatly assisted me with proof-reading at the time of publication. Our collaboration over the past 12 years and mutual support is most precious to me.

The Editor of the Catholic News, Fr. Peter Nicholson C.S.Sp. for agreeing to publish part of this work in the columns of the Catholic News, which has suscitated keen interest among its readers, and for granting permission to use some of the photographs of the Catholic News Library.

The photographer of the Catholic News, Tony Forte, for the excellent photographs he has contributed towards the illustration of this book.

Ms. Gloria Baptiste for her kindness and flair in unearthing relevant documents in the West Indian Collection of the Library of the St. Augustine Campus, University of the West Indies.

Mrs. Vere Achong, Director of the Medical Library of the General Hospital, Port of Spain, for permitting and assisting my research into Hansen's disease.

Ms. Lucia Philip for also assisting my research in the Library of the Parliament of Trinidad and Tobago.

Dr. Walter F. Van Crosson, Messrs. Sultan Khan and Arthur Ramsammy for their interviews about life at Chacachacare.

Defence Chief of Staff Commodore Mervyn Williams, Lieutenant Commander, St. Clair Grant and Coast Guards for their determination in locating, restoring and maintaining the Chacachacare cemetery at Marine Bay where ten of our Sisters are buried.

Author Gaylord T.M. Kelshall for his valuable information and documents concerning the War Years and the effects they had on Trinidad and Chacachacare.

Publisher Gerry Besson, typesetter Angela Richards and graphic designer Sue-Ann Gomes for their diligence, interest and co-operation in the making of this book.

Last but not least, the group of Past Pupils of Holy Name Convent School, led by Mrs. Paula Craig (née Lanser) who all worked very hard to raise funds needed for the publication of this book.

To each one I say a hearty 'THANK YOU' and may God bless you all.

Sr. Marie Thérèse Rétout O.P.
St. Augustine
September 1987

Marie Thérèse Rétout O.P.

Note about the author

Some may wonder why young men and women leave their home, family and country to go to other lands and spend their lives at the service of God and people. From what the author revealed about herself — and she is one of them — it shows clearly that it is all God's work.

A call to follow Christ can sometimes come very early in life. In the case of the author, she dates this call from the age of seven on her First Communion day. Life for her was not to be a bed of roses as two years later her mother, at the age of 32, died shortly after losing a baby son, her third child. For the young girl, the following years were spent in a boarding school in Burgundy, the country of her birth (Chalon-sur-Saône is her birthplace) with no home as such until the second marriage of her father whose family was gradually increased by three children.

The next trial was the Second World War and the four years of ruthless Occupation of France by the Germans which brought suffering and much fear. It was also a time of deep crisis of Faith for the author. In the midst of much spiritual darkness and doubt she heard again the early call. It was hard for her to believe in God and for two years the author struggled against the divine attraction. Finally, she had to surrender. God then made her meet the Dominican Sisters of Bonnay and she felt drawn to their way of life.

On February 2, 1948 — a gloomy winter day — she entered the Dominican Novitiate at Etrépagny in Normandy. Six months later, on July 29, she was given the Dominican habit and then started her period of Novitiate. During that year, letters sent by the Sisters in the Trinidad convents used to stir in her a desire to offer herself to go there to help. She knew by her own experience the heartbreaks of an orphan and she wanted to love those children in this far away land. But on second thought the sacrifice of leaving her country was too great and she tried to forget this desire. However, just before making her first religious profession the urge to offer herself for Trinidad and Tobago returned irresistibly. She, therefore, wrote her application to the Prioress General, '. . . to please the Lord' as she put it.

On August 5, 1949 she was sent to the Sisters' convent in Paris to pursue her studies and formation as a Junior Professed Sister. On the Saturday of the last week in September, at around 1.30 p.m., the author remembers that she was busy peeling potatoes in the cloister when a Sister came to her and said, "Mother General wants to see you at once." Thinking that the Prioress General was going to announce to her may be the death of her father or of her brother Michel, she went to her with great apprehension. The fact was that the Mother Superior wanted to let her know that she had accepted her for Trinidad but first of all she wanted her to go to England so as to familiarise herself with the English language.

The author arrived in Trinidad on March 8, 1952 and in the 35 years she spent in Trinidad she has given nearly 20 years to educating children at St. Dominic's Home and 13 years to journalism as a full-time reporter and feature-writer for the Catholic News.

At one time or another, she assumed the responsibilities of Novice Mistress, Prioress and Counsellor. In 1973, the author applied and was granted the citizenship of Trinidad and

Tobago, a nation she has adopted as her own.

In 1974, on a journalistic assignment which lasted two years, she visited all the 61 parishes of the Catholic Church in Trinidad and Tobago. This long 'BEAT' now lives on in her book 'PARISH BEAT' (1977) — a milestone in the history of the Catholic Church in this country. Although writing in a foreign language is much more difficult than in one's own mother tongue, she has tried to use this calling to the fullest and continues to do so at the Catholic News and in producing, in 1984, another book, about the St. Augustine Campus of the University of the West Indies entitled, 'A LIGHT RISING FROM THE WEST'. And now, 'CALLED TO SERVE' is here, her third book in ten years.

Gerard A. Besson
January, 1988

History is often described as a teacher of justice and truth.
It is moreover a school of wisdom.

Yves Congar O.P.

Chapter
1.

The French
Revival of the 19th Century

*Silent witnesses of the past when France was dotted
with Monasteries and Convents, the strongholds of
Christianity and Centres of Spiritual Life.*

*The cloister of the St. Vincent Cathedral (14th-16th cent.)
in Chalon-sur-Saône, France.*

Writing the history of the Dominican Sisters in Trinidad and Tobago cannot be done without reference to the French Dominican Sisters of St. Catherine of Siena. This Congregation, founded in France in 1854, has passed on the religious Dominican way of life to young women in these the most southerly islands of the Caribbean archipelago, Trinidad and Tobago.

The understanding of the foundation and growth of this religious history is partly obtained in the establishment of its development. The epoch was the 19th century, a century which marked France a spirit of renewal and discovery.

The great French Revolution of 1789, which aimed at bringing about a new social order for the benefit of the working class, had a tremendous effect not only on France but on the whole of Europe. The political turmoil brought in its wake an industrial revolution through the development of the applied sciences. Biology was put to the service of medicine thanks to Claude Bernard and, even more, Louis Pasteur. Research in physics led to the use of electricity. A new technique was invented to transform cast-iron into steel.

The discovery of steam power led to new modes of transportation: the steam locomotive and steam ships both of which allowed for communication with the ouside world.* Karl Benz (1844-1920) invented the motor-car. Steam also facilitated the development of industry, increased production and opened the possibility of exports. This intense commercial activity characterised the 19th century.

Another form of communication expanded when the electric telegraph was placed at the service of the public in 1851 and the following year the first dirigible airship was built and flown by Gifford. Agriculture was considerably improved by the manufacture of fertilisers.

In politics, Napoleon III, no less ambitious than Napoleon I (Bonaparte), seized power in 1848 and re-established the Napoleonic Empire. From 1852 to 1860 the new Emperor ruled France with absolute power which he relaxed 10 years later during the period known as the Liberal Empire. In order

*In the 19th century the state subsidised three large shipping lines — Le Havre/New York; St. Nazaire/Guianas; Bordeaux/Brazil/Argentina.

to obtain the support and co-operation of the working class, Napoleon III undertook major public works such as the reconstruction of Paris. He also encouraged the development of agriculture, industry and commerce and founded a number of benevolent institutions.

The Emperor then sought to win the favour of the Catholic Church which had been terribly impoverished by the Revolution and whose freedom of worship had been seriously restrained. All monasteries and religious houses had been closed down and nationalised; religious vows were abolished and religious men and women had to return to civilian life. The law of the new civil organisation of the secular clergy was passed by the National Assembly on July 12, 1790. In other words, nothing was left of the original structure of the Church in France.

Napoleon III, in order to ensure the total submission of French Catholics to his imperial power, applied in full the Concordat, signed on July 16, 1801 by Napoleon I and representatives of the Church. This Concordat granted religious freedom to French citizens as well as the right to re-open monasteries and convents. Former members of religious orders and congregations availed themselves of the authorisation and, little by little, resumed their religious life in the new foundations they established. In Burgundy, Henri Lacordaire (1802-1861) restored the Dominican Order in France in 1839. He became one of the most illustrious orators of the 19th century.

In March 1850, the Legislative Assembly, after long and stormy debates, succeeded in passing the Loi Falloux which recognised two types of schools, the "public schools" controlled by the State and the "free schools" run by an individual or a religious community free from state supervision. This law, even in these present times of secularisation, continues to be enforced today and is the cause of many conflicts between State and Church.

The unbounded ambition of Napoleon III, who wanted to impose his hegemony over Europe, led him and the country to military disasters in 1870. He died in 1873 thus bringing an end to the Napoleonic era.

While in Eastern Europe a political philosopher, Karl Marx, (1818-1868) was spreading his ideas and theories designed for the integral reorganisation of society, in France, committed men were at work propagating the social teaching of the Catholic Church. Among those were Louis Veuillot, an outstanding journalist and author, Charles Montalembert, leader of French Catholics and defender of religious freedom, and Frederick Ozanam, a scholar and the champion of the cause of the poor.

The French revival was such that, during the 19th century, 400 congregations for women were founded in France. Religious orders flourished and, with the development of maritime shipping lines, missionaries went to other continents in keeping with the injunction of Christ: "Go and teach all nations." The Foreign Missions of Paris alone sent over 2000 missionaries to Asia, this immense territory entrusted to them by the Holy See and this during a period of only 50 years. The impact was such that it has deeply marked Catholicism. The Catholic Church, through its numerous works of mercy, impressed the civil power and on more than one occasion solicited assistance to undertake similar work in French colonies. Such was the case of Anne Marie Javouhey, (1779-1851), the founder of the Sisters of St. Joseph of Cluny. In 1867 parts of Africa were being explored by Stanley and Livingstone. In 1868 Msgr. Charles Lavigerie and a band of volunteers walked in the footsteps of the explorers bringing the Gospel message to African peoples.

This 19th century revival was also manifested in France through a holy priest, in the small village of Ars, St. Jean Marie Vianney (1786-1859), who exercised an extraordinary spiritual attraction leading many converts to God. In 1854, Pope Pius IX proclaimed that the Blessed Virgin Mary was born free from original sin and made this belief an article of faith for the members of the Catholic Church throughout the world.

In 1858, the Blessed Virgin Mary appeared to a young girl, Bernadette, at Lourdes in the south of France and confirmed Pius IX's declaration when she said to her: "I am the Immaculate Conception." Since then Lourdes, the Marian shrine par excellence, has attracted millions of people.

This spiritual revival has also had its influence on French society as a whole. More and more humanitarian and philanthrophic movements, such as the one for the Abolition of Slavery, sprang up and expanded. In England as well, an Act of Parliament in 1833 gave freedom to slaves in British colonies, chiefly in the West Indies, Guiana and Mauritius.

After this brief survey of the situation in France in the 19th century, we can now look at the foundress of the Dominican Sisters of St. Catherine of Siena, Marie Thérèse Joséphine Gand (1819-1907).

Chapter
2.

Birth and Vocation
of a Courageous Woman

*Church of Saint Pierre in Chalon-sur-Saône,
the Parish of the Dominican Sisters in which
their Convent was situated.*

In the East of France at Boulay in Lorraine, a general forester, August Gand, married to Victorine née de Saint Hillier, was already the father of three sons, and one daughter when baby Marie Thérèse Joséphine was born on July 16, 1819. Gand was not only a staunch Catholic but also an ardent supporter of the French monarchy.

After three transfers on his job in 1821, 1825 and 1831 he was promoted to the rank of inspector of forests and went to live in Thionville (Lorraine) with his family. It was there that Marie Thérèse made her first holy communion on April 18, 1831. The Gands were deeply united in their faith and love of God and this was their strength in facing the dangerous days of their time.

The aftermath of the 1789 Revolution was still felt in many ways, particularly in movements aimed at repressing royalists and Catholics. This was exactly the position of August Gand. Consequently, he was denounced for his royalist sympathies and his belief in God. In 1832 he and his family were banished from Thionville to Colmar in Alsace and then to Chalon-sur-Saône where they finally settled.

August Gand had a sister, Amelie, who was a Benedictine nun in a monastery at La Rochette near Lyon. One day he took his young daughter Marie Thérèse to visit her aunt. The nuns had a boarding school. August and Amélie arranged for Marie Thérèse, aged 13, to pursue her education with the nuns. But no matter how lovingly the aunt looked after her niece, the latter grieved so much over the separation from her family that her parents recalled her to Chalon.

However, in 1835 Marie Thérèse paid a visit to her aunt to tell her a secret — she too wanted to become a nun. Surely aunt Amélie must have thought that one day her dear niece would become a Benedictine nun like herself; but God had other plans.

Before the 1789 Revolution, Chalon-sur-Saône, 50km north of Cluny — the cradle of monasticism in France — situated at a short distance from the famous vineyards of Beaujolais, was a stronghold of Christianity. There had been a bishop attached to the ancient cathedral of St. Vincent and no fewer that 17 religious orders and Congregations had houses in Chalon, a town of about seven to eight thousand inhabitants.

It was in 1621 that the Dominican nuns of Dijon had established a foundation in Chalon. The Revolution closed down all the monasteries and convents on August 18, 1792 and all religious had to go either into exile, return to their families, or live in hiding because most of them refused to take the oath of "Freedom and Equality" demanded of them by the revolutionaries.

Four Dominican nuns of Chalon chose to live in hiding. One of them was denounced and imprisoned on May 3, 1794. Their hardships were somewhat forgotten when Pope Pius VII stopped at Chalon on his way back to Rome from Paris where he had gone for the consecration of Emperor Napoleon I, and spent the Holy Week in Chalon (April 9 to 15, 1805). The Pope had been preceded by the Emperor himself who stayed two days in Chalon (April 6 and 7).

In 1810, a kind and wealthy Madame de Villeneuve bought a large house in the heart of the town for the nuns who had been dispossessed of their convents and who wanted to resume their religious life. At once 20 of them answered her invitation — four Dominicans, ten Carmelites, four Clarisses and two others. They organised themselves as best they could for a time until other accommodation could be found, though it was extremely difficult. Finally, the Dominicans remained alone in the house.

On the death of Madame de Villeneuve in 1820 and with the help of benefactors, the nuns bought the house. Their community was duly approved by an ordinance from King Charles X of France on April 25, 1827. They were by then materially secure but their other great need was to find a spiritual guide to help them to live their Dominican religious life.

To this effect, and at the request of the parish priest of St. Pierre, three nuns from a newly restored Dominican monastery in Langres came to Chalon to help the Dominican nuns. The group adopted the official title of "St. Dominic's Monastery". Unfortunately, the three nuns from Langres were not the most capable for the task and they caused much confusion. The nuns opened a school to ensure their livelihood and exercise an apostolate.

It was at that time that Marie Thérèse became acquainted

with the Dominican nuns and felt the call to join them. Great was her difficulty to obtain the consent of her father. As she later recalled:

"I was fully aware of the life of insecurity into which I was entering. The community as such was not properly founded, therefore, I was not surprised by my father's hesitation in granting me his authorisation to join this group of Dominican nuns. I even entered before the day that had been fixed by my parents. Though the situation was confused, I felt attracted to this life because, I reasoned with myself, if no one devotes herself to the task who then will begin?"

Marie Thérèse Gand entered the Chalon monastery on August 3, 1838 with the mysterious presentiment of being in the right place to do God's will. She was given a new name for her religious life, Sister Dominic of the Cross. In the community there were already two novices and two postulants.

The Prioress, Mother Stanislaus, who must have been a very impulsive person, subjected the nuns of her community to all her whims and fancies. She was impressed by the young postulant, Sr. Dominic who was then 19 years old. One day she imposed an impossible order on her, namely, to write the future Constitutions of their community and also to teach in the school. This came as a double shock to the young inexperienced postulant who had to develop her own method of teaching in order to fulfil the task imposed on her.

On March 19, 1839, Sr. Dominic received the Dominican habit from the hands of the bishop of the diocese and this brought to an end all her doubts about staying in the monastery. Her postulancy and novitiate were made in uncertainty and confusion. When it was time to take religious vows, Mother Stanislaus refused to listen to the bishop or to Mr. Gand who were in favour of having the young novices first take temporary vows, for a period of five years, renewable on a yearly basis.

Mr. Gand had to abide by the decision of the Prioress and Sr. Dominic, aged 21, took her perpetual vows on March 21, 1840. Four months later her family returned to Lorraine leaving Marie Thérèse in Chalon. Her mother died in 1850 and she was not to see her father until 1852. Many a time the heart of the young nun ached but she was convinced that she was in the place chosen for her by God.

Tension within the community became intolerable as Mother Stanislaus, who had come from the monastery of Langres, tried to impose on the community the strict monastic rule of the Second Order for the contemplative life.

However, the Dominican nuns in Chalon had determined to become members of the Dominican Third Order, a blending of contemplative and active life.

Mother Mugnier, the eldest of the original community, stood up for the nuns who opposed the dictates of Mother Stanislaus. At the request of the parish priest of St. Pierre, Abbe Compain, the bishop of the diocese had to intervene and ordered Mother Stanislaus to return to her monastery in Langres. She left on October 5, 1840.

The following years were crucial for the Community. The nuns were held in suspicion by the bishop, the parish priest and the population of Chalon. All sorts of rumours were circulated by the parents of the pupils at the nuns' school. To make matters worse, two terrible floods from the river Saone forced them to seek refuge in 1840 and again in 1844. The poor nuns suffered great poverty and even destitution during those years.

It was when the crisis was at its worst that Divine Providence intervened. The owner of a spacious house, situated on the heights of Chalon, offered it to them in exchange for their monastery built in the heart of town. The proposal was accepted and Sr. Dominic of the Cross played an important part in the reorganisation of the monastery and the school. The foundation must have been solidly implanted because the Dominican nuns remained in Chalon in this house until 1980.*

During the years of confusion, Mother Stanislaus had imposed various spiritual directors on her Community. One wanted the nuns to follow the rule of St. Ignatius and another that of St. Francis de Sales. Patiently they endured many trials putting their trust in God that one day, a son of St. Dominic would come to teach them the Dominican way of life.

* *After a span of six years, the Dominican Sisters are back in Chalon-sur-Saône at the same address, No. 7 Avenue de Paris.*

Their endurance was rewarded when the Dominican Father Alexander, Vincent Jandel O.P. was sent to Chalon by Fr. Henri Lacordaire to preach a Lenten mission in St. Pierre's parish. He visited the nuns in their convent and from then the Dominican Fathers took charge of their Sisters. The training the latter received from the former was so thorough that newly restored Dominican communities called on the one of Chalon to help them. Such was the case with the Dominican nuns of Nay (1850), Carcassonne and Nancy (1851).

On February 4, 1850, Sr. Dominic of the Cross was appointed Novice Mistress in addition to her duties as Principal of the school. In June of the same year, the Prioress, Mother St. Augustin, fell ill and the responsibility for the Community, the novitiate and the school were entrusted to Sr. Dominic.

In 1851, political events shook France once more when Louis Napoleon seized power. Loyalties were very much divided and the community went through difficult times.

In 1852, the bishop of the diocese, Msgr. de Marguerye, asked Sr. Dominic of the Cross, then Prioress of the community, to accept for a few weeks, the three Bonnardel sisters, who had come from Bonnay, a small Burgundian village close to Cluny. A new turn of events was to bring about a complete change in the life of Sr. Dominic.

Chapter
3.

The Foundress

Sister Dominic of the Cross Gand as a young professed.

Nine kilometres from Cluny is the little Burgundian village of Bonnay — a corruption of the word meaning "good water". In the 1850's there were approximately 600 inhabitants. Bonnay had its castle in Chassignoles which was bought by Pierre Bonnardel after the 1789 Revolution.

At his death in 1840 his widow was left with their seven children — four sons and three daughters. The eldest son, Francois, qualified as a physician; the two after him became priests and the youngest a sculptor. Before his death, Mr. Bonnardel told his three daughters: "Do not marry, stay together and devote yourselves to helping the poor."

One night Louise Bonnardel, the eldest of the three sisters, had a dream. In it she saw nuns dressed in white showing her their religious habit. Perplexed about what this dream could mean, she consulted her parish priest and then a saintly priest in the village of Ars, Curé (parish priest) Jean Marie Vianney.

To whatever she told the latter he replied: "Do not leave Bonnay; join a Third Order but before doing this consult your bishop and do whatever he tells you." Then, as though the holy priest was seeing something in a vision, he exclaimed: "Oh! How beautiful! O my God, what beautiful work! Much glory will then be given you, O my God!" The prophetic words were of great comfort to Louise and her sisters.

The three Bonnardel sisters completed their education and one of them obtained her teaching diploma in 1851. They undertook the teaching of catechism to little children and visiting the sick in the village of Bonnay.

Considering their good works, their mother foresaw the need of a house and land to open a school. She, therefore, bought a vineyard in Bonnay. However, the three sisters wanted to be more than teachers, they wanted to become nuns. In view of this, they sought the advice and guidance of the bishop of the diocese, Monsignor de Marguerye. Their mother and brothers being willing to assist them financially, the foundation stone of the future convent-school was laid on June 8, 1851 in the newly acquired vineyard.

In the meantime Msgr. de Marguerye contacted the Dominican Sisters in the Chalon monastery and asked them to receive the three Bonnardel sisters into their community for a period of three months in order to initiate them into the religious life.

The Bonnardels went to the monastery in Chalon towards the end of 1851. After their three months of initiation, they returned to Bonnay and supervised the construction work on the school which was opened in November 1852. The three sisters kept in touch with the Novice Mistress of the Chalon monastery, Sr. Dominic of the Cross Gand.

On February 10, 1853 Msgr. de Marguerye accepted the three Bonnardel sisters into the Dominican Third Order. He allowed them to wear a religious habit and granted them permission to accept postulants. A year later, the Bonnay foundation comprised Louise, Eugénie and Marie Agnés Bonnardel and five postulants and the school had an enrolment of 50 pupils. All were filled with zeal and eagerness but there was no rule to follow.

The bishop, who was keenly interested in the foundation, asked that under obedience, Mother Dominic of the Cross be sent to Bonnay to help the fledgling Community. On March 4, 1854 she arrived at Bonnay and stayed until the end of the month. The Novitiate was canonically begun on March 7. Mother Dominic assigned each one to various duties in the house and initiated them in personal and choral prayers. Although she had to return to her monastery in Chalon she felt that she was still needed in this foundation.

The bishop having imposed on Mother Dominic of the Cross a moral and spiritual obligation to look after this young community, she returned once more to Bonnay on April 20, 1854 to prepare the postulants to receive the religious habit from the hands of the bishop. The ceremony took place on May 5 and Msgr. de Marguerye granted the wish of the nuns to have St. Catherine of Siena as their special patroness. Sr. Marie Dominic Bonnardel was appointed Prioress of the community and Mother Dominic of the Cross returned to her monastery in Chalon.

The task of leader of the community proved to be too much for Louise Bonnardel who requested Mother Dominic to come back, but without success. She then appealed to her two brother-priests to help to secure her return. The matter was put before the bishop who then pleaded with the Chalon community to release Mother Dominic from their monastery and allow her to remain in Bonnay permanently.

This favour was granted on October 2, 1854. On that day, for the last time, Mother Dominic of the Cross travelled the 40 kilometres between Chalon and Bonnay and took her place in the Bonnay community. On October 10, Msgr. de Marguerye arrived unexpectedly and canonically instituted Mother Dominic of the Cross as Prioress of the community.

The first concern of the new Prioress was to establish a link with the Dominican Order. For this she wrote to Fr. Danzas, the Prior of Flavigny, near Dijon, and asked him to send a preacher to the Sisters. On January 6, 1855 feast of the Epiphany of the Lord, a young Dominican Friar, Fr. François Balme aged 27, arrived at Bonnay, sent by the Master General of the Order Rev. Fr. A.V. Jandel. For 45 years this priest was to devote himself to the spiritual welfare of the Dominican Sisters of Bonnay and to become the sure and wise guide of the Foundress, during the crucial first five years of the new Congregation.

On May 14, 1855 the three Bonnardel Sisters made their religious profession and Bishop de Marguerye instituted a council comprising Mother Dominic of the Cross, Prioress and Novice Mistress, and the three Bonnardel sisters as counsellors.

To pursue their experience of religious life within the Dominican Order, it was absolutely necessary for the Dominican Sisters of Bonnay to draft their own Constitutions. Once more the onus was put on Mother Dominic of the Cross. On this occasion she had Fr. Balme at her side to guide her. The task was a particularly difficult one because there were no written Constitutions for the Third Order (the first Order is that of the Friars Preachers and the second that of the enclosed nuns vowed to a contemplative life).

The Dominican Sisters of Bonnay were opening a new way which combined a life of prayer with the discharge of works of mercy. This was in keeping with the Dominican motto: "To contemplate and to give to others the fruits of one's contemplation."

Mother Dominic set to work writing the Constitutions of the Sisters of St. Catherine of Siena. On May 5, 1858, the first draft was approved by the Master General of the Order, Fr. Jandel, and on February 2, 1859 by the bishop of Autun, Msgr. de Marguerye. On July 28, 1859 the community was declared a Congregation under the name and patronage of St. Catherine of Siena. In 1861, after the necessary amendments, the Constitutions were presented to the Holy See for approval. The Sisters had by then a rule of life according to the Dominican tradition. This represented over 20 years of work by their Foundress.

The works of the Sisters of Bonnay were gradually transforming the village. In those early days of the foundation, material difficulties abounded. The Bonnardel family had invested much money in the land and construction of the first building and was no longer in a position to continue financial assistance. Whatever works the Sisters did brought little gain since they were helping the poor. As a result, they themselves suffered much privation and their health declined causing great anxiety to the Foundress. However, God is not outdone in generosity and benefactors came forward to assist with the material aspect of the foundation and vocations came as well.

On August 13, 1857 the foundation stone of a convent was laid, and in April 1858 construction of a new chapel commenced. It was completed in 1859 and Fr. Danzas O.P., the Prior of Flavigny, himself an artist, made very beautiful stained glass windows for the chapel which was built in the Romanesque type of architecture.

News of the Bonnay foundation spread far and wide and as a result appeals were made to the Sisters for help for other Dominican communities. In 1857, Mother Dominic of the Cross travelled to Paris and Sens to assist two such new communities. On her return to Bonnay, she received the visit of a Miss Van den Schrieck who brought her a letter of recommendation from Fr. Danzas. The purpose of her visit was to ask Mother Dominic to assist her in establishing a Dominican community in Louvain, Belgium. For this Miss Van den Schrieck was asking that three Sisters be sent to them. After reflection and consultation this was granted with a certain reluctance and for a period of three years only.

The original Dominican convent and chapel of Bonnay.

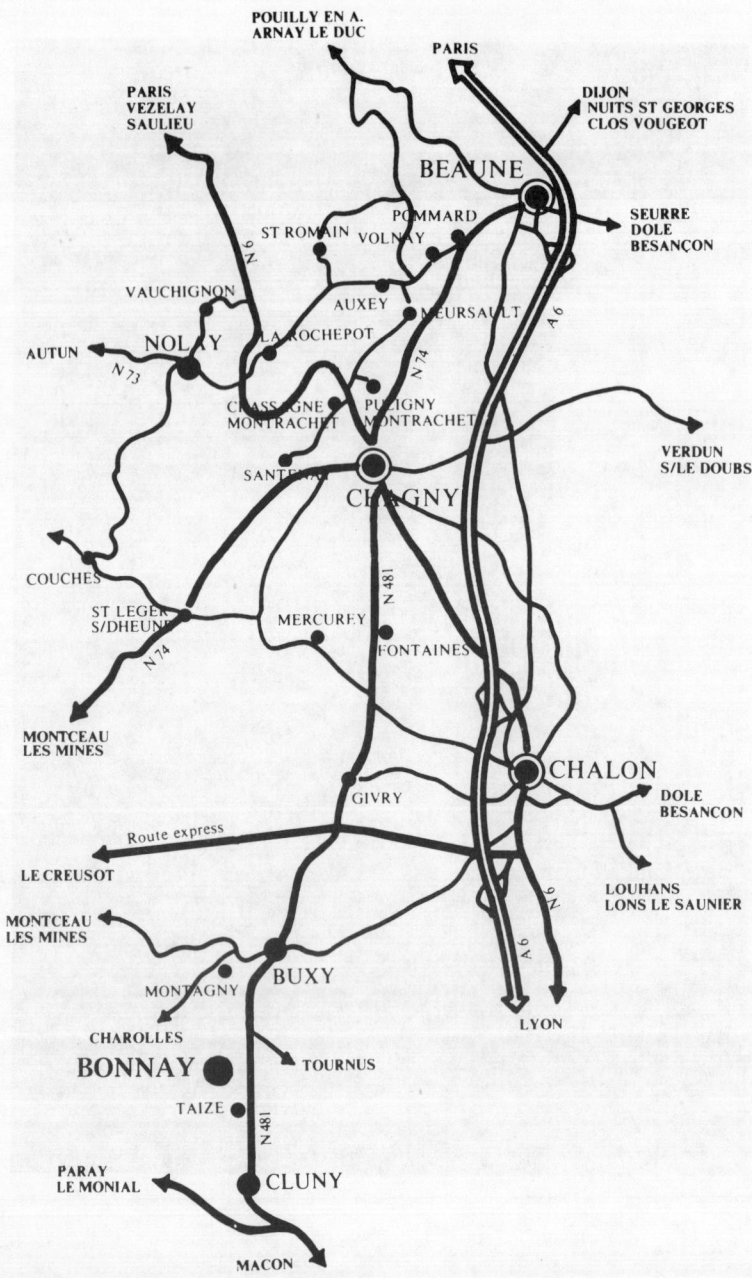

Map showing part of the province of Burgundy where
Chalon-sur-Saône and Bonnay are situated.

Chapter
4.

New Foundations

On July 9, 1858, in answer to a request by Miss Van den Schrieck from Belgium, at the foot of the stone cross erected on the roadside close to the convent in Bonnay, five Dominican Sisters said goodbye to the cradle of the Congregation and set out for the long journey to Louvain via Chalon and Paris. They were met in Belgium by Miss Van den Schrieck and four postulants with whom she wanted to establish a Community. By December there were seven more.

The house having become too small, Miss Van den Schriek bought a larger one in the town of Terbank. The transaction was made in the names of four French and two Belgian Sisters. Mother Dominic went to pay a visit to the new community and ratified the deal.

On her return to Bonnay, the Foundress of the Dominican Sisters of St. Catherine of Siena had the great joy of receiving a decree from the Holy See in Rome, dated July 28, 1859, which approved the Congregation of St. Catherine of Siena of the Regular Third Order of St. Dominic; it declared the convent of Bonnay the Mother-house of the Congregation and Mother Dominic of the Cross Gand, head of this Congregation.

A request for a second foundation was granted by the Prioress General and her council on August 28, 1859 to take charge of a home for destitute children situated in the village of St. Nicolas, diocese of Strasbourg in the East of France. The wealthy and generous Keller family had built a convent next to the children's home to receive the Sisters.

Once more the Foundress left Bonnay accompanied by six Sisters assigned to the new foundation. She organised the life of this new Community, entrusted everyone to the Lord and returned to Bonnay. This foundation was so successful that up to the present day the Dominican Sisters are still in their convent in St. Nicolas and looking after emotionally disturbed children.

In Belgium the foundation turned out to be a disaster. In making her religious profession, the foundress of the Belgian community, Miss Van den Schrieck, had formally declared that it should be part of the Congregation of the Dominican Sisters of Bonnay, but one year later she was dead. Sr. Marie Dominique Bonnardel was instituted Prioress of the community to succeed Miss Van den Schrieck.

Cardinal Sterkx, Archbishop of Malines, made it clear to Sr. Marie Dominique that he wanted an exclusively Belgian community and entirely under his jurisdiction. This was contrary to the Constitutions of the Congregation and, as a consequence, divisions appeared in the community; to these were added financial difficulties.

A real storm broke out when politicans meddled in the internal conflict. Soon it became the gossip of the town and insidious attacks were made on Mother Dominic and the French Sisters. The contention was between the Cardinal, who demanded full jurisdiction over the community, and the Foundress who maintained that the Holy See had given her full authority over the Congregation which she had founded.

No reconciliation appeared possible, therefore after undergoing many trials, Mother Dominic of the Cross recalled her Sisters to Bonnay in 1867. As she was about to write a letter of protest to Cardinal Sterkx there came news of his death on December 4, 1867.

Another foundation near Lyon was also a failure. In 1861 two young women, recommended by some Dominican Fathers of Lyon, came to see Mother Dominic in Bonnay; they wanted to join the Congregation. One had her own school and was offering it to the Congregation; the other was prepared to stand the expense of founding a convent in Charpennes near Lyon.

Everything seemed favourable for this other foundation: the Dominican Fathers had recommended the two candidates and the bishop of the diocese had expressed his willingness to have the Dominican Sisters. However one mistake was made in that the Foundress failed to ask the bishop for his written authorisation to settle in his diocese.

This caused great embarrassment. Finally the bishop, Msgr. Ginouilhac, gave his written authorisation, though with a certain reluctance.

Other problems arose, this time with the candidate who had proposed to finance the foundation. The conditions she laid down were so unreasonable that Mother Dominic had to ask her to leave the community. As a result, through the signatures they had affixed to a deed, the Foundress and the three Bonnardel sisters had contracted a debt of 55,000 francs for the purchase of a piece of land on which to build the convent!

The school never flourished, and as a consequence, the means of the Sisters' livelihood were so low that they suffered many privations. Conflicts between the bishop, the parish priest and the Sisters never abated; this was a constant strain on the community. Suspicion everywhere was making life unbearable.

Finally, the Sisters had to be recalled to Bonnay. However, the Charpennes foundation had had one special blessing, namely, the acquaintance of the Sisters with Madame Isabelle de Vatimesnil who, in later years, became the most outstanding benefactress of the Congregation. At her own expense, she built the handsome convent of Etrépagny in Normandy which, in 1882, became the Mother-house of the Congregation and still is today.

In the midst of many sorrows and tribulations, Mother Dominic of the Cross had the consolation of receiving from the Holy See on May 5, 1864 the decree "Ad laudandum" of the Constitutions of her Congregation, the first step towards definitive approval. The Holy See put aside the Dominican Fathers' jurisdiction over the Congregation and placed the Institute under the government of a Prioress General, except the jurisdiction of the Ordinaries.*

In other words, the weight of most of the responsibility for governing the Congregation was placed on the shoulders of the Foundress, Mother Dominic of the Cross Gand.

Tribulations continued to test the Foundress' resilience and her faith in God. In Bonnay, Dr. Francois Bonnardel had died suddenly on February 21, 1861 leaving the family affairs in utter confusion and the affairs concerning the foundation in Bonnay in which the Bonnardels were deeply involved.

In November 1864, a typhoid epidemic broke out in the village of Bonnay and 15 Sisters in the convent contracted the disease. Within one week four Sisters, aged 22 to 26, died and were followed by two more a week later. Great was the sorrow of the poor Mother who had already seen 13 of her daughters die since the beginning of the foundation.

The First General Chapter of the Congregation took place in Bonnay in 1866. It was presided over by Msgr. de Marguerye, bishop of the diocese. Unanimously Mother Dominic was elected Prioress General of the Congregation. Fr. Francois Balme O.P. attended the Chapter and helped with the writing of the capitular decrees. The Congregation then numbered 60 choir Sisters and 18 lay Sisters. Most of them were young women.

At the end of the Chapter, Fr. Balme declared to the Prioress General and the Sisters: "In spite of all human conjecture, God has not only made your Congregation grow in numbers but also in strength; a strength drawn from the example of Christ who won his final victory on the Cross." This statement must have influenced the Foundress in selecting the following motto for her Congregation: "In Cruce Vita" — In the Cross is Life.

* Bishops of dioceses where the Congregation would establish foundations.

Above: Mother-House of the Dominican Sisters at Etrépagny in Normandy, France.
Below: View of the entrance of the chapel.

The convent of St. Nicolas near Belfort, East of France.

Chapter
5.

The Call From Trinidad

The Leprosarium at Cocorite in 1869.

In 1866, shortly before the celebration of Christmas, Mother Dominic of the Cross received a letter from the Master General of the Dominican Order, Rev. Fr. Alexander, Vincent Jandel, her old acquaintance from the days at Chalon in 1845. In his letter he had enclosed one from the Most Rev. Louis Joachim Gonin, O.P., Archbishop of Port of Spain, Trinidad, which invited Mother Dominic to send some of her Sisters to take care of the patients at the Leprosarium in Cocorite.

The idea of having religious Sisters perform this outstanding work of charity had come from the British Governor of the Colony, Sir Arthur Hamilton Gordon, later Lord Stanmore. He had suggested to Archbishop Gonin that he use his office to obtain Sisters to revive the run-down institution.

Although Fr. Jandel was confident of Mother Dominic's willingness to accept this difficult and far-away mission, the failure of the two previous foundations in Belgium and in France made the Foundress somewhat hesitant about another one at that time. She sought enlightenment and finally took her decision.

By mid-January 1867 Mother Dominic wrote to both Fr. Jandel and Archbishop Gonin telling them that she accepted the foundation in Trinidad but under one condition, i.e., that she be given one year to prepare her Sisters for the task ahead. This was agreed upon though with some regret, and the Sisters who had volunteered to go to Trinidad were sent to a hospital, the 'Antiquaille' in Lyon which specialised in tropical diseases, to receive basic training.

The departure of the first five Sisters destined for Trinidad took place on March 8, 1868. Four more followed them on November 8 and six others early in 1869. This was an act of faith and trust in God of great magnitude because all of them, the Foundress and the pioneers, were launching into the unknown. The only comfort Mother Dominic had came from the fact that some Dominican Fathers of the Lyon Province were already in Trinidad since the Holy See had entrusted the Trinidad Mission to them. Mother Dominic was certain that they would look after their Sisters well.

Archbishop Gonin himself was a Dominican and the fourth Archbishop of the Metropolitan See of Port of Spain which had been established by the Holy See in 1850. When the Dominican Fathers arrived in 1864 there were only four R.C. priests in Trinidad. Archbishop Gonin stayed in office for 26 years. Archbishop Finbar Ryan, O.P., his third successor, wrote the following about him "His Gallic progeniture fitted him admirably to conciliate the large French element in the community, and his legal acumen, (for he had been a lawyer before he joined the Dominican Order), to take in hand the administrative consolidation of the archdiocesan resources."

What was Trinidad like in the 1860's? Parry and Sherlock in their Short History of the West Indies, Chapter 16, recall that to solve the problem of labour shortage as a result of Emancipation (1834), a "satisfactory scheme of immigration had been devised and a rising tide of East Indian labour was flowing into Trinidad and British Guiana. By 1870 there were 28,500 East Indians in Trinidad and by 1883 the number had risen to 48,000 — about one-third of the island's population."

Thanks to this imported labour, sugar estates expanded and the road to prosperity was once more opened. This showed in 1869 when sugar represented 75 percent of the total value of exports. Land was made available to peasants and "this led to an increase in the number of small holders and in their economic importance."

Transport was facilitated when, on March 5, 1859 the Cipero Steam Tramway was opened to the public. A Collegiate School was established in 1859 in Port of Spain and four years later, St. Mary's College was founded by the French Holy Ghost Fathers. In 1869 the British Colonial Office deputed Dr. Patrick Keenan to assess the education system in Trinidad. The gentleman recommended, after a thorough investigation, the use of the vernacular language in primary schools with English coming in the later stages as a second language. He also envisaged the feasibility of a "University of the West Indies". These developments signalled a revolution in the education system of Trinidad.

It was in 1813 that a few cases of leprosy were discovered in Trinidad, but it was not before 1845 that a Leprosarium was established in Cocorite, situated on the coast three miles north-west of Port of Spain. Supported by government funds, this institution was managed by paid employees who had primarily their salary in view.

On August 30, 1854, with a population of a little over 70,000, a cholera epidemic broke out in the country. It lasted for about two months and claimed over two thousand lives. The number of deaths was so high that many burials had to be made in trenches. During the epidemic, Archbishop Vincent Spaccapietra distinguished himself by his untiring ministrations to the victims. He established an hospice for the sick which, for a long time, carried his name. Today, it is known as 'L'Hospice' and is run by the Carmelite Sisters on Observatory Street, Port of Spain.

The epidemic must have precipitated the decision to build a General Hospital in Port of Spain: work began in 1854 and was completed in 1858. The inauguration took place on September 1 and a few days later, the Lunatic Asylum in Belmont was opened on September twenty-seven.

While the Dominican Sisters of Bonnay who had volunteered to come to Trinidad* were taking training in nursing,

---

*   From the very beginning of the Mission in Trinidad and Tobago, Dominican Sisters who were sent from France, were volunteers. In all, since 1868, 138 Sisters worked very hard in Trinidad and Tobago. More offered themselves but were not sent. For instance, between 1910 and 1965, 159 Sisters expressed their desire to go to Trinidad but were not accepted by the Authority within the Congregation. At the cemeteries of Lapeyrouse in Port of Spain and on the island of Chacachacare the remains of 81 French Sisters rest in peace along with 19 others who, though members of the French Congregation of St. Catherine of Siena, belonged to other nationalities, namely: Austria, Belgium, Canada, England, Germany, Poland, Portugal, Switzerland, Venezuela and the Caribbean (Grenada, Guadeloupe and Martinique). All these Sisters laboured in our country for many years.
There are also those (19 Sisters) who, after having spent the best years of their lives in Trinidad and Tobago, returned to France where they died and are buried.
Finally, today in France there are 19 retired Dominican Sisters who altogether gave almost 500 years of dedicated service to the people of this nation.
May God bless them all and reward them for their generous service. They left their homeland, prepared the ground in the land to which they were sent, planted the seed which today produces a good harvest. It has been as St. John put it in his Gospel (12 : 24) ". . . unless a wheat grain falls on the ground and dies, it remains only a single grain; but if it dies, it yields a rich harvest." (Author's note)

there was much exchange of correspondence between Archbishop Gonin in Port of Spain and Mother Dominic in Bonnay.
The Archbishop informed the Prioress General about what the
Colonial Government was prepared to offer the Sisters and
what would be required of them. He wrote in 1866:

"The Government would give them the use of a separate
dwelling near that of the patients and a salary sufficient for
their support. The Leprosarium has 52 patients of both sexes,
37 are Catholics, 11 Protestants and four Moslems. It is the
new Governor, Sir Arthur Gordon, who conceived the idea of
confiding to the care of the nuns patients suffering from leprosy.
Though a Protestant, he seems to evince Catholic inclinations
and sympathies, unhappily not shared by those around him.
Sir Gordon ardently desires that the Sisters should start as
soon as possible, his reason being that he might die or be
transferred to another post or that the Minister for the Colonies might change his mind."

In the exchnage of letters there was a point on which
Archbishop Gonin and Mother Dominic could not agree. The
Archbishop wanted to have full control over the Sisters once
they settled in Trinidad, but the Prioress General had to
defend the unity of her Congregation and told him that she
had been given power by the Holy See to govern her Congregation with the help of a Council.

Finally, it was agreed that no definitive contract between
the Colonial Government and the Archbishop on the one hand
and the Prioress General on the other should be entered into.
Rather, a temporary commitment should be made for a period
of three years after which a mutual decision would be taken.
The government also agreed to give a lump sum of money to
the Sisters for their work — about 10,000 francs — and to provide them with food, house-linen etc. Entire freedom would be
given to them for operating the institution but one condition
would be imposed on them, i.e. that they refrain from trying
to convert Protestant patients.

Mother Dominic sent a manuscript copy of the Constitutions of her Congregation to Archbishop Gonin to inform him
about the way of life of the Dominican Sisters of Bonnay and
she also asked him to kindly see that the Sisters be provided
with a chapel in Cocorite and that he appoint a priest to minister to them and to the R.C. patients.

Chapter
6.

Arrival of the First Dominican Sisters in Trinidad

A Dominican Sister with patients at Cocorite.

On March 26, 1868, the first five Dominican Sisters reached Trinidad having left the port of St. Nazaire eighteen days earlier. Their arrival was the principal event of the year in the country. Sr. Marie Dominique Bonnardel, Sr. Marie Osanna Brevet, Sr, Marie Augustin Cartier, Sr. Catherine Lucie Glasersfeld and Sr. Marie Guichardon were accompanied by Fr. Raphael Pierrez O.P., a volunteer for the Trinidad Mission, and a pious widow, Madame Corberon.

Three Dominicans, Frs. Bion, Sebastien and Greenough went to meet the travellers on board ship and they were all brought from the steamer to the Port of Spain wharf by the agent of the Royal Mail Company, Mr. Scott. Taken first to the Cathedral presbytery, they met Archbishop Louis Joachim Gonin who welcomed them and introduced them to the community. The Sisters were then led to their temporary residence in Marine Square, now renamed Independence Square.

The Governor, Sir Arthur H. Gordon, had rented a house on one of the islands to enable the Sisters to get acclimatised a little. Many had reproached him for bringing out nuns for the Leprosarium; it was felt that he was sacrificing them. However, the Governor's firmness and his desire to bring relief to the poor patients, physically and morally, triumphed over all obstacles.

In his defence he said: "I have always thought that to cure such ills, of soul as well as body, something more is needed than paid-for devotion; to my mind it seemed that it required Christian charity, the charity which sees above all in the sick and the poor the living members of our Lord Jesus Christ".

Sir Arthur suggested that the Sisters take a month's rest in the house he had rented for them, but they stayed only two weeks. Archbishop Gonin was not in favour of seeing them settle in the Leprosarium right away as the house reserved for them was undergoing repairs. He would have liked them to reside for sometime at L'Hospice in Belmont. Sr. Marie Dominique thanked both the Archbishop and the Governor for their kind disposition towards the Sisters and remarked, "As much as we came to bring relief to these poor people it is to them that we must go without any more delay, the good Lord will protect us".

On Holy Thursday, April 9, 1868 the Dominican Sisters were taken to Cocorite and shown their quarters which consisted of four rooms above the pharmacy and store-room of the Leprosarium. Their task was to clean the place and make it habitable. The flooring boards were all disjointed and the gallery was termite-eaten.

The next day they took up their duties at the Leprosarium; it was Good Friday, and at 3 p.m. they started dressing the patients' hideous wounds. The wards were very dilapidated, (repairs were not done before 1877), the whole place was insanitary and badly kept; the patients had no bed linen, only rags; dirt was everywhere and a putrescent odour filled the air.

It did not take long for the Sisters to win the hearts of the people. The female patients called them "Sesees" meaning dear little Sisters, and the males "Mamans". Sr. Marie Dominique, the Prioress of the community, was appointed Superintendent of the Leprosarium and Fr. Raphael Pierrez, O.P., Chaplain.

Medically speaking, nothing was known about leprosy until 1873 when a Norwegian physician, Dr. Armauer Hansen, discovered the bacillus responsible for the disease which he named *Mycobacteria leprae*. M. Elizabeth Duncan, in her *Historical Review of Social and Clinical Aspects of Leprosy* published in the *Leprosy Review* of June 1985, remarked that the earliest indubitable references to leprosy come from India and go back to 6 B.C. The parts of the body which are usually damaged by the disease are the hands, feet and eyes. The crippling is caused by germs attacking and damaging nerves which normally carry messages to and from the brain. There are several types of leprosy, some more severe than others. In Trinidad it has been estimated that approximately one-third of patients suffering from leprosy had the severe type.

Infection can spread when an untreated patient coughs and sneezes, especially if he suffers from the severe type. Air can spread germs to others. However this disease — called after the name of its discoverer, Hansen — is not easily passed from one person to another; it is even considered the least catching of all communicable diseases. It is not inherited and is not a curse from God, as biblical stories would have us believe.

Since the cause of the disease was not known, in the early days no remedy could bring a cure. *Chaulmoogra* oil was used on the wounds but it was ineffective. In Cocorite an attempt was made to heal the wounds with cod liver oil adding to the air another odour which Shakespeare described as "the rankest compound of villainous smell that ever offended nostril".

At the turn of the last century some new drugs were tried such as *streptomycin* and *cycloserine* but they were eventually discarded as ineffectual. In the 1940's sulfones had a beneficial influence but they caused dreaded reactions; the same happened later with *rifampicin* or *rifadine*. More research and experiments were carried out and new drugs manufactured: *clofazimine, dapsone, lamprene, rimactane and hansolar;* these, so far, have been so successful that now new patients cannot spread the Hansen disease if they follow their treatment.

Hansen patients need not be isolated anywhere for any time. In Trinidad and Tobago, Hansen's disease has almost been eradicated thanks to the new drugs, vigilant supervision and regular treatment.

But let us go back to 1868 when the situation at Cocorite was heart-rending. As the Sisters went·on organising the work at the Leprosarium they became acutely aware of the need to have more hands to cope with the situation. To this effect they wrote an appeal to Mother Dominic of the Cross in Bonnay to send more Sisters. Four more volunteered to go to Cocorite and on November 8, 1868 they arrived in Trinidad. Two days later, Fr. Etienne Brosse O.P. came as chaplain to the Asylum as a replacement for Fr. Pierrez who was obliged to return to France on account of ill health. Fr. Brosse was to remain in the post for 25 years.

In the 1860's there were four institutions established for the relief of·the sick, namely, the Colonial Hospital in Port of Spain, the Cocorite Leprosarium, the Lunatic Asylum in Belmont and the Ariapita "Town Hospital" (also called "Shine") catering for the needs of infirm paupers. The latter was maintained by the Port of Spain Borough Council. The "hospital" was composed of several small wooden huts, with very little light inside and much dirt which offered a repulsive aspect to those who visited it for the first time. The occupants had no bed linen only rags, and all they had to hold their food in was a calabash.

One of the Borough Council members pleaded with the Sisters in Cocorite to take charge of the Ariapita Asylum. The matter was communicated to Mother Dominic in France and she gave her consent. On May 12, 1869, two Sisters took up their duties at the Ariapita Asylum. There, as well as in Cocorite, the Sisters were subjected to much provocation on the part of the Protestants who felt that too much was put in the hands of the Catholic nuns.

At Cocorite there was a school for East Indian children but they were very much left to themselves. One of the major difficulties in operating this school came from the fact that the children spoke different languages, the main one being Hindustani. Fr. Brosse, whose heart went out to these children, undertook the learning of this language and mastered it well. He wanted one of the Sisters to help him but they were already so overworked that they could not give him satisfaction.

Consequently, another request was made to Mother Dominic to send more Sisters to Trinidad and it was favourable received. She sent six more Sisters; on June 24 1869 they landed in Port of Spain. Fr. Mariano Forestier welcomed them at the wharf and took them straight to Cocorite. These new Sisters brought valuable help to Cocorite, Ariapita and the East Indian school. For important reasons, however, the latter could not be maintained for long because it was too tiring for the Sisters to walk from Cocorite to St. James daily and the school was too isolated.

On July 29, 1869 a sinister rumour spread like wildfire in Port of Spain: "Father Trouche is dying!" After only four days of painful illness he was no more. He had fallen a victim to the terrible epidemic of yellow fever. On August 7 it was the turn of Fr. Ceslaus Mentel. Both had died at the Cathedral presbytery in Port of Spain. Who was to be next?

Chapter
7.

The Plague

The community of the Dominican Fathers at the presbytery of the Cathedral of the Immaculate Conception in Port of
Spain, and the population of the city as a whole, were still
painfully impressed by the rapid deaths of Fathers Michael
Trouche and Ceslaus Mentel due to yellow fever when, suddenly, more alarming news came from Cocorite. Like a thun-
derbolt the dreadful epidemic struck there.

In July — August of that year (1869) some of the Dominican Sisters working at the Leprosarium and the Ariapita
Hospice felt extremely tired. Debilitated by the humid and hot
tropical climate, the change of diet, their heavy clothing
unsuited to the tropics and the insanitary surroundings in
which they lived; their physical resistance therefore gave way.

Sr. Marie Jean Vanconpenhoudt a Belgian, who had
arrived in Trinidad at the end of June 1869, was the first to
succumb to the deadly plague: she died on September 8, 1869
in the flower of her youth. Sr. Agnes du Rosarie Villeneuve,
who had been working with Sr. Marie, also fell ill and died
three days later. Born in France, she was 28 years old.

Then Sr. Marie Madeleine Mortel, who had made a trip to Port of Spain, returned to Cocorite feeling ill; she too was suffering from yellow fever and died on September 14 at the age of 32. On that very day, another Sister took ill; she was Sr. Catherine Lucie Glasersfeld, born in Austria, well-educated — she could speak several languages. Sr. Catherine died on September 23 at the age of 32. The next day she was followed by Sr. Josephine du Rosaire Mery who died at the age of 42.

That September 24, 1869 was a most cruel day because not only did Sr. Joséphine die but also Mother Marie Dominique Bonnardel, the Prioress of the community. She died at the age of 51. She had been so grieved by the deaths of her dear Sisters that she had no resistance left to fight the disease.

The following day, death struck again and took away two more Sisters: Sr. Marie Osanna Brevet, aged 51, and Sr. Marie du St. Sacrement Guichardon, 28. The ninth and last victim of the yellow fever epidemic at Cocorite was Sr. Marie Hyacinthe Seurre, aged 30, the seventh French Sister victim of the plague. With the holy man Job it could then have been said: "The Lord gave, the Lord has taken back. Blessed be the name of the Lord." (Job 1:20).

It was found that no other cases of yellow fever developed in the Mucurapo Ward in that year 1869, except for one male patient at the Leprosarium who died of it, as revealed my research at the office of the Registrar General of Port of Spain.

On September 23, 1869 Archbishop Louis Joachim Gonin wrote the following letter to the Prioress General in Bonnay, Mother Dominic of the Cross, which she received on October 19.

"My Very Rev. Mother, I have a sad duty to fulfill towards you. You may have learned that the yellow fever epidemic, which had not appeared in Trinidad since 1852, is now causing havoc in the Antilles. Two of our Dominican brethren, Frs. Trouche and Mentel, who were teaching at St. Mary's College, and one Sister of St. Joseph of Cluny were the first victims. The plague has just reached your community at Cocorite and I must tell you that it is causing a disaster. Four of our Sisters have already died — Sisters Agnes, Madeleine, Marie de St. Jean and alas, today, our much regretted Sr. Catherine Lucie.

"Sadly enough this is not all. Five are still very ill and at this moment two are close to death, Rev. Mother Prioress and Sr. Marie Osanna. It is only by the next sea-mail that you will be able to know more about the issue of their illness.

"I fully understand how cruel such news will be to your motherly heart; however, I hope that Our Lord will give you all the necessary graces of resignation and courage which you will need. I am convinced that everything will arrange itself with time and that God will draw good out of this evil. It is a time to rekindle our faith in His divine promise, 'Blessed are those who weep for they shall be comforted'.

"P.S. I re-open my letter, September 24, to inform you of something which will be most painful to your heart: two more Sisters died yesterday; one, alas, is Mother Prioress and the other Sr. Josephine. Let us renew our faith and repeat from the depth of our hear, 'Lord, thy will be done'. Let us have full confidence in Him; He will console us in due time and will give us back even more than what we have lost."

Fr. Etienne Brosse, Prior of the Dominican Fathers in Trinidad, also wrote to Mother Dominic to relate the very sad news. "They died like saints!" he stated, adding, "Your Sisters joyfully offered their lives to God." When the epidemic broke out there were 24 members of the Dominican Order in Trinidad; death, through this yellow fever, took away almost half of them: two Fathers and nine Sisters.

The tragic situation at Cocorite in that month of September 1869 could easily be imagined. Medical doctors gave orders to have the sick evacuated to the Colonial Hospital but some of the Sisters were already so weak that they could not be moved. As a precaution, in order to avoid the spread of the epidemic, a doctor sent some of the Sisters to one of the islands off the north-west coast of Trinidad but it was all in vain; one of them died there and the others had to be brought back to Cocorite.

Then began the unforgettable week when every day, from September 23 to 27, one or two Sisters died. The remains of these heroic victims of Christian charity were laid to rest in a small cemetery forming part of the large burial ground in Port-of Spain — the Lapeyrouse cemetery.

The whole population of Port of Spain mourned the deaths of the Sisters. Records do not say if the epidemic spread to other wards of the country. In his brief history of Trinidad from 1797 to 1897, *100 Years Together,* H.C. Pitts does not mention it, whereas he notes the other terrible epidemic of Asiatic cholera in 1854.

After the deaths of the Sisters many people spontaneously offered their services to look after the patients at Cocorite, proposing to take turns working at the Leprosarium. However, the authorities thought it better to entrust the material care of the patients to paid nurses under the surveillance of a director. Fr. Brosse remained as chaplain of the Leprosarium to the R.C. patients.

At the Ariapita or Shine hospice, several young women undertook to replace the Sisters. They belonged to the Society of the Nativity of the Blessed Virgin Mary. They intended to act as nurses in turns until other Dominican Sisters came from France.

The Sisters who had survived the epidemic found strength in a new leader, Mother Catherine Dominique Vanrouchoudt, who had manifested exceptional courage during the tragedy. It was not before October 26, 1869 that finally Mother Dominic of the Cross received all the letters addressed to her bringing the terribly sad news of the deaths of nine of her daughters in Trinidad. The poor Mother grieved so much that all she could write afterwards about that moment was, "Silence at the foot of the Cross was the only consolation in our sorrow."

Many testimonies of sympathy from France, Rome, Belgium, England and Germany comforted her. About these Mother Dominic remarked: "This was the greatest homage which could have been paid to their sacrifice." In less than eight months, 15 of her daughters had left her: six who chose to be secularised from the convent in Belgium and nine who died in Trinidad. The Cross was heavy indeed!

In Cocorite, the survivors had been compelled to take some rest. The Governor, Sir Arthur Gordon, who had taken upon himself the responsibility of establishing the nuns at

Cocorite, decided that certain sanitary improvements would be gradually effected; this was started by the planting of trees in swampy areas bordering the sea.

In Bonnay, at the call of Mother Dominic, several volunteers came forward among the Sisters to go to Trinidad and continue the work started by the deceased Sisters. On October 28, 1869, Mother Dominic assigned Sr. Catherine Dominique in Cocorite as Prioress of the Mission in Trinidad. The colonial authorities in Trinidad also appointed her Superintendent of the Leprosarium.

The Prioress General of the Congregation then informed Archbishop Gonin that, considering the small number of Sisters left, she could no longer send Sisters to the Ariapita hospice.

Her decision displeased the Archbishop because he had made plans to reorganise the life and works of the Dominican Sisters in Trinidad. The inmates of the hospice were nonetheless not abandoned; the young women who had volunteered to replace the Sisters at the time of the epidemic continued to devote themselves at the hospice. After a few years, Archbishop Gonin formed them into a regular Congregation for the Archdiocese with the name "Petites Soeurs des Pauvres" or "Little Sisters of Charity".

On April 8, 1870 four Dominican Sisters from Bonnay embarked at the French port of St. Nazaire and landed in Trinidad on the 25th of the same month. They were given a grand welcome by their Sisters in Cocorite, the six survivors of the epidemic, who had resumed their work on December 1, 1869 after a period of rest. Life continued with God's blessings and the kind co-operation of many.

VERITAS

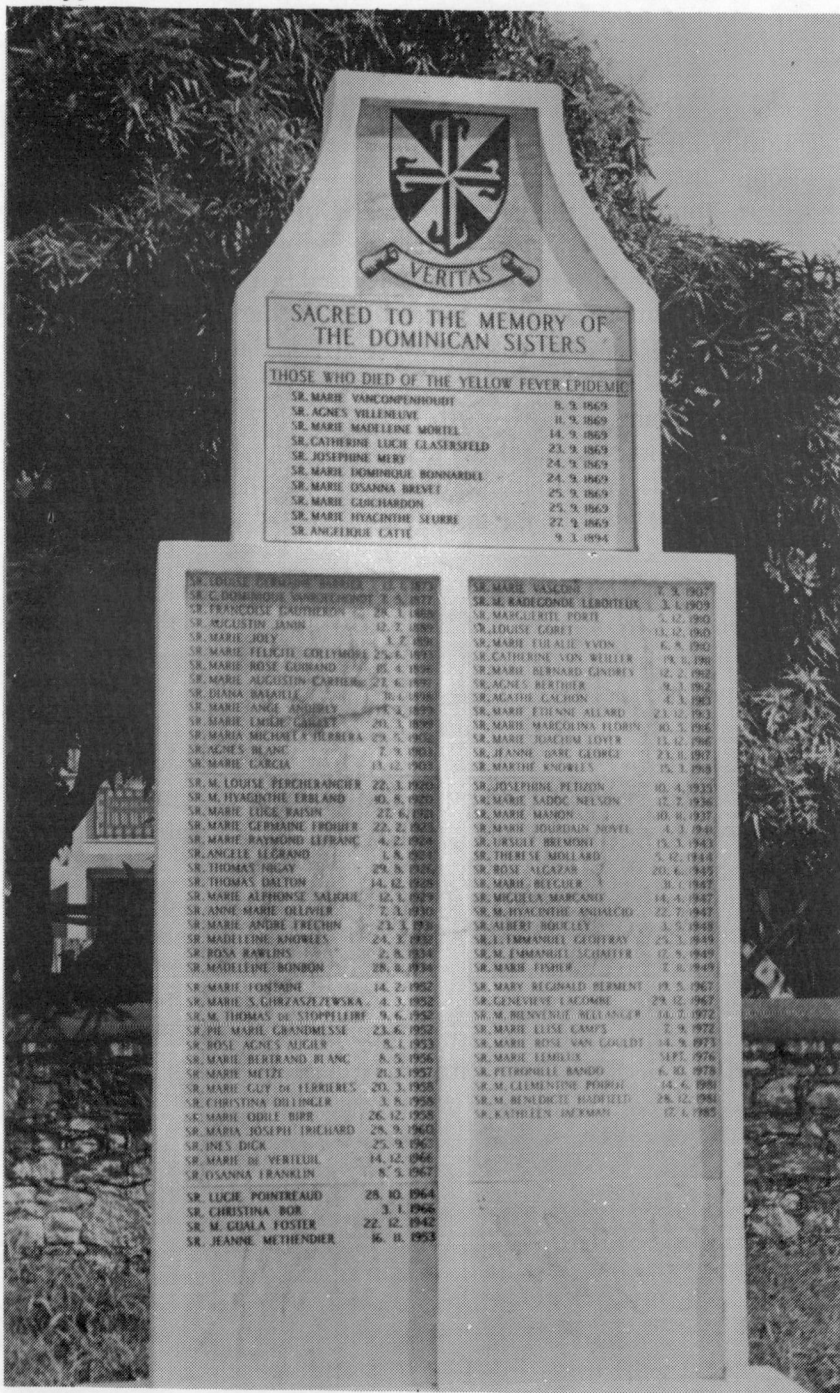

SACRED TO THE MEMORY OF THE DOMINICAN SISTERS

THOSE WHO DIED OF THE YELLOW FEVER EPIDEMIC

SR. MARIE VANCOMPENHOUDT	8. 9. 1869
SR. AGNES VILLENEUVE	11. 9. 1869
SR. MARIE MADELEINE MORTEL	14. 9. 1869
SR. CATHERINE LUCIE GLASERSFELD	23. 9. 1869
SR. JOSEPHINE MERY	24. 9. 1869
SR. MARIE DOMINIQUE BONNARDEL	24. 9. 1869
SR. MARIE OSANNA BREVET	25. 9. 1869
SR. MARIE GUICHARDON	25. 9. 1869
SR. MARIE HYACINTHE SEURRE	27. 9. 1869
SR. ANGELIQUE CATTE	9. 3. 1894

The commemorative monument erected at the Lapeyrouse cemetery in Port of Spain in remembrance of the deceased Dominican Sisters.

Chapter
8.

Tragedies, Conflicts and Distress

The year 1869 was a year of tragedies for the Dominican Congregation of St. Catherine of Siena in Bonnay with the death of nine Sisters in Trinidad from the yellow fever epidemic and the defection of six others from the Belgian convent of Terbanck; alas, the year 1870 was again to be a sad one not only for the Congregation but for the whole country of France.

From July 19, 1870 to May 1871 France and Germany were at war because of a dispute·between the leaders of these two countries over a successor to the throne of Spain. The contention surrounded Leopold of Hohenzollern, a relative of William I of Prussia. Bismarck, the Prussian Chancellor, had urged Leopold's acceptance of the Spanish throne. The French were opposed to Hohenzollern. The immediate cause of war was the publication of the famous *Ems Dispatch* announcing Prussia's refusal to grant a French demand that no Hohenzollern would ever accept the Spanish throne.

Before publishing the Dispatch sent by the French Minister of Foreign Affairs, Bismarck edited it in such a manner as to arouse war-fever in both countries. When the edited Dispatch was seen in Paris on July 14, 1870, it so provoked public opinion that the French Government declared war against Prussia on July 19. The Dispatch had the effect that Bismarck intended, "a red flag for the Gallic bull".

The war went against France from the very beginning. Germany was ready for war, France was not. The over-ambitious Napoleon III, after several retreats of the French troops, foolishly gave orders to engage the Germans at Sedan on September 1; that was a most disastrous defeat. Thousands of men died in the mad strategy. The rest of the French forces was sent to defend Paris which was threatened by the German invasion.

As a result of the Sedan defeat, a Republican Government headed by Adolphe Thiers was proclaimed in Paris on September 4 to pursue war against Germany. But the well-trained and disciplined German army continued to capture one town after another and then laid siege to Paris itself. The city held out until January 28, 1871 when the starving people, (they had been reduced to eating rats!), freezing in the bitter winter, finally surrendered.

The French capitulation cost a very high price. By the terms of the Treaty of Frankfurt, France had to cede to Germany the whole province of Alsace and part of that of Lorraine. In addition, a compensation of five billion francs was to be paid to Germany. A German occupation army remained in northern France until the indemnity was fully paid in 1873. To make matters worse, a civil war broke out in France, known as the "Commune"; it was led by revolutionaries who committed many massacres.

The convent of the Dominican Sisters in St. Nicolas, Alsace, was only 14km from the German border. German troops arrived in the valley on November 2, 1870. From that day on the Sisters and children of the orphanage suffered a great deal from lack of food, fear of the occupants and separation from the rest of France.

With the advance of the Germans, the French population had to evacuate towns and villages. This was the case with the village of Bonnay and a little later that of Charpennes.

Mother Dominic found herself obliged to scatter her daughters to various places to ensure their safety. She sent two to England to live with the Dominican Sisters of Stone; two others went to the convent of Terbanck in Belgium and all the others, including the novices, headed for Switzerland where some stayed with the Dominican Sisters of Schwitz and the others with the Franciscan Sisters of Verroliez.

Mother Dominic herself was obliged to leave Bonnay in December 1870. Accompanied by a Sister she also made her way to Switzerland but on the road she was overcome by illness and was given hospitality by a good Christian family living close to the Swiss frontier. The poor Mother had lost everything: her daughters were all dispersed and she had news neither from them, nor of her family in Lorraine. She was ill, without money and no means of livelihood.

"My soul is like that of the woman of Canaan," she said, "I do nothing but cry to the Lord; my prayer is a cry of distress and of suffering. I have nothing but Him, all human means are wanting . . . but He is there."

After some time, communication was re-established and through correspondence Mother Dominic was reassured about the situation of each one of her daughters. From England she learned that the two Sisters had settled among their English Dominican Sisters. One of them, Sr. Dominique du Rosaire, was even translating into French the history of the life of their foundress, Mother Margaret Hallahan. The translation of the book was published in 1875.

This fraternal collaboration established strong links between the two Dominican Congregations. In Switzerland, the French Sisters were shown much affection and esteem by their host communities and they did their utmost to help them in their work.

After expressing deep gratitude to the family who had taken such good care of her during the crucial months of exile, Mother Dominic travelled to St. Nicolas where she was overjoyed at seeing her daughters once more. From there she recalled all those she had sent to Switzerland and England; the novices were to go to the convent of Terbanck with some professed Sisters, the others were to come to St. Nicolas until further arrangements.

Great was their joy when news arrived that the new border,

(after the armistice), was fixed just beyond the property of the Kellers, the Sisters' benefactors in St. Nicolas. In thanksgiving to God for remaining on French soil, Mr. Keller with his family, the Sisters and the children renewed together in the chapel of the convent the consecration to the Sacred Heart of Jesus, placing their persons and places under his protection.

At the same time a storm was brewing in Bonnay. The parish priest of the village — a Bonnardel — who had been put in charge of the family patrimony after the death of his brother François, was determined to exercise all his power to have the bishop of the diocese declare the Dominican Sisters of Bonnay a diocesan Congregation under the sole authority of the bishop. The Congregation was still indebted to the Bonnardels for the construction of the convent and this made the situation more complicated.

A group of Sisters returned to Bonnay in 1872 with Sr. Marie Agnés Bonnardel as Prioress. This was the year to convene the General Chapter of the Congregation Fr. Bonnardel, who had had his way with the bishop of the diocese, conveyed the bishop's order to the Sisters that the Chapter was not to be held in Bonnay that year. Msgr. de Marguerye's reason was that his resignation had been tended to the Holy See and, therefore, the Sisters would have to wait for his successor.

The only authorisation he gave, through the intercession of the Dominican Provincial, was to hold an "extraordinary Council" in Bonnay which took place on December 11, 1872. This was the occasion which revealed to the Foundress the unrest which existed in the Bonnay community. Not only had Fr. Bonnardel won the bishop to his side but his two sisters Agnés and Eugénie as well and the latter in turn had influenced eight Sisters of the community to oppose Mother Dominic. They had supported the views of the priest that the Bonnay community had to become a Diocesan Congregation under the jurisdiction of the bishop only.

Mother Dominic felt that she was no longer wanted in Bonnay when 18 years earlier the same Bonnardel sisters had begged her to leave her convent in Chalon and come to Bonnay to help them in forming a religious community. They were regarding her with suspicion now. Strange destiny! Alone in her room she wrote:

"I prayed at length, prayed my Rosary and opened the book of the Imitation of Christ. An image fell from it. It represented Christ alone in a prison cell, his hands bound. Below the picture it was written: 'I fed them and they have all abandoned me.' It gave some comfort to my soul."

In a letter dated December 30, 1872 she remarked, "This year 1873, I wonder where we will finish it?" At this painful time, when she needed more than ever her wise and faithful adviser, Fr. Jandel, she heard the news of his death on December 11, 1872.

The third General Chapter opened in Bonnay on August 5, 1873. The new bishop of Autun, Msgr. de Lezeleuc, adopted the same hostile attitude of his predecessor towards Mother Dominic. Her opponents had hoped that she would not have been re-elected as Prioress General at the Chapter but she was, unanimously.

Following the Chapter, life continued in the Bonnay community but with a certain amount of uneasiness. It was on March 31, 1874 that the storm broke. Sr. Marie Agnés Bonnardel had reached the end of her fourth term as Prioress of the community and, according to the Constitutions she could not be re-elected. Bishop de Lezeleuc died more or less at the same time.

The Episcopal See being vacant, and acting upon the advice of her brother, Sr. Marie Agnés, and the Sisters who supported her, appealed to the Holy See stating in their report that if their Prioress was not maintained in her post they would form a Community of their own.

Meantime, the Council of the Congregation with the Prioress General used their rights and assigned a new Prioress. The dissident Sisters refused to obey her. The Holy See appointed Msgr. Perraud as Bishop of Autun. Mother Dominic informed him of the situation in Bonnay. At first favourable to her cause, he nonetheless changed his mind three months later.

On August 22, Bishop Perraud came to the convent of Bonnay for a canonical visitation. On hearing the many accusations laid against her, Mother Dominic realised that no hope was left for the unity of the Congregation. The situation became untenable for her. Finally, on August 24, 1874, following the counsel of her advisers, she departed from Bonnay.

It was a very sad day for her and she never returned to the birth-place of her Congregation. She went to Belgium where more sorrow awaited her as she had to close down the Convent at Terbanck. Afterwards, she travelled to St. Nicolas where she met Fr. Balme who advised her to go to Rome to defend the cause of the unity of her Congregation.

At the Holy See, Mother Dominic of the Cross Gand was known as the promoter of the first Congregation of Dominican Tertiaries in France. From there she gained full support for her cause. The Constitutions of her Congregation had been approved by the Holy See and therefore the professed Sisters were under serious obligation to live according to these Constitutions. Pope Pius IX himself spoke with Mother Dominic no less than six times during her stay in Rome and gave her the assurance that the unity of her Congregation would be preserved.

In the months that followed, the Holy See was put to great embarrassment by the attitude and actions of Bishop Perraud. What saved the situation was the heroic humility of Mother Dominic who chose to abandon the convent of Bonnay to the Bonnardels for the sake of peace. Authorisation was granted her to transfer the novitiate of Bonnay to the convent of St. Nicolas. The departure of the novices accompanied by the Sisters faithful to Mother Dominic took place on March 21, 1876. The Holy See allowed the dissident Sisters to stay together in a house, dependent on the bishop of the diocese. An order was given them to cease wearing the Dominican religious habit and adhering to the Constitutions of the Congregation, since they were no longer members of this religious institute.

In 1916, after the death of their leader, Sr. Marie Agnés Bonnardel, the dissident Sisters, who had continued to live in Bonnay, asked to be re-admitted to the Congregation of Mother Dominic of the Cross. They were gladly accepted by her successor. Mother Dominic had died in 1907.

In 1878, Mother Dominic and her Sisters of the Congregation of St. Catherine of Siena had taken possession of their

new and beautiful convent at Etrépagny in Normandy, the gift
of a most generous benefactress, Mrs. Isabelle de Vatimesnil.
This was the new Mother-house of the Congregation and has
remained so to this day.

*Mother Dominic of the Cross
rejected by some of her
Sisters suffers in silence.*

*Saint Dominic in prayer
at the foot of the Cross
Fra Angelico.*

Chapter
9.

1871 - St. Dominic's Orphanage
Founded in Belmont

First houses of the St. Dominic's Orphanage in the late 1870's.

In the Trinidad of the 1860's and early 1870's, distressingly sad was the sight of poor, abandoned children — some not older than three or four years — roaming about the streets of Port of Spain, hungry, half-naked, rummaging in the garbage and stealing in order to eat.

In 1857 some members of the Anglican Church in Trinidad founded an orphanage for East Indian children in Tacarigua near the Orange Grove sugar-cane plantation where many East Indians were working. These people had volunteered to leave their motherland, India, and come to Trinidad as their government had presented them with an "Indentured System" whereby they would give five years of their labour, under certain conditions, after which time they would be offered either a free passage to return to India or a parcel of land in Trinidad where they could settle.

After the Emancipation of African slaves in Trinidad (1834) there was a serious shortage of labour on the plantations which sustained the economy of the country. The Colonial Government, therefore, decided to import people from other lands. In 72 years (1845 - 1917), 141,615 East Indians came to Trinidad. After a long and trying sea voyage, the indentured were called to take over the strenuous work in the cane fields.

Because of the harsh conditions, many became ill, the chief diseases being dysentry, malaria, tuberculosis and leprosy. The Cocorite Leprosarium received many new patients, including children. The disease spread rapidly: from 49 patients in 1862, the number increased to 210 in 1891.

The French priest, Fr. Mariano Forestier, O.P. was one person in Trinidad who wanted to imitate the Anglicans in their work of charity with abandoned orphans. Fr. Forestier was born in 1831 and became a diocesan priest before joining the Dominican Order in the convent of Santa Sabina in Rome at the age of thirty-one. After his religious formation he offered himself for service in Trinidad and arrived in Port of Spain in 1864 in the company of Fr. Andre Violette shortly before the feast of Christmas.

Fr. Forestier was entrusted by his superiors with the construction of the first Rosary church on Park Street, Port of

Spain. To accomplish this task he gave himself unsparingly. Helped by many kind friends he made never-ending collections, knocking at every door, remembering the words of Christ, "Ask and you shall receive." He found, and managed to pay off all the debts of the church before he could turn his thoughts and ardent zeal to another great project – the foundation of a Catholic orphanage.

Two cases urged Fr. Forestier to take action. One day, while on one of his rounds as chaplain of the Colonial Hospital, he saw a dying mother entrusting her little son to a kind-hearted woman telling her, "Take good care of my little Augustine." These were her last words. Then a few days later, a four-year-old girl child was found lying beside the dead body of her mother who had been murdered by her father. Fr. Forestier's main concern was the plight of so many children. "What to do with them?" was his torment. He began to look for a house.

Behind the Colonial Hospital, the Belmont Ridge, (below the Laventille Hills), covered several acres of land. This was the property of a Portuguese Protestant minister which had been put up for sale along with a small house. Fr. Forestier cast a longing eye on this piece of land—it was just what he needed. However, he did not know where to find the money to buy it. "I haven't got a cent," he told his faithful friends. Time was pressing and he could not let this unique opportunity pass by. He prayed in great earnest asking the Lord to help. Help indeed came in the person of Louis Alexandre Le Roy, a respected gentleman in Port of Spain and member of the Legislative Council.

Le Roy, born in Ajaccio (Corsica) in 1820 came to settle in Trinidad in 1839. Married to a devout Trinidad Catholic lady they both excelled in charitable works. Mr. Le Roy bought the Belmont property in his own name for $2,000 and later donated it to Fr. Forestier. The good gentleman died while on a trip to France in 1883. In his will he had requested that his body be brought back to Trinidad and buried close to his dear orphans. His wife and his sister Marie continued the good work of their beloved deceased. They were buried side by side with Louis Le Roy in the Rosary church. A wall plaque in the chapel of the Holy Face keeps their memory alive.

Fr. Mariano, now assured of a site for his orphanage, began a quest for funds to enable him to start building. He preached everywhere and appealed for help. The population responded enthusiastically and generously: money, jewellery and other items, were given in exchange for construction materials. As a result, a wooden house was built for orphan boys as well as a temporary chapel. The girls were to be accommodated in the existing house on the ridge.

A most kind lady, Mrs. Casimir Alcazar, who had already taken into her home the two orphans found by Fr. Forestier, came to his assistance. She cooked meals for the builders every day. Work began in March 1871 and was completed on September 11 of that year. The new orphanage was blessed and opened by Archbishop Joachim Louis Gonin who placed it under the protection of St. Dominic. Two months after the opening, there were already 18 orphans in St. Dominic's. Miss Stephanie Blanc a devoted parishioner of Rosary church, agreed to take charge of the Orphanage. She was to spend all her time and energy in the interest of the children for the next 25 years.

Survival in those early days was almost a daily miracle. Mrs. Alcazar could be seen every day in the streets of Port of Spain with baskets on her arms, going from door to door begging the day's food for the children. It was also a common sight to see Fr. Forestier going through the town in a buggy drawn by a donkey led by one of the older boys, seeking food and alms for the children. He always expressed deep gratitude to his benefactors. Fr. François Balme, on a visit to Trinidad, declared that Fr. Forestier was "the hardest worker, the biggest beggar and the best understood person in Port of Spain".

Fr. Forestier had no rest until his orphanage was granted government recognition as a public utility. This he obtained towards the end of the year 1871. The grant consisted of four dollars per child per month up to the age of sixteen.

Numbers increased rapidly. In 1874 there were over 50 orphans with a greater proportion of boys than girls. A group of kind-hearted women, with whom Fr. Forestier established the first fraternity of Dominican Tertiaries, took charge of construction work on another house with the help of the children themselves. Their names deserve mention here: Mesdames Alcazar and Bideau, Stephanie Blanc, Asperie Bernard and Nancy Winniet, Leontine de La Bastide, Maria Joseph Rodriguez and Rose Ramsey. Surely God has given them a great reward in heaven!

Fr. Forestier would sometimes return from various parts of the country where his ministry took him, with abandoned children he found on his way and bring them to the Orphanage. He was regarded as the St. Vincent de Paul of Trinidad. The number of children kept growing and the grant was insufficient to feed them all. There were days when Stephanie Blanc and her assistants, having distributed among the children the last bit of food collected, would have nothing to eat till the next day. Miss Blanc used to go barefooted because she could not afford a pair of shoes. Heroic times!

The Founder felt most distressed about the situation at the Orphanage. He thought that the only way to keep it going would be if he could obtain some of his Dominican Sisters to look after it. More prayers were addressed to God for this intention. Finally, after a thousand and one vicissitudes, his desire was granted.

In 1875 the Co-adjutor of Archbishop Gonin, Msgr. William O'Carroll, on a visit to France called to see Mother Dominic of the Cross in Bonnay. He pleaded the cause of the little orphans of Fr. Forestier so well that Mother Dominic granted his request. Four Sisters assigned to take charge of the Orphanage, arrived in Trinidad at the end of October 1875 accompanied by two Dominicans, Frs. Laurent Henocq and Hilaire Arnaud. Due to some difficulties, however, the Sisters had to stay at Cocorite for a few months. Their official appointment at St. Dominic's Orphanage was on February 24, 1876. The Prioress of the community was Mother Marie Thomas Nigay.

Regretfully, Fr. Forestier was not there to see his dream come true, that is to say, his Orphanage in the care of his Dominican Sisters. His health had broken down and he was sent to France for a complete rest. When he returned to Trinidad Fr. Violette had taken over from him.

Nonetheless, in 1880 Fr. Forestier took up residence at St.

Dominic's in a small house built especially for him, but he often slept in the boys' dormitory to help with supervision. He died in the presbytery of Santa Cruz on April 20, 1901 at the age of 70, surrounded by his beloved orphans, after blessing them for the last time. What a welcome Our Lord must have given him in heaven. He who said: "Whoever receives such little children for my sake, receives Me." (Matthew 18 : 5).

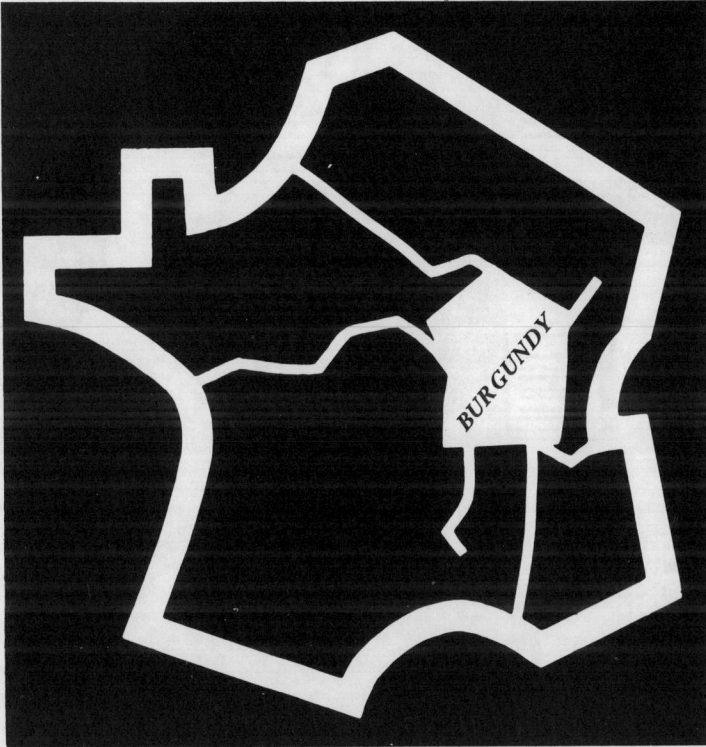

This is a map of France showing the province of Burgundy.

Group of first girls at the Orphanage with two Dominican Sisters and some of the kind ladies who cared for them.

Group of first boys at the Orphanage with Fr. Hilaire Arnaud O.P. (left) and Fr. Andre Violette O.P.

Chapter
10.

Years of Growth
at St. Dominc's Orphanage

❀

One of the oldest houses of St. Dominic's, Bethlehem for little girls.

Two problems caused the newly arrived Dominican Sisters to wait in Cocorite instead of going straight to St. Dominic's Orphanage in Belmont, Port of Spain, to assume responsibility of the establishment. First of all, there was no room to accommodate them because whatever space was available had been occupied by a group of Venezuelan Dominican nuns. These had been expelled from their monastery in Caracas by a government hostile to the Church and personified in its president, Guzman Blanco.

Banished from their country they found refuge in this city of Port of Spain and entrusted themselves to the care of their brethren in St. Dominic. They reached our shores on October 25, 1874 and Msgr. William Dominic O'Carroll, himself a Dominican and co-adjutor of Archbishop Gonin who was in Europe at that time, welcomed them to Trinidad. They were temporarily accommodated at St. Dominic's Orphanage.

On his return to Trinidad, Archbishop Gonin did not wish the nuns to stay there unless they were willing to take charge of the Orphanage. This type of work being incompatible with their monastic vocation, the nuns declined and left the Orphanage after spending 15 months there. They went to live in a place called "Calvary" until they found a suitable building in which to settle. It was in 1888 that they took possession of Rosary Convent situated next to Rosary church on Park Street, Port of Spain.

The Archbishop of Port of Spain, the Most Rev. Joachim Louis Gonin O.P., was the cause of further delay. Contrary to all expectations, the Archbishop insisted that the Dominican Sisters could assume responsibility of St. Dominic's Orphanage on condition that they clear the institution's $3000 debt and open a school in San Fernando.

Mother Dominic of the Cross, being fully aware of the heavy commitments of each Sister, felt that it was impossible at that time to establish a school in the South of Trinidad and told the Archbishop just this. Archbishop Gonin wrote back to express his displeasure at her refusal.

Fr. François Balme, O.P., sailed from France to Trinidad to discuss the issue with the Archbishop who finally agreed to dissociate the two foundations. Consequently, Mother Dominic accepted responsibility for St. Dominic's Orphanage and sent Mother Thomas Nigay as Prioress of the new community which she was to form with Sr. Marie and Sr. Jeanne.

On February 24, 1876, as the three Sisters, who had been lodged at Cocorite for the past four months, were about to leave for the Orphanage, a letter from Archbishop Gonin announced to the Prioress of Cocorite and Vicaress of the Prioress General in Trinidad that he had changed his mind and that the two foundations in Belmont and San Fernando had to be accepted together by the Dominican Sisters.

The *volte-face* of the Archbishop, to say the least, was incomprehensible. The long distance between Trinidad and France did not permit rapid communication with the Prioress General. The Vicaress of the Mission, knowing the mind of Mother Dominic about the situation and the crying needs at the Orphanage, took the decision to proceed with the work at St. Dominic's and sent the three Sisters there with the mission to take charge of the establishment. Two more Sisters joined the pioneers a little later.

In retaliation, the Archbishop refused to grant the right of canonical institution to the Dominican community until, he stated, the Sisters were willing to accept the San Fernando foundation. The two sides remained adamant in their respective positions and eventually the San Fernando foundation was taken over by the Sisters of St. Joseph of Cluny who opened a school there in 1882, and are still in San Fernando up to the present time.

Fr. Mariano Forestier had offered the ownership of the land of the Orphanage to his Dominican Sisters as he was confident that one day they would take away from him the heavy task of caring for the children. However, the Sisters did not think it right to accept the offer. Fr. Forestier then turned to the Archbishop and laid the matter before him. Archbishop Gonin bought the property under contract (registered No. 425 of 1871) in the name of the diocese on June 2, 1871.

At the Orphanage, the Sisters lost no time in reorganising the institution which comprised 66 children. The dedication of the staff could not be equalled. Financial assistance came from the Colonial Office grant, public charity, sale of agricultural produce grown on the property itself and, through Fr. Balme, within generous donations from Catholics in France interested in the welfare of the children. One year only, half of the debt had been repaid. The morale of the Sisters, staff and children was excellent. Msgr. O'Carroll compensated by his kind concern for the coldness of the Archbishop towards the Sisters.

The Governor of Trinidad, Sir Henry Turner Irving (1874-1880), on visiting the Orphanage was shocked at the dilapidated state of the shanty "cottage" in which the children and Sisters lived. Construction of a large and permanent dwelling was then decided upon. The Governor promised to make his contribution and a public subscription was opened.

Levelling of the ground was done by the Department of Public Works assisted by the senior boys. The work was very hard and the labourers few but God inspired generous men with the idea of lending a hand. They came from Belmont and from Maraval, five miles away. Bands of workers were formed — 88 men on the first expedition, 250 on the fifth and last one, comprising men, women and children.

This was the schedule each day: at 5 a.m., a small cannon gave the signal for Holy Mass in the Maraval church; afterwards they formed ranks outside in the church yard. The beloved pastor of Maraval, Fr. Alvarez, opened the march at the head of the first column; his people followed, the men carrying tools slung over their shoulders. By 7 a.m., the small battalion of God's workers had reached Belmont. After a short rest, the "captain" blessed them all and work started. Pickaxes struck the rebellious soil and spades gathered in heaps what had been dug out. Women and children removed the heaps with the help of wheelbarrows and buckets.

A bell announced the midday meal; there was a pause and work resumed until 3.30 p.m. Then Msgr. O'Carroll gave them Benediction of the Blessed Sacrament and all went back with their Padre to Maraval singing the Litany of Our Blessed Lady. The orphans accompanied them up to the St. Ann's Road junction. This wonderful gesture was repeated for five consecutive days and the residents in the neighbourhood of the

Orphanage followed the Maraval example.

On September 14, 1879, all three buildings comprising a house for the children, a small convent for the Sisters and a chapel, were completed. The construction had lasted a little over nine months. Ardent thanksgiving was offered to God for this remarkable work which He had obviously blessed.

Archbishop Gonin seized this occasion to impose on the Sisters a new system of administration of the Orphanage. The new rules were contained in a draft regulation which he presented to the Sisters. In this system the Sisters were to be reduced to the rank of salaried employees who could be dismissed according to his judgement. Without any warning, Archbishop Gonin imposed it on the Community during the absence of the Prioress who, due to illness, had to return to France for some rest.

The new system was to be operational within three weeks and if the Sisters complied with it the Archbishop was willing to give them canonical approval for their convent. The Sisters were dismayed; they managed to inform their Prioress General quickly who wrote the Archbishop to let him know of her disapproval of this system. The Archbishop was highly displeased. Fr. Balme once more sailed to Trinidad and saved the situation.

Msgr. O'Carroll, (who died in 1880), had donated a small house to the Dominican Sisters, situated next to the chapel of Laventille on Morne Leotaud, to enable them to rest in this pleasant area. The Sisters made good use of it. Suddenly, in 1886 Archbishop Gonin reproached the Sisters for leaving their convent and going to Laventille without his permission. He went so far as to forbid them from going to Laventille and should they disobey his instructions he was prepared to send them away from the diocese!

In the months that followed, some Sisters fell ill and had nowhere to go for a rest. Mother Dominic was told about the situation. Her concern was such that since the house belonged to the Sisters she gave them orders to go back to Laventille for a rest and she informed the Archbishop about her decision.

Until the death of Archbishop Gonin, which occurred in 1889, the situation between himself and the Sisters remained critical for he could not accept the authority of the Prioress General of the Congregation over the Sisters established in his diocese.

Archbishop Gonin was succeeded by Most Rev. Patrick Vincent Flood O.P. from Dublin, Ireland. He was the fifth Archbishop of Port of Spain. The Laventille house was repaired in 1906 and put up for sale in 1909.

At St. Dominic's, work increased year by year. The number of orphans kept growing. Between 1878 and 1913 the number doubled and reached 200. More houses had to be constructed. Each time Divine Providence sent generous benefactors to assist the Sisters and children.

Father François Balme O.P. the devoted friend and counsellor of the Foundress and of the Congregation for 45 years.

Chapter
11.

Reorganisation of
the Leprosarium at Cocorite

Mother Thomas Nigay O.P.
the great woman of Cocorite.

In 1897, while Sir H.E.H. Jerningham was Governor of Trinidad, the house occupied by the Dominican Sisters at the Cocorite Leprosarium was reconstructed and from then on the situation greatly improved. The convent stood in the centre of the 12 wards built around it. All in all, there were 252 patients and 13 Sisters. Between 1901 and 1904, ten more Sisters came from France to Cocorite. In 1921 the Leprosarium had 500 patients looked after by a staff of 23 Sisters and about 30 lay persons.

On April 9, 1906 the Port of Spain Legislative Council passed the following regulations for the management of the Leprosarium (Ordinance No. 194, section 6): "The nurses shall be chosen among the Sisters of the community and shall be under the direct authority of the Resident Superintendent who will be in every way responsible for their conduct and the manner in which they discharge their duties.

"The Resident Superintendent shall be under the immediate direction of the Medical Superintendent; she shall reside on the premises. In the absence of the Medical Superintendent she shall be first in authority and she shall see that all the instructions of the Medical Superintendent are carried out and shall be responsible to him for the good order, cleanliness and general discipline of the establishment, immediately reporting to him any matters of serious importance." These regulations were observed for many years.

A day in the lives of the Sisters was divided between prayer and work. Rising time was 4.30 a.m., followed by one hour of private prayer and Holy Mass. After breakfast, the Sisters started their work in the wards until noon. Prayer, lunch, a short recreation and then back to the wards until 4 p.m., when they gathered in the chapel for Vespers. Back to the wards again until the prayer of Compline at 6 p.m., followed by the Rosary, supper, recreation and the prayer of Matins at eight. Around nine p.m., was bed-time.

Every Monday some Sisters made themselves available to listen to people who came to the convent door asking for prayers. Sometimes as many as 60 would come to seek relief from their problems so great was their faith in the Sisters' prayers.

One of the Sisters, Mother Thomas Nigay, stands out for her extraordinary capability, zeal and devotedness as Superintendent of the Leprosarium, a post she held for 28 years. Having reached Trinidad on October 24, 1871, she went to Cocorite where she stayed for five years. In 1876 she was appointed Prioress of the St. Dominic's Orphanage in Belmont when the Dominican Sisters began to assume the responsibility for the establishment.

On May 14, 1885, Mother Thomas went back to Cocorite and the superintendence of the Leprosarium was entrusted to her with the charge of the priorship of the community. In all her 55 years of service in Trinidad, Mother Thomas returned only once to her native land, France, where she took a few months rest.

In September 1911, Dr. Fernand A. de Verteuil of Vancouver, British Columbia, Canada, wrote the following testimony about the work of the Dominican Sisters at Cocorite and of Mother Thomas in particular: "For six months I had the opportunity of working at the Asylum with my father, Dr. F.A. de Verteuil, the Medical Superintendent (for 15 years). I have seen these ladies day after day, without a word of complaint, with cheerful smiling countenances, dressing foetid ulcers, fleshy stumps — remains of what were once hands and feet — work from which even the most stouthearted would recoil in horror.

"Were there any experiments to be made and new drugs or treatment to be tried, any observations to note, they were ready and eager to devote to these extra hours of labour from a day of which almost every hour was already fully occupied. They carry out their work so quickly and unostentatiously, that apart from the yearly reports of the Medical Superintendents, little is heard of their doings even in the very island in which they labour. They shun all publicity, are reluctant to an extreme degree of allowing anything to be said or published in praise of their glorious, I should almost say divine, mission.

"Many have received during that memorable occasion — the coronation of King George V — honours and decorations. I venture to think that in the whole worldwide dominions of His Majesty there could not be found one worthier to receive some distinction than the head of the Trinidad Cocorite Asylum, Mother Thomas Nigay."

The cause had been well pleaded by the distinguished physician and it had its results in subsequent years. On December 16, 1921 the Superintendent of the Cocorite Leprosarium, Mother Thomas Nigay, was elected Honorary Serving Sister of the Grand Priory of the Order of the Hospital of St. John of Jerusalem in England. On February 3, 1914, she had also been awarded the gold medal for Public Assistance by the French Government.

Mother Thomas, according to Dominican Fathers Cothonay, Arnaud, Bariou, Bugnon, Guillet and Bisquey, her contemporaries in Trinidad, . . . "enjoyed the esteem, respect and affection of all. Protestants as well as Catholics incline profoundly before her who is in the eyes of all, the personification of religious virtue and Christian charity."

Two other Sisters, Rose Vebert and Marie Louise Percherancier, also received silver medals from the President of the Republic of France in 1919 and 1921 respectively.

Another person who can be singled out for the yeoman task he did at the Leprosarium was Fr. Etienne Brosse O.P., the second chaplain. Fr. Brosse came to Trinidad in 1867 and was appointed chaplain of the Leprosarium on November 10, 1869. During the 25 years he spent there this distinguished linguist, (he learned Hindustani and was fluent in it), did tremendous work both in ministering to the patients and Sisters as well as by his writings.

In 1879 his book *"La Lèpre est-elle contagieuse?"* (Is Leprosy Contagious?) was published and it caused great excitement in scientific circles. His description of leprosy gives an idea of the courage that was required to nurse patients affected by the disease in those days. He mentioned that one of the greatest discomforts was the offensive odour coming from the exhalations of putrefied wounds. The smell used to cling to the clothes, the hands and the entire body. Even after the changing of clothes the smell remained and after washing several times with vinegar it still persisted.

The works of Fr. Brosse, *"Le Site d'Eden"* (The site of Eden); *"L'Aurore Indienne"* (Indian Dawn); *"L'Inde Incon-*

nue" (Unknown India) and the *"Chamites"* were all treatises on comparative philology which were "much more serious" wrote Fr. M.J. Guillet O.P., in the 95th article of his series *"Fragments of the Past"* (1864-1914)" than those of a scholar who knows languages only from books and writes about them shut up in his room. Fr. Etienne received them from living beings, heard and took down the words from their mouths. One can understand, therefore, the words of praise of the celebrated English orientalist, Sir W. Monier Williams, who said on the publication of *"Les Chamites"* that the author was "20 years ahead of the science of the present day".

On January 22, 1894, Archbishop Patrick Vincent Flood O.P., removed Fr. Etienne from his position as chaplain of the Leprosarium: he was then 74 years of age. He spent the remaining seven years of his life in the Cathedral presbytery in Port of Spain giving much of his time to hearing confessions in the cathedral. Fr. Brosse died peacefully on November 18, 1900. During his 33 years in Trinidad he had not returned once to visit his homeland, France.

Chapter
12.

The Birth of Holy Name Convent
in Port of Spain

*The old Bolivar College which became the
Holy Name Convent in 1890.*

The Archbishop, The Most Rev. Patrick Vincent Flood, well disposed towards the Dominican Sisters and their Prioress General Mother Dominic Gand, wanted with their co-operation to reorganise the St. Dominic's Orphanage in Belmont.

The Colonial Government was pressing for the foundation of a reformatory for boys, and the Archbishop thought that the best place would be on the grounds of the Orphanage. However, to put this plan into action it was necessary to remove the girls, and the Archbishop, who was about to depart for Europe, was hoping to find there some male religious Congregation willing to take charge of the boys. Once more, Divine Providence intervened in the planning.

In the Port of Spain of the 1880's there lived a kind and wealthy widow, Hannah Campbell, nee Murphy, who had suffered the cruel death of her husband in 1884. Her only consolation was his conversion to the Catholic faith shortly before his death. In thanksgiving to God for this extraordinary favour, after making a retreat with the Dominican Sisters in Belmont, Mrs. Campbell resolved to devote herself to works of charity.

In the course of a trip to France she paid a visit to the Dominican Sisters at their new Mother-house in Normandy. Their beautiful convent in Etrepagny was the treasured gift of a young widow, Isabelle de Vatimesnil, whose husband returned to the faith in tragic circumstances. After his death, she used some of her wealth to build a convent for the Dominican Sisters.

On hearing this, Mrs. Campbell was struck by the similarity of her life with that of the French lady and decided to imitate her. On her return to Trinidad, after learning that Archbishop Flood wanted to reorganise the Orphanage and that the Sisters and the girls would need a new place, Mrs. Campbell began to look for a house for them.

At No. 32 St. Ann's Road, bordering part of the large Savannah of Port of Spain was a college known as "Maison Bolivar" which eventually became the property of Dr. Pedro Luis Montbrun. It measured 348 metres in length and 44 metres in width. In later years, the St. Ann's Road was renamed

'Queen's Park East' and the No. 2 was designated to the site of the "Maison Bolivar". In 1889 it was put up for sale.

The property consisted of a handsome dwelling house (14 by 7 metres), a hall (85 by 27 metres) and a house for boarders (27 by 10 metres). The entrance was enhanced by a large portal which opened on a 50-metre driveway leading to a fountain in front of the main house. The houses were in need of repair. Mrs. Campbell found that the property was suitable to house the Sisters and the girls of the Orphanage and bought it for the sum of 15,300 pounds sterling. In a letter to Archbishop Flood, dated April 18, 1889, Mrs. Campbell wrote the following:

"It is my wish that the Bolivar College should become the Private property of the Sisters and be handed over to them absolutely with the sole condition that during their stay in Trinidad some charitable work is to be carried on by them there. Should the Sisters be recalled to France they can sell this property and take the proceeds with them."

Without delay, Mrs. Campbell engaged herself in the transformation and repairs of the houses. The main dwelling house was to become the convent; the boarders' house was to be for the girls and the hall was to be used as a chapel. Fr. Kurman C.S.Sp., gave her all his assistance in artistically arranging it as a place of worship and he himself built the altar. The chapel was blessed on June 28, 1889, for the feast of the Sacred Heart. On that day the "Maison Bolivar" had become the Holy Name Convent; however, the Sisters did not take possession of it immediately.

On his return from Europe, Archbishop Flood expressed his regret at not having been able to find a male Congregation of Religious willing to take charge of the boys of St. Dominic's. From Etrépagny, Mother Dominic wrote the Archbishop to propose to him that only the senior girls should be transferred to another house (Holy Name Convent) and that the Orphanage should then be re-organised to suit his plan. The solution was accepted by the Archbishop.

The transfer of property and the inauguration of Holy Name Convent took place on March 21, 1890, the date chosen to coincide with the 50th anniversary of the religious profession of Mother Dominic of the Cross. For this very special occasion she decided to come to Trinidad. For 25 years she had dealt with some of the religious affairs of this distant country: she had sent out a number of her daughters, some of them had died heroic deaths, it was time, therefore that she herself got to know this beloved country and its people. Her heart lept for joy at the thought of it.

At the age of 70 Mother Dominic sailed from France on September 26, 1889 to Trinidad where she was going to stay for six months. She was accompanied by Sr. Marie Patrice Andre, one of the first vocations from Trinidad, if not the first.

On her arrival, Mother Dominic was overjoyed at seeing her dear daughters, their works, their many friends and the people of Trinidad as a whole. The English newspaper of the day, *The Public Opinion,* had these comments about the visit of the Prioress General: "The good Mother seems to enjoy our climate; she likes the Creoles' character, a character which is open, frank and sympathetic. This is what she has had many occasions to notice during her stay among us. On our side, we have greatly appreciated the pleasant and religious manners of this distinguished and revered Mother Superior."

After visiting the three convents of the Congregation in Trinidad and witnessing the grand celebrations to mark her golden jubilee and the inauguration of Holy Name Convent, on March 21, 1890, Mother Dominic and her companion embarked on the "Venezuela" on April 7 Easter Monday. They arrived in France safely on April 24. On August 15 of that same year, the foundress had another great joy, that of receiving from the Holy See in Rome final approval of the Constitutions of her Congregation. Had she then completed the work the Lord had chosen her to do? Not yet; she was given 17 more years to live, which time she occupied in consolidating whatever had already been accomplished.

The beginnings at Holy Name Convent were marked by austere poverty. To give an idea — the menu on March 21, day of the grand celebrations, consisted of an omelette, salt-fish and potatoes. Mrs. Campbell, having been informed of this, sent her coachman to the convent with a large salmon deliciously prepared!

Among the Sisters, there were some artists who used their talents to make a living. The sales of their paintings, embroidery and handicraft brought some modest revenue to the Community. They also taught these skills to the girls, and Holy Name Convent became renowned for artistic works.

In those days there was no boundary between the convent and the Colonial Hospital situated side by side. The Sisters petitioned the Governor to have a wall built between the two properties. The request was granted and a wall was constructed in April 1890 at a cost of 229 pounds sterling; half of the sum had to be paid by the Sisters.

In the early 1890's, Archbishop Flood asked the Sisters to help Fr. Sutherland O.P., to run the Catholic Printery founded in 1881. The Sisters accepted and the printery was set up on the grounds of Holy Name Convent. Fr. Sutherland and a tradesman initiated into the printing work some of the Sisters and 20 girls who had been transferred from St. Dominic's Orphanage to Holy Name. At that time, the Catholic Printery was producing catechims, (an average of 300 a week), in Spanish and Hindi, as well as invitations, poems, missals and the Archbishop's pastoral letters in Spanish and English.

Archbishop Flood was concerned that there were only Protestant newspapers in the country and was anxious to start a Catholic newspaper for the archdiocese. This he did with the help of Fr. Hilaire Arnaud O.P., The first editor was a layman, Charles J. Williams and the first six-page edition came out on May 6, 1892 at a cost of one penny. Sr. Rose de Ste. Marie Vebert was then in charge of the printery.

On January 31, 1910, the printery was transferred to No. 34 Belmont Circular Road, in a wooden building situated at the foot of the hill of St. Dominic's Orphanage. From then on until 1974 when the printery was closed down, apprentices were recruited from the senior boys of the Orphanage and the printing of the *Catholic News* has continued all through these years. From 1974, to the present day, the *Catholic News* has been printed by other printeries but is still published by the Roman Catholic Archbishop of Port of Spain.

Four young women from Venezuela were among the first vocations to join the Dominican Sisters in Trinidad.

The benefactress, Mrs. Hannah Campbell, lived close to the Sisters and frequently visited them taking a keen interest in all their works as well as in their health. Until her death she continued to procure for them the necessary means to complement what they and the girls earned for their livelihood. In 1891, invited by Fr. Hilaire Arnaud, the Sisters undertook the visiting of patients at the Colonial Hospital, a work particularly dear to the heart of Mrs. Campbell and which they continued for many years. In 1894, there was another outbreak of the dreaded yellow fever epidemic and one of the Sisters fell victim to it. Archbishop Flood ordered that all the Sisters and the girls at Holy Name Convent evacuate the premises at once.

They moved to the Sisters' house at Laventille where they stayed while the Health Office had the houses of Holy Name Convent fumigated.

Memento of Mother Dominic's
Golden Jubilee of religious profession.

Mother Dominic of the Cross renews her vows on the day of her Golden Jubilee at Holy Name. Behind her is Mrs. Hannah Campbell, the benefactress.

The façade of the Bolivar College which became Holy Name Convent, with the chapel at right.

Chapter
13.

Volcano of Death Stirs Life - a New School Opens

*The Devenish house bought by the Dominican Sisters in 1907
to establish a school named 'Notre Dame'.*

As related by H.C. Pitts in his *100 Years Together*, the end of the 19th century and the beginning of the 20th were marked by important events in Trinidad, and in the Eastern Caribbean as well. On January 1, 1889, an Order in Council uniting the British colonies of Trinidad and Tobago came into effect. That same year, the first aeronautical experiments were made in Trinidad and witnessed by large crowds at Shine's Pasture during the month of November when a member of Donovan's Circus, then visiting the country, ascended in a balloon to a height of 500 feet.

October 28, 1890 was declared a public holiday to celebrate the opening of Trinidad's first great industrial exhibition. Thousands crowded the vicinity of the Princes Building where Governor Sir William Robertson performed the inauguration ceremony. The exhibition consisted of a wide range of agricultural and industrial displays.

At Cocorite, celebrations were held on April 12, 1893 to mark the 25th anniversary of the arrival of the Dominican Sisters in Trinidad for the management of the Leprosarium. The sole survivor of the original group of Sisters was presented with a purse and an address.

On March 4, 1895, at about 4.30 p.m., while most of the town was watching cricket played by an English team versus "All Trinidad", huge clouds of smoke were seen coming from the premises of Messrs. James Todd & Sons situated between Henry and Frederick Streets, Port of Spain. The Fire Brigade was slow to arrive and when they did, some time elapsed before water could be obtained.

The flames soon crossed both streets and the heart of the town was consumed by fire. So enormous was the fire that 300 sailors and marines were landed from H.M.S. "Buzzard" and the U.S. cruisers "New York", "Cincinnati" and "Raleigh" then in port. Strong measures were necessary to clear the streets of thousands of excited citizens.

When water and other usual means were found ineffective, the men from the ships blew up several buildings with explosives and so eventually managed to check the devastation. A count on the morning of March 5 revealed that 57 business houses and residences on Frederick, King, Queen, Henry and

Chacon Streets had been burnt. Damage was estimated at 750,000 pounds sterling. The origin of the fire remained a mystery. Despite the great fire the "All Trinidad" team won the cricket match!.

On that March 5, 1895, at 8.30 p.m., the streets of Port of Spain were lit by electric light for the first time. Electricity changed the mode of transport when new electric trams were tried on May 18, (at midnight), to replace the traditional mule cars. Lady Broome, wife of the Governor, formally opened the Belmont Tramway Line on June 26, 1895. The three carriages of the company were gaily bedecked for the occasion and the press remarked that "the rate of speed was very high, fully 15 miles an hour"!

In the Caribbean island of Martinique there had also been a huge fire on June 22, 1890 but the disaster was nothing compared to the formidable eruption of Mount Pelée volcano on May 8, 1902 which destroyed the city of St. Pierre killing some 40,000 people. The only survivor, a man named Siparis, was found in a cell in the city prison. The Soufrière volcano on the island of St. Vincent erupted as well. News of both eruptions reached Trinidad on May 11 and three days later there was a solemn requiem Mass in the Cathedral of the Immaculate Conception for the repose of the souls of the victims.

One of the repercussions of the volcanic eruption in Martinique was felt in Trinidad at Holy Name Convent. Shortly after the cataclysm, Mr. Soleau, a Frenchman, a friend and benefactor of the Sisters, brought a young girl, Leonie Marie Raynaud, to the convent; her parents and relatives had perished in the eruption. Mr. Soleau entrusted Leonie to the care and protection of the Sisters who undertook the responsibility for her education.

Very soon, news spread in Port of Spain and environs that the Dominican Sisters of Holy Name were giving private lessons to a young Martiniquan girl. Several parents, who wanted to give a French education to their daughters petitioned the Sisters to start a private school. Their request was granted. The numbers kept increasing; from 10 pupils in 1904 to 22 in 1905 and 30 in 1908. The private school was indeed established in 1902. It was registered as a Private School much later, on May 8, 1936.

The presence of the Dominican Sisters at No. 32 St. Ann's Road had drawn many people to their chapel; and with the addition of pupils from the school, it became imperative to build a new and larger chapel. But where would they find the funds for construction? That was the big question.

Mother Rose Vébert, then Prioress of Holy Name Convent, launched a campaign of prayers among the Sisters and the children. Our Blessed Lady was declared "Heavenly Treasurer" of the project. Not only did donations arrive but voluntary service as well, professionals such as from Mr. Baccarcich, a government architect; Mr. Barsotti, also an architect from Italy, and a friend of the former; and Mr. Cazabon who designed the beautiful interior decoration of the chapel.

On December 8, 1904, the foundation-stone of the new chapel was laid. While men were at work on the construction site, Sisters and children kept praying the Rosary in turns. Generous benefactors brought many donations: Mrs. Cipriani donated the fine black and white tiles, which were imported from Barcelona. Her husband, Mr. Eugene Cipriani, offered a bell which was named after them — "Charlotte-Eugenie" and blessed by Archbishop Flood on February 4, 1907. Mrs. Hannah Campbell, who was then suffering with ill health, put her last resources towards the purchase of a superb marble altar ordered from Carrara and columns of red marble from Verona, Italy.

The construction of the Holy Name chapel, regarded as a gem of architecture, was not without its moments of great sadness, such as when Mr. Baccarcich, who had climbed onto the roof to inspect the work, fell to his death. Soon after, Mr. Cazabon was overcome with fever and died on November 30, 1905, fully resigned to God's will. Many prayers and Masses were offered for the repose of their souls and the consolation of their families.

Sorrows however, were followed by many joys. Construction and decoration work was coming to an end but donations continued to pour in for the furnishing of the chapel. Three ladies particularly were outstanding in their generosity — Mesdames Cipriani, Agostini and Johnson.

The solemn blessing of the new chapel took place on February 11, 1906. Archbishop Flood celebrated the Eucharist on the exquisite marble altar for the first time with a special remembrance for Messrs. Baccarcich and Cazabon. The chapel in all its whiteness was like "a bride adorned for her spouse" and the Archbishop blessed both inside and outside its walls. Many priests, religious, friends and benefactors were present at the celebration and rejoiced with the Sisters for this sacred edifice.

But more sorrow came when a telegram arrived announcing the death of the venerated Foundress, Mother Dominic of the Cross Gand. After a long life of struggle, (she was 87 years old), Mother Dominic entered her eternity in total peace and serenity, when the morning bell of the Angelus rang on February 2, 1907. Her death in France was followed on March 17, by that of Miss Le Roy in Trinidad, the devoted friend and benefactress of St. Dominic's Orphanage, and the following day it was the turn of Mrs. Hannah Campbell to go to her God. She died in her sleep.

Finally, on May 17, 1907, Archbishop Flood died on his return from Toco where he had gone to administer the sacrament of confirmation. This prelate had made a great impact on the Church by his powerful preaching. He had been the Archbishop of Port of Spain for 18 years and it was during his time that the Archbishop's House, at No. 27 Maraval Road, was built.

At No. 33 St. Ann's Road, adjoining the Holy Name Convent, was the Devenish property. It consisted of a solid dwelling house 16 metres by 6 and was built in the 1840's; close by were the servants' quarters. An ornamented portal opened on a long drive bordered by beautiful trees ending at a fountain surrounded by rose beds in front of the house. Behind the house there was an orchard with many fruit trees, and further down, towards the Dry River, the area was forested.

The Dominican Sisters really needed a house for their school which was growing and they were hoping and praying that one day they could acquire this fine property. Their prayers did not remain unanswered. Mr. J.B.D. Sellier, a friend of the school and an experienced solicitor, successfully con-

ducted the transaction and Mrs. Marie Devenish finally agreed
to sell her property to the Sisters for the sum of $16,000.

The Deed of Conveyance was signed on July 27, 1907. To
raise the necessary funds, the Sisters were authorised by
the Holy See to take a $10,000 loan from a bank, and the land
and house at Laventille were sold to pay part of the debt.
Later on when the street was renamed, this property became
No. 3 Queen's Park East.

The organisation of the school on its new premises
started with the opening of a door in the fence between the
two properties to establish communication. The house was
named "Pavillon Notre Dame" and the elegant structure
embellished with fretwork was admirably suited for this
purpose.

The Holy Name Printery was installed in the servants'
quarters. With the help of the senior girls of the Holy Name
Training Centre and some senior boys of the St. Dominic's
Orphanage, (everyday some came to the printery to learn the
trade); a vegetable garden was started which became a real
bread-basket in subsequent years.

Tracks were cut in the forested area and cocoa, coffee
and banana trees were planted. Within a few years the whole
property had become very productive. Elderly Sisters of today
still remember the delicious fruit they enjoyed at Holy Name
Convent.

Group of pupils in the 1920's with Sr. Marie Yolande O.P.

Group of pupils with Sr. Genevieve and Sr. Marie Elise Camp O.P.

Chapter
14.

Two World Wars

Life at the Holy Name Convent School in Port of Spain was inevitably bound to national and international events of importance. On July 31, 1914 news reached Trinidad that war had been declared between France and Germany. As the German armies invaded Luxembourg; England and Russia joined in the battle.

Because of its magnitude, this war was to be called the First World War and it had its repercussions in Trinidad and Tobago. On August 3, 1914, a German ship moored at the Port of Spain wharf and the captain asked that he be provided with coal. Enraged by a refusal by Order of the British Governor, Sir John Chancellor, the German captain declared: "Then we will take it!"

Three days later, martial law was proclaimed in Trinidad and Tobago and as a result 1,000 men were recruited and submitted to intense training to guard the port. A few days later, two German warships were sighted in the Serpent's Mouth near Icacos; but the presence of two American destroyers protected Trinidad.

Isolation on account of the war caused food shortages
throughout the country and prices of goods escalated. The
lack of communication with France made the Dominican
Sisters anxious about the safety of their families and convents
in France.

On September 1, 1914, the Notre Dame School was
reopened but with fewer pupils because a number of them had
gone to Venezuela with their families for security reasons. On
September 4, the news that the Germans were marching on
Paris and that some of the sons of French families in Trinidad
had either died or been captured in France, brought much sadness to the population here.

In 1915, Mr. Eugene Cipriani died and the following
year, his widow. Both had left legacies to build a new convent
for the Dominican Sisters at Holy Name as the old Bolivar
House was falling into ruins.

After four years of cruel war, during which over three
and a half million men died on battle-fields, France emerged
victorious but bleeding. She had lost the flower of her youth.
Communication with Trinidad and Tobago and the outside
world was gradually re-established.

A young professed, Sister Thomas of the Rosary, born
and educated in England, had joined the French Dominican
Sisters in Etrepagny, France, and volunteered to come to Trinidad. She arrived at Holy Name Convent after the war and
was put in charge of the Notre Dame school. She organised the
curriculum in such a way as to prepare students for the Cambridge Examinations affiliated to that University.

In order to compare the standard of studies in Trinidad
with the corresponding forms in the schools in England, Sr.
Thomas had the students tested by the Sheffield Board of
Examinations and this proved to be a real stimulus for them.
This arrangement lasted until communications with Europe
were once more disrupted by another war — World War II
(1939 - 1945). In 1925 the first candidates presented at the
Cambridge examinations were all successful at the Junior
and Senior levels.

On the feast of St. Joseph, (March 19, 1920), the Sisters
at Holy Name had the scare of their lives. At 4.00 a.m., just

across Memorial Park, strange crackling noises awoke them. The whole sky was red with sparks flaring upwards. The Victoria Institute was ablaze, and in less than an hour, it was reduced to ashes. All the precious collections — a wealth of national heritage — had been destroyed. A terrible loss.

In 1926, to satisfy the needs of parents asking for a boarding school, a one-storey house was built quickly at the back of the 'Pavillon Notre Dame' to accommodate the Community during the demolition of the old convent, (the Bolivar House), and the construction of the new one. The same architect, Mr. Newbold, who had just completed the new convent for the Dominican Sisters at Chacachacare, was retained to build the one at Holy Name. The foundation stone was laid on February 25, 1927.

Within 18 months the convent was completed, and the blessing, by Fr. Casey O.P., Vicar General of the Archdiocese, took place on September 25, 1928. Soon the Sisters settled into their new home and the boarding school opened its doors to 15 boarders for the beginning of a new term on January 1929.

Sr. Thomas, who had done so well in reorganising the school, fell seriously ill; but the Lord provided a replacement. The Prioress General, Mother Therese Isabelle, sent six Sisters to work in Trinidad and five of them were assigned to Holy Name Convent. Among them was Sr. Marie Benedicte, a refined English lady, who had all the qualifications to manage the school. A true sports-woman, a born teacher, an artist, a most lively person, Sr. Marie Benedicte soon became the favourite of the pupils. When she returned to France in 1931, the Holy Name School numbered 134 day pupils and 28 boarders.

It is interesting to note that in the 1930's the Holy Name Community consisted of 21 Sisters from the following countries: France (13); England (2); Switzerland (2); Trinidad and Tobago (1); Venezuela (1); Algeria (1) and Egypt (1). A mini multi-ethnicity United Nation's and very typical of Trinidad.

The year 1928 was marked by a dreadful hurricane which, on September 12 and 13, caused 1,000 deaths and rendered 1,500,000 people homeless in Guadeloupe, Saint Lucia, St. Kitts, Haiti and Florida. A few days later, on September

26, Trinidad was rocked by a prolonged earthquake which caused much fear but claimed no victims. There was only minor damage.

Among the five Sisters newly arrived was Sr. Jeanne Emmanuel Barrière from Paris. She was then 26 years old and was asked to teach at the school shortly after her arrival. In 1938, Sr. Jeanne Emmanuel accepted the post of School Principal. To obtain the necessary qualifications she resumed her studies under the most trying circumstances. After four years of persevering efforts, she succeeded in her final exams and received the Bachelor of Arts degree with Honours.

Sr. Jeanne Emmanuel carried the responsibility of the school with great courage and efficiency for 23 years. During that time many improvements were made and extra-curricular activities were innovated. "Mother Jeanne", as the pupils called her, left her imprint on Holy Name Convent School as well as others as we shall see later.

Once again there were rumours of war in Europe. On September 1, 1939, the troops of Adolf Hitler of Germany invaded Poland. British and French armies went to the rescue of the Polish people. War was practically on without being officially declared. France and England gave an ultimatum to Hilter to withdraw his troops from Poland. On his refusal, on September 3, 1939, France and England declared war on Germany. On September 11, Canada joined these two countries in the fight against Germany.

In Trinidad and Tobago precautions were taken in case of air bombardment. Every night at 9.00 p.m. there was to be complete darkness. At the sound of the sirens, all lights were to be camouflaged and the population went through a drill for 15 minutes.

At sea, ships were torpedoed, and as a result, maritime traffic came to a halt. There were German submarines in the Caribbean Sea. Archbishop Finbar Ryan, who was in Europe at the declaration of war, made an attempt to return to Trinidad by sea but the ship on which he was sailing was stopped at the Azores and the passengers trans-shipped to Lisbon in Portugal. However, four Dominican Fathers managed to reach Trinidad via New York. They had taken a great risk.

In 1940, because of the importance of its oil industry, Trinidad was considered vulnerable to enemy raids. The presence of German submarines - the redoubtable 'U-Boats' — in the Eastern Caribbean Sea was a serious threat to navigation. According to information received, a loop system of anti-submarine detection was installed to control the Serpent's and Dragon's Mouths. Submarine networks were set in Bocas One, Two and Three of the Dragon's Mouth blocking the three Passages permanently. The nets were anchored in the seabed and held up by buoys on the surface.

There was need for constant maintenance on account of the strong currents in this area. When clearance for entry into the Gulf of Paria was given, ship convoys passed through the Boca Grande, between Chacachacare Island and the Venezuelan coast. There was the case of a German submarine which, must have sneaked past under a ship and which afterwards sank two ships at the Port of Spain anchorage. No one ever heard how the submarine escaped, presumably the same way as it had come in.*

News from Europe became all the more alarming when Italy entered the war in June 1940 and German troops were only 70 km from Etrépagny. All the Sisters' minds were on what could happen to their French Sisters there. Fervent prayers were offered for them asking God to protect them in a very special way.

On June 14, 1940, the Germans were marching in the direction of Paris but they were prevented from reaching the capital by the Americans; and the French Resistance army, under the command of General Charles de Gaulle, attacked the Germans at strategic points. Germany was defeated. On May 8, 1945 at 9.00 a.m., sirens and church bells in Trinidad announced the Armistice. However, joy was mixed with sadness because the Americans were still at war with Japan and three months later there was to be the horrible nuclear holocaust of the cities of Hiroshima and Nagasaki by the American Air Force.

After the armistice had been signed, the Sisters in Trini-

*   For full details see book "U-Boat War in the Caribbean" by Gaylord T.M. Kelshall — Paria Publishing Co. Trinidad — 1988.

dad began to receive news from France. They learned with great sorrow how their Sisters had suffered. Etrépagny had been bombed by the Germans, the convent included. The Sisters, young and old, had to flee for safety and found themselves among the thousands of refugees making their way, often on foot, to the south of France where they took refuge. On the roads they had been exposed to bombing and strafing.

They all had gone through most crucial times but none of them had been killed or seriously injured. Sr. Marie Benedict Hadfield who was in France during the Second World War was imprisoned by the Germans on account of her British nationality. Three of the convents had been damaged and occupied by German troops; and, even after their repair, it took the French Sisters months to return to normal living.

The post-World War II era was to be quite different from previous times, as we shall see further on.

Principal Sr. Jeanne Emmanuel, Sr. Monique Moniquette, teachers and pupils of Holy Name in the late 1940's.

Map of the Caribbean War by Gaylord T.M. Kelsball.

SHIPPING LOSSES — TRINIDAD AREA
1942 – 1943

SUNK ●
DAMAGED ⊕

ATLANTIC OCEAN

CARIBBEAN SEA

WAIN RIVER

ORINOCO DELTA

DRAGON'S MOUTH

SERPENT'S MOUTH

ST. LUCIA CHANNEL

ST. VINCENT PASSAGE

MARTINIQUE PASSAGE

GALLEONS PASSAGE

CITY OF MELBOURNE
WEST KEHAR
KLUBEN TIPTON
BAGHDAD
PRIMERO
APALOIDE
ROTHLY
TORTUGAS
NURMAHAL
ATHELEMPRESS
BARBACENA
EMPIRE STARLING
CRANFORD
BILL
DRACO
SIR HUON
ESSO COPENHAGEN ⊕
STEEL TRAVELLER ⊕
MAKY
STRABO
COLLINGSWORTH
SAN EMILIANO
ALIPORE
ANTONICO
BIRMINGHAM CITY
STEEL AGE
BAYOU
FRANK SEAMENS
MONTE GORBEA
THELMA
MOENA
BRITISH COLONY
WEST IRA
REGISTAN
ESSO HOUSTON
LA CORDILLERA
KENTAR
CLAN MAC NAUGHTON
TRICULA
BETH
POLYBIUS
TREMINARD
FARNAHYBA
WEST LASHAWAY
BRENAS
WINAMAC
HAVSTEN
PLAVE
PIAVE
WEST CHETAC
SOLON II
MINOTAUR
REEDPOOL
NORFOLK
PENELOPE
LIHUE
NORMAN PRINCE
DELPLATA
PRESIDENTE TRUJILLO
TORONDOC
BLAKELY ⊕
LADY NELSON ⊕
UMTATA ⊕
CGC
MTB
ALEGRATE
WATSONVILLE
MONTE GORBEA
LEIV ERIKSSON
CORNWALLIS
KORTHION
ANDREA BROVIG
LILIAN
MONA MARIE
STAR OF OREGON
KASTOR
GLACIER
COMRADE
WEIRBANK
CHALLENGER
SANDAR ⊕
KING ARTHUR
GILBERT B. WALTERS
ACHILLES
TELAMON
TRINTADON
CITY OF BAYAMO
EMPIRE CROMWELL
WEST ZEDA
GEORGE G. HENRY
TORRAIN
ALCOA TRANSPORT
CITY OF RIPON
PRESCODOC
NIGERIAN
LENNOX
MONT LOUIS
MAE
FLORENCE M. DOUGLAS
EASTERN SWORD
PRESIDENT KOPATIC
WILLIAM A. MC KENNY
CARIBSTAR
ANDROID
EMPIRE FENNYSON
LINDVANGEN
ALCOA ANTIGUOUS
ALCOA MARINER
CLAN MAC FAYDEN
TAMBOUR
ATHELBRAN
NORLANTIC
NATHANIEL HAWTHORNE
HEINRICH VON REIDMAN
EMPIRE LUGGARD
THORSHAVET
GYPSUM EXPRESS
WEST CELINA
KAHUKU
LINDENHALL
COLD HARBOUR
SCOTSBURG
THOMAS B. SCHALL
FRED R. KELLOGG
SURINAME
ELLIOT
VILLA
C.S. FLIGHT
M.F. ELLIOT
UNIWALECO
EMPIRE CLOUD
CIR. KAMPMANN
HAN SADAAM
BRITISH CONSUL
SAN VICTORIA
HARRY G. SEIDEL
CIRCLE SHELL
LEDA
BRABANT
MOKIHANA
BRITISH CONSUL
FAN GULF
MACABI
SYLVAN ARROW
WEST HARDAWAY
AMSTERDAM
MARGARETA
CARONA
EMPIRE EXPLORER
NIDARNELAND ⊕
QUEBEC ⊕
VINDALE
TAMANDARE
CAPE VERDE
FLOTO
GEO. W. MC KNIGHT
WINONA
CASTLE HARBOUR
BEACONLIGHT
ARUCA
CITY OF CORINTH
CAPO OLMO ⊕
BONAYANIA
WARRIOR
OCEAN VANGUARD
PADEREWSKI
SORHAULT
NIMBA
COMMERCIAL TRADER
TELMWORLS
SAN GASPER ⊕
STANVAC MELBOURNE
OREMONSSON
HAVARD
HARBOROUGH
OCEAN JUSTICE
NORDVANGEN

Chapter
15.

Life in the 1900's
at the Leprosarium in Cocorite

*New convent for the Dominican Sisters at Cocorite built by
the Government in 1897. At right, the chapel.*

What was life like in the Cocorite Leprosarium in the
1900's? Thanks to the Sisters who were keeping a diary of
events, we are able today to have a glimpse into those days.

First of all, the Sisters recorded their appreciation for
their new convent which had been built by the government in
1897. It was situated in the centre of the institution and
adjoined the chapel. Another improvement was an adequate
supply of potable water. For 38 years, the Sisters had suffered
from a serious water shortage, especially during the dry season,
by 1906 however, they were able to enjoy a shower bath
instead of using the traditional bucket and calabash.

Safety was also ensured for them when barricades were
affixed to the doors of their dormitory to protect the Community against nocturnal incursions by mentally sick patients.
A house had been built for a warden responsible for the security of the Asylum. Rose trees, planted by the 'green' fingers
of a Sister, bloomed at the entrance of the institution. An
average of 300 patients were accommodated in 12 wards and
the community consisted of 15 to 17 Sisters.

In 1905, and again in 1906, over 100 patients asked to
return to India and the Government of Trinidad acceded to
their request. Before leaving the Leprosarium, though Hindus,
they all went into the chapel and asked the chaplain's blessing
for their long journey.

The Sisters, who used to pray the Rosary with patients
in the Hindi language — one decade in the following languages:
Latin, French, English and Hindi — sang the hymn "Ave Maris
Stella" in Hindi for them. This hymn implores Mary to be the
"Star of the Sea" for voyagers. How patients suffering from
leprosy, even if the disease was in the first stages, could be
allowed to travel in such a condition is beyond comprehen-
sion. The fact is that they *did* leave Trinidad for India, the
voyage lasting about two months at that time.

In 1910, Governor Sir George Le Hunte, a friend of the
Leprosarium, said to the Sisters in the course of one of his
regular visits: "This institution brings a pleasant remembrance
to me. I began my career 35 years ago as private secretary of a
governor who had previously been in Trinidad — I refer to Sir
Arthur Gordon, now Lord Stanmore — and I will not fail to

tell him how he is still remembered here."

"Recently when I saw him in England he told me of the wretched condition in which he found this Asylum in 1866, and how, after consulting the Archbishop of Port of Spain, he asked for nuns to take charge of it. His request was fulfilled and succeeded beyond expectation."

The Sisters taught handicraft and embroidery to those patients who still had the use of their fingers. In 1910 they established the first praesidium of the Legion of Mary in the Leprosarium. The same year a new medical doctor was appointed in the person of Dr. Ferdinand de Verteuil; his son, Dr. Fernand A. de Verteuil, established in Vancouver, Canada, came to assist him for a few months as bacteriologist during which time he trained a Sister for laboratory work. At that time the drugs used to fight the disease were "Mastin" and another called "606".

Patients had done so many excellent works in the year 1921 that it was decided to hold an exhibition of garden produce, handicraft, honey, wax and eggs. The patron was the Governor himself who received a rousing welcome by the band conducted by one of the Sisters, Sr. Marie Emmanuel, a gifted musician who could play almost any instrument.

Life at the Cocorite Leprosarium had by then become so well organised that it seemed it could continue for ever. However, the year 1915 saw the beginning of drastic changes. An important medical conference had been held in Bergen, Norway, where it was declared that leprosy was a contagious disease necessitating the segregation and isolation of patients suffering from it. This declaration had its repercussions in Trinidad and Tobago.

On September 1, 1915, the Colonial Government passed a law requiring all persons suffering from leprosy to be either isolated in their own houses or to seek admission at the Cocorite Leprosarium. Those found outdoors were forcefully taken to the institution. From then on the number of patients at the Leprosarium kept increasing (71 admissions between September 1 and December 31, 1915). The government then allocated funds for the construction of three more wards, one for females and two for males.

An amusing incident was entered in the Sisters' diary: "The beginning of 1922 marked the election in Rome of another successor of St. Peter. It was on February 6, 1922 at 7.30 a.m. that the radio announced that Pius XI was the new Pope of the Catholic Church. Filled with joy, the Sisters rang their convent bell to pass on the news which quickly spread throughout the patients' wards.

"However, in passing the word someone made a distortion and the message 'Pius XI is the new Pope' became 'Fire in the children's ward'! This of course caused a panic; cries and more cries were heard and in the haste to reach there one could not find his clothes, another his crutches etc. Some were smelling smoke and others seeing flames! Fortunately the truth came out and this gave rise to peals of laughter!"

In 1922, among the patients admitted was Fr. Julien Bouche, a well known Dominican priest. Fr. Bouche was born in France in 1857. He became a member of the Dominican Order in 1876 and volunteered to come to Trinidad where he arrived in 1892. After four years of ministry at the Cathedral of the Immaculate Conception, he was appointed Chaplain of the Cocorite Leprosarium and Vicar of St. James' parish.

As there was no Catholic church in St. James, he had one built, as well as two schools. He learnt Hindi and a Chinese dialect which helped him in his ministry to the patients. After spending six years at Cocorite and St. James, Fr. Bouche, who was fluent in Spanish, was sent to Cuba in 1902. Called back to France, he pleaded to return to Trinidad and was again in Port of Spain in 1909.

On his return, it was discovered that he had contracted leprosy. Dr. Raoul Scheult, who was then Medical Superintendent of the Leprosarium, allowed Fr. Julien to retire to St. James in a house near the church he had built. There he lived by himself spending much time studying. On visiting him, Archbishop John Pius Dowling, O.P., was moved with compassion and offered to take him to his own house which he accepted.

Fr. Julien was accommodated in a room in the tower of the Archbishop's House and every day the Archbishop took his meals with him. Archbishop Dowling was keenly

interested in the linguistic works of Fr. Julien who had trans-
lated the catechism manual of the archdiocese from English
into Chinese and Indian dialects. Together they sang hymns
accompanied by the Archbishop's own harmonium which he
himself played. As Fr. Julien Bouche's condition deteriorated,
he was admitted to the Cocorite Leprosarium on September 8,
1922. When he arrived there he said to Mother Thomas Nigay,
the Superintendent, "Today is the anniversary of my religious
profession. I have come to achieve my sacrifice." He asked to
be put in a ward close to the patients. A bed was prepared for
him in Ward 9.

He could hardly walk, his feet having been eaten up by
the disease. After a few days his condition grew worse; and his
suffering was so intense that his cries could be heard from afar.
Finally he became unconscious though his body was shaken by
fits. His lips were moving. Archbishop Dowling came to see
him and Fr. Julien recognised him. He said, "I have a lot of
pains." The Archbishop comforted him.

During the night that was to be his last on earth, the
Sisters watched over him and prayed with him. They sang
the "Hail Holy Queen". When they reached the words "O
clement", their dying Dominican brother opened his eyes
which had a heavenly look; smiling he said, "O Purissima!"
(the "All Pure" as he used to call the Blessed Virgin Mary).
She had come to introduce him to the heavenly mansions.

Fr. Bouche's funeral Mass took place at the Rosary
Church in Port of Spain and he was buried in the Lapeyrouse
cemetery. His funeral was attended by large crowds.

"Here at the Asylum," wrote Sr. Rose de Ste. Marie
Vebert, "death is a friend who is welcomed; one gets ready
for her as for a fete!" This Sister who had also contracted
leprosy three years before was admitted to the Leprosarium.
Her slow agony was going to last 15 more years. Like the
other patients, she was destined to go into exile on the island
of Chacachacare.

Chapter
16.

Drama - Exodus to Chacachacare

View of the Hansenian Settlement in Chacachacare.

At the beginning of the year 1921, the population of Trinidad and Tobago was shocked by an advertisement which appeared in the *Trinidad Guardian* announcing the proposed establishment of a Leper Settlement on the island of Chacachacare. Immediately the project was met by strong opposition which, as reported in the *"West Indian Committee Circular"* of February 3, 1921, ". . . culminated in the dispatch of an influentially signed petition protesting against it to the Secretary of State for the Colonies".

Why this opposition? Because this scenic island of Chacachacare bordering the Boca Grande of the Dragon's Mouth, north-west of Trinidad, being within easy reach of Port of Spain, was used by citizens as a holiday and health resort. The Surgeon General at that time, Dr. K.S. Wise, was strongly opposed to turning Chacachacare into a western Molokai; he suggested instead that the Leper Settlement be relocated on the island of Patos.

According to records of the religious history of Chacachacare — a name which was said to suggest the cries of some of the many birds living on the island — some 400 people formed its population. In the 18th century, there was a cotton plantation owned by Don Santiago Mariño de Acuña. Besides cotton harvesting, fishing and gardening were the main occupations of the people. Their spiritual needs were taken care of by the priests of Carenage.

However, towards the end of the 19th century, the people having fallen out with the parish priest, the Archbishop sent a Dominican, Fr. Hyacinthe Bariou, to Chacachacare on March 15 1884. Thanks to his zeal and activity, he managed to build a small church dedicated to St. Catherine, a presbytery and a school.

In those days, island steamers linked Port of Spain with Chacachacare three to four times a week and the voyage lasted three to four hours. In 1901 the Dominican Fathers ceased ministering to the people of Chacachacare and they were succeeded by the Holy Ghost Fathers who had a rest house on the island.

The reasons which compelled the authorities to transfer the Leprosarium from Cocorite to Chacachacare came from

the fact that the disease was spreading in alarming proportions. From 1895 to 1914, the number of admissions to the
Leprosarium had been 1537 and from 1915 to 1918, 743
patients were admitted but no fewer than 375 had been registered as "discharged or absconded". There existed then a
grave laxity in dealing with this particular problem and responsible for the spread of the disease.

Another reason was the growth of the population. Cocorite had become a suburb of Port of Spain and it was felt, as
Algernon Aspinall put it in an article published by the *"West
Indian Committee Circular"* of July 21, 1921, that "the presence of the Leprosarium was a grave menace to the health of
the capital and the island generally, and a positive scandal".

Despite the many protests, the colonial authorities
pressed on with the preparations for the transfer of the Cocorite Leprosarium. In December of that year 1921 a press
release informed the population that the government had
imposed an income tax increase to defray the cost of construction of the new Leprosarium on the island of Chacachacare.

On May 20, 1921 paper No. 58 was laid before the Legislative Council for the removal of the Cocorite Leper Asylum
to the island of Chacachacare.

Next came the publication of an eviction order for the
people living on Chacachacare. It was issued by the acting
Governor, T.A.V. Best on December 29, 1921 and it read:
"Notice is hereby given that in pursuance of the authority
vested in me by Clause 6 or Ordinance No. 42 (Revised Edition) ALL THE LANDS (exclusive of the property of the
Roman Catholic Church) situated in the island of Chacachacare in the ward of Diego Martin, which are not already Crown
Lands, have been appropriated for the purpose of establishing
a Leper Settlement."

Needless to say this eviction order, as some senior citizens recall today, was deeply resented by those concerned.
They had to abandon their lands and houses and seek accommodation either in Teteron, Chaguaramas or Carenage, and
some even went to Venezuela.

The date of the first transfer of patients to Chacachacare was kept as a state secret. It was May 10, 1922, recalled

the Dominican Sisters in their diary. On that day at 6 a.m. patients were seized with horror when news spread throughout the wards that several medical practitioners escorted by policemen were on the grounds of the Leprosarium. All of a sudden, the whole place was surrounded and cordoned off by policemen on foot and on horseback.

The poor patients understood the situation. In their panic they attempted to escape but were prevented by the police force. There was general consternation. A dead silence set in. Then the Chief Superintendent, holding a list in his hand and accompanied by policemen, entered each ward and called out the names of those who had to go — 25 were called out that day. At once, a guard stood by each one while the patient gathered his belongings.

Since it was impossible to escape, all had to be resigned to their fate. Some were sobbing, others fainted and others again were seized with fits. Even the policemen were moved with compassion. The parting with their friends was most poignant. The Dominican Sisters could hardly bear the sight of the distress of their beloved patients.

A crowd of curious onlookers had gathered outside the institution to see the patients being escorted by policemen to the Cocorite pier where a steamer took them to Chacachacare. The crossing took two hours and the patients were given a meal on their arrival. Those who had been selected were in the first stages of the disease and still able to give assistance in the construction work of the settlement.

Anxiety set in among the remaining patients at Cocorite; each one wondered when the next departure would take place. Was it in view of somewhat dispersing the gloom which had set in over the institution that on May 24, 1922, a treat was offered to the youngsters — a small relief. The respite, however, was of short duration.

July 28 was the date fixed for the second departure to Chacachacare. Some patients had secretly prepared hide-outs and managed to escape (one hid in a coal heap!). In August again there was another departure but this time it was to India and not Chacachacare. Forty Indians (34 males and six females) preferred to go back to their motherland and they were allowed to do so. The voyage was to last at least six weeks in the least comfortable part of a ship, enough to make one wonder how many survived the ordeal.

Successive departures reduced the number of patients at Cocorite and increased the population at the Chacachacare hospital. In September, Mother Thomas, the Resident Superintendent of Cocorite, accompanied by a Sister, went to Chacachacare to visit their patients. Already 100 of them had been resettled. The Sisters were agreeably surprised by the progress of the construction of small cottages which made the place resemble a village. The stronger patients were working alongside employees of the Public Works Department.

In the night of July 28-29, 1923 there was a near tragedy at the Cocorite Leprosarium when a bandit attacked the chaplain, violently hit him on the head and almost killed him. In December he was replaced by the former Dominican Provincial of Holland, Fr. A. Ter Maat who after spending eight years in Curacao had volunteered his services for the Cocorite Leprosarium. He spoke French and English fluently and through his many Dutch friends he was to bring great help to the patients.

The exodus to Chacachacare continued during 1923. A road had been built from the pier along the sea in order to go from one bay to another (Sander's Bay for females and Coco Bay for males). The new settlement comprised a hospital, an infirmary and a common refectory, a bakery, kitchen, storerooms and the patients' cottages. A concrete jetty had also been built and plans were afoot for the construction of two chapels, one for the Roman Catholics and one for Protestants.

The new chaplain, Fr. Ter Maat O.P., paid regular visits to the patients at Chacachacare. The government had bought a private house to be used as a guest-house for visitors who had to overnight on the island.

At the end of 1923 the Sisters were overworked with less personnel and patients who were very ill and demanded much care. Some of them were making novenas requesting death rather than go to Chacachacare.

What about the Dominican Sisters, would they also go into exile on Chacachacare?

Chapter
17.

The Dominican Sisters
Follow Their Patients Into Exile

The convent of the Dominican Sisters at Marine Bay (top) the chapel and chaplain's residence and the Convent of the Sisters of Mercy.

The Government authorities were rather hesitant in asking the Dominican Sisters to go to the island of Chacachacare where the new Leprosarium settlement was being built. But when the question was put to them as to whether they would be prepared to go there, they replied without hesitation, "The destination of our patients will be ours, we are ready to go to Chacachacare."

On March 30, 1926 the Medical Superintendent, Dr. K.S. Wise, wrote to Mother Therese Isabelle, Prioress General of the Congregation:

"I know that H.E. the Governor Sir Horace A. Byatt will be glad to learn that the arrangements made at Chacachacare have been acceptable to you. I have to assure you that the single-heartedness and self-sacrifice of the Sisters and nurses of your Order for the work at Cocorite has been the admiration of all in Trinidad and the Medical Department regards itself as very fortunate in having their sympathetic and skilled assistance in doing all that is possible for these unfortunate people.

"I cannot help feeling that the removal to Chacachacare is the beginning of a new era in the history of the disease for the public. You will realise, therefore, how anxious I am that the Sisters and nurses feel themselves so placed as to be able to continue that exceptional record of devoted work and cheerful self-sacrifice that brings such great consolation to the inmates and which will, I know, contribute in a material degree to any success that improved conditions at Chacachacare may achieve."

Among the arrangements mentioned by Dr. Wise was the plan of building a convent for the Sisters at Chacachacare. Governor J.R. Chancellor had proposed to Archbishop John Pius Dowling O.P. that "the Church should retain possession of the property that it owns on Chacachacare on the south-eastern extremity of the island and that the buildings on that property be altered at the expense of the Colonial Government so as to provide suitable accommodation for the nuns who would supervise the work of the Asylum."

The acquisition of land on Chacachacare dated back to the 19th century when on February 4, 1842, Emilie Marin-

Birotte donated to Bishop Patrick Smith and Abbé Christophe 26 quarrées (80 to 84 acres) of land valued at $17,000 for the use of the R.C. Church. It was on this land — overlooking "Embarcadère Corbeaux" — that Fr. Hyacinthe Bariou, O.P. had a church, a presbytery and a school built in the 1880's. The bay on this southern part of the island was then called "La Chapelle". This church land was sold to the government on January 21, 1956 after the departure of the Dominican Sisters from Chacachacare which took place in 1950.

The architect who drew the plan of the Chacachacare convent was Mr. Newbold; he worked in close co-operation with the Sisters as this was a rather peculiar type of work for him. He succeeded so well that he was also given the contract to build another convent at Holy Name on Queen's Park East, Port of Spain in 1927. Started at the beginning of 1926, the wooden structure was completed by October of the same year.

In the course of the construction the devoted architect almost lost his life. The day was February 17, 1926 and it was Ash Wednesday as reported in the Catholic News of February 20, 1926. The government gulf steamer "Naparima" was on her way back from Chacachacare to Port of Spain shortly after 3 p.m. At the second Boca, a luxury ship, the S.S. "Vandyck" of the Lamport & Holt Line came into view from Gasparee Island and, sweeping round in a semi-circular curve, gave the signal that she intended to go through the second Boca. The signal was duly answered by the Naparima.

What took place afterwards could only result from a navigational miscalculation of distance and speed. The "Vandyck" crashed into the stern of the "Naparima" which, in about 12 minutes, sank beneath the waves. As a result of the collision, nine persons perished at sea and three could not be resuscitated from drowning.

Among the survivors were the Chaplain of the Leprosarium, Fr. A. Ter Maat, and the architect. The impact of the collision had been such that the priest was thrown overboard into the sea where he managed to hold on to a piece of wreckage. He and others were rescued by boatmen of the island of Huevos and crew members of the "Vandyck". The Dominican

Fathers of the Cathedral presbytery were stunned when they saw their Fr. Ter Maat arriving at 8 o'clock at night dressed as a sailor!

While the Sisters were making preparations to leave Cocorite, Mother Thomas Nigay, who for 36 years as Resident Superintendent of the Leprosarium had done noble work for a noble cause, was dying.

Her death occurred on August 29, 1926. She was born in 1843 in Burgundy, France and arrived in Trinidad in 1871 where she spent the rest of her life at the service of patients at Cocorite and children at St. Dominic's Orphanage.

The Dominican Sisters began moving their belongings from Cocorite to Chacachacare in September 1926. Their new convent was dedicated to Our Lady of the Rosary and the place was renamed "Marine Bay". On October 2, 1926 there was the last transfer of patients. Some had to be carried to the Cocorite jetty on stretchers.

October 16 was the last day of the Sisters at Cocorite. The Prioress, Mother Marie, was very ill. The Medical Superintendent, Dr. Welch, and two wardsmen assisted her from the convent to the launch named after her. The sea was calm and the boat arrived at Marine Bay at 11 a.m. Three months later, Mother Marie was the first of ten Sisters to be buried in the little Marine Bay cemetery.

The official inauguration of the "Hansenian Settlement" on Chacachacare took place on November 18, 1926 and was attended by many visitors from Trinidad. The old Cocorite Leprosarium lay desolate. The following year it was entirely destroyed by fire, the cleansing element. For the Dominican Sisters this act was like a holocaust which sealed the 59 years of dedication they had given to this place.

Today life has returned to this very site and dedication to the relief of human suffering is perpetuated thanks to two worthy organisations: the Lady Hochoy Home for Mentally Retarded Children and the Community Hospital of the Seventh Day Adventists.

In Chacachacare the Sisters met a number of difficulties in organising their life. Besides a shortage of water — the island is very dry and the only supply comes from the rain, so cisterns had to be built to collect water — there was no electricity on the island and the main problem was transport to go across from Marine Bay to Sander's Bay, a distance of about three-quarters of a mile. No proper boat arrangements had been made with the authorities in Port of Spain and this took a little time.

Meantime the Sisters had to find temporary accommodation at Sander's Bay when they could not return to Marine Bay in the evenings and when the condition of the sea was unfavourable for navigation. The crossing took approximately 15 minutes.

Finally a small convent and a chapel were built in Sander's Bay and Archbishop Dowling came to Chacachacare to bless them on November 30, 1927 and administered the sacrament of confirmation. He also gave a special blessing to one of the Sisters, "Mother Rose", who had contracted leprosy and was living in a small cottage in Sander's Bay which the people had called the "Santa Casa" because in her they had found God.

Dominican Sisters of Cocorite who followed their patients into exile on the island of Chacachacare in 1926. Second from left (sitting) Mother Marie who died three months later; extreme right (sitting) Mother Rose who contracted leprosy, in the middle (sitting) Mother Thomas who died before the transfer to Chacachacare.

Chapter 18.

A New Foundation - "The Good Shepherd"

As early as 1878, the Governor, Sir Henry T. Irving, had asked Archbishop Louis Joachim Gonin to establish an Industrial School for delinquent girls whom he would have liked to see in the hands of the Dominican Sisters. The Governor had offered a loan at most advantageous conditions to build a house for this purpose but a piece of land was needed.

For 10 years negotiations went on between Archbishop Gonin and the civil administration. Finally it was agreed that a large house would be constructed on the grounds of the St. Dominic's Orphanage which had become the property of the archdiocese. Archbishop Gonin was not in favour of entrusting this work to the Dominican Sisters and he turned to the Sisters of the Congregation of the Good Shepherd in Angers, France. These religious Sisters were founded in 1641 by St. Jean Eudes under the name of "Our Lady of Charity Refuge". In 1814, Marie Euphrasie Pelletier reformed this Congregation and the name was changed to "Our Lady of the Good Shepherd of Angers".

As the name indicates, this Congregation manifests God's

mercy and compassion in the form of rehabilitation for repentant unprincipled women through living with religious Sisters; the latter providing them with the means of recovering their respectability by a life of Christian morality. When Mother Euphrasie died on April 29, 1868, the Congregation numbered 2067 professed religious Sisters scattered in 110 convents throughout the world.

The Mother Superior agreed to send some Sisters to make the new foundation in Trinidad. For this, English-speaking Sisters were chosen from their houses established in the United States of America, and arrived in Trinidad in 1890. For 12 years they developed and consolidated the Good Shepherd Industrial School which was built on Church lands at No. 32 Belmont Circular Road.

For reasons which have never been made clear, the Sisters were recalled by their Superiors to the United States; they left Trinidad on July 4, 1903. Then Archbishop Patrick Vincent Flood, who had succeeded Archbishop Gonin, asked the Dominican Sisters if they would continue the work. The Prioress General gave authorisation to accept it for a period of six years as a start. The "Good Shepherd" then became a sort of annexe to St. Dominic's Orphanage. In order to establish communication between the two institutions, a door was opened in the wall bordering the Industrial School.

The spacious house could accommodate 70 girls. In 1903 there were only 25 with a few Catholics among them. The girls worked in a public laundry forming part of the establishment, which brought them about $40 a month. To this was added an allowance of $24 per girl paid by the government, up to the age of 16, and a grant of $1400 annually. The building was solidly erected and maintained at government expense. Admission was arranged through a magistrate and delinquent girls had to be over 10 years of age.

The Sisters had a chapel within the house and the Holy Ghost Fathers of St. Mary's College took charge of the ministry. Between 1890 and 1914 no less than 217 girls had passed through the Good Shepherd Industrial School.

The first six years (1903-1909) of the Dominican Sisters at the "Good Shepherd" having given satisfaction to all con-

cerned, the contract of administration was renewed. Regretfully, the war years (1914-1918) brought a strain on the Trinidad communities as no French Sisters could come to Trinidad
during those four years.

In 1919, Archbishop John Pius Dowling, feeling the great
need for more religious Sisters in the archdiocese, invited the
Corpus Christi Carmelites, who had recently been founded in
England, to come to Trinidad and take charge of the Spaccapietra Hospice situated on Observatory Street, Port of Spain.
The Sisters accepted the offer and the pioneers arrived that
very year.

Again in 1922, Archbishop John Pius Dowling O.P. asked
the Mother General of the Carmelite Sisters if she could help
him by taking over the management of the Industrial School
for girls. The French Dominican Sisters were in need of more
Sisters to pursue the works they had undertaken in Trinidad
since their arrival in 1868 and therefore begged leave to withdraw from the Industrial School. Mother General accepted the
administration of the School and sent several of her Sisters to
learn management skills from the Dominican Sisters. The
transfer of the Industrial School to the Carmelite Sisters
took place in 1923. Years later it was renamed 'St. Jude's
Home'. The Sisters are still in charge today (1987).

The Good Shepherd Convent.

Chapter
19.

Reorganisation of
St. Dominic's Children's Home

The new (1954) St. Martin's Nursery School.

On April 20, 1901, the founder of St. Dominic's Orphanage, Fr. Mariano Forestier O.P., died in Trinidad and two years later, on September 7, 1903, the one who could be regarded as the co-foundress, Miss Stephanie Blanc, a Dominican Tertiary, also died. For 25 years this mother-substitute to the children had devoted herself to their care with an indefatigable zeal for which God alone could reward her. On her death, there was a total enrolment of 189 children (94 boys and 95 girls) in the orphanage. The buildings consisted of two houses named "Nazareth" for the boys and "Bethlehem" for the girls as well as two schools, one for the boys and one for the girls.

In 1909 Archbishop John Pius Dowling decided to transfer the Catholic News Printery from Holy Name Convent at 2 Queen's Park East in Port of Spain to the grounds of St. Dominic's Orphanage. A small plant was built to accommodate it on the left side of the main entrance at No. 34 Belmont Circular Road and some senior boys of the home were employed as apprentices. The first boy to work at the printery was Francis Emmanuel Joseph who is still alive today (1987) and the first foreman was Joseph Peschier.

The years of the First World War brought increased poverty to St. Dominic's. The children's clothes had to be made out of flour bags; footwear could not be afforded so children went barefooted, and every day their feet were examined for "jiggers" (insects which penetrate into the flesh causing infection). The harsh economic conditions in the country caused more and more children to be sent to the two orphanages by the courts. In 1919 the total number had reached 215 (124 boys and 91 girls).

From heaven, the good Fr. Forestier must have pleaded for his beloved children because a noble woman in the person of Mother Marie of the Assumption was sent in 1924 to take the management of St. Dominic's in her hands. For the next 20 years she transformed the orphanage to the point where she could be regarded as its second foundress.* Archbishop Dowling approved the construction and expansion projects she

---

* *Mother Marie of the Assumption who was born in France gave 58 years of sterling service to Trinidad. She died on February 14, 1952 at the age of 90.*

proposed to him but his condition was that the community would have to find the necessary funds for these projects.

Undaunted, the Sisters soon engaged in all sorts of fund-raising ventures, the first being a grand Nativity Play in the open air on the hilly grounds of the orphanage. So successful was this play that it became a traditional feature in Trinidad, sometimes attracting as many as 3,000 people at one performance.

Then there were bazaars and sales of flowers. By special permission of the civil authorities, the children were allowed to sell their "buttercups" on a particular day in the streets of Port of Spain; while some boys would play their instruments on a truck to attract the attention of passers-by. Old boys and girls sent donations. For the actual construction work, the children did their best in transporting whatever material they could carry.

God was served first and the new chapel was blessed by the Archbishop on the feast day of St. Dominic, August 4, 1930. Afterwards, expansion work continued so as to provide accommodation for the ever-growing number of children at St. Dominic's. When in 1943 Mother Marie was struck by an attack of hemiplegia, there were 604 children at St. Dominic's (362 boys and 242 girls). The next nine years of her life were years of intense suffering which she bore with admirable courage. She died at Holy Name Convent on February 14, 1952. Surely God must have given her a wonderful reward.

Archbishop Dowling, relying on the excellent qualities of Mother Marie, had instituted a Board of Visitors in June 1935 "to assist the Manager in her arduous duties". Appointed were Captain Matthew Costelloe, Alderman H.A. de Freitas and Dr. C.F. Lassalle, M.D. They were given power to co-opt one or more other members as they deemed necessary or useful. Their powers were "consultative, advisory, inspectorial — singly or collectively — of all people connected with the St. Dominic's Orphanage and all parts of it assigned to children, masters, lay mistresses or superintendent and monitory of same persons". This Board of Visitors has been in existence ever since.

On August 26, 1946, Archbishop Finbar Ryan, after visit-

ing the orphanage wrote the following to the Manager who was
then Sr. Marie Benedict : "The Board of Visitors has no function other than that of an advisory body. The members are
appointed directly by the Archbishop in order that the Orphanage may have the benefit of expert business and professional
counsel and also that an efficient buffer or liaison (as may be
needed) may be established between the Institution and the
Social Service Department of the Government. The Archbishop's Deputy is the chairman of the Board and he draws up
the agenda."

"The Orphanage schools are run in connection with the
Board of Education. The spiritual care of the children is the
chief concern of the chaplain of the Orphanage; it is his duty
to arrange for the administration of the sacraments and the
official instruction of the children. The Sisters are to co-
operate with him."

"It must be obvious that the Archbishop as official
owner of the Orphanage and, in case of difficulty or dispute,
the last court of appeal, cannot be expected to intervene in
the day-to-day affairs of the Institution. It is equally obvious
that the Prioress and/or the Manager, may need the backing of
his authority in cases of emergency, particularly such as may
arise in connection with externs. It is to assure to the Prioress
and Manager the support and advice they may need, that I
have named an official Deputy. He has authority, subject to
such limitations as I have indicated, and subject to the principle of subsidiarity to supervise all the departments of the
Institution."

The Second World War had prevented Dominican Sisters
from coming to Trinidad. As a result, there was a shortage of
religious personnel not only at St. Dominic's but in the other
convents as well. However, in May 1945 five Sisters were on
their way to Trinidad via New York. Among them was Sr.
Catherine Dominique who, in 1939, just before the declaration of war between France and Germany, had been sent to
England to familiarise herself with the English language.

When war broke out on September 3, 1939, she found
herself cut off from France and spent nearly six years with the
English Dominican Sisters. The painful separation from her

native country was to be later on a gain for Trinidad. Shortly after her arrival, Sr. Catherine Dominique, a most vivacious and dynamic person, was appointed Prioress of the community of Sisters and three years later, Manager of St. Dominic's.

She had had time to assess the situation and to make plans for the future. She was impressed by the family spirit that existed in the place not only among the children in care but among the old boys and girls who would continue visiting St. Dominic's after they had left the institution at age 16.

But Sr. Catherine Dominique Viau was stunned by the primitive living conditions: wooden houses, children sleeping on boards, poorly clad yet looking happy and showing an affectionate attachment to the Sisters. The latter were not better off in their cramped rustic quarters of the convent.

Sr. Catherine Dominique's special mission for which she was naturally well equipped was to be that of a builder and innovator of new pedagogic methods. With the savings of the community and some donations, she had a new wing added to the old convent. Then she turned her attention to the infants and in 1950 the enterprising Manageress had a nursery built for them on top of the hill. The St. Theresa's Residential Nursery was blessed by Archbishop Finbar Ryan O.P.

Then Sr. Catherine Dominique envisaged a new approach to education in institutions such as St. Dominic's. With the help of Sr. Marie Thérèse Rétout, who had spent two years in England studying this new type of management of "Children's Homes", the implementation of the new plan began in 1954 with the inauguration of a new building for a residential Montessori nursery school.

As good as the formula seemed to be, it was, however, unsuccessful. These children needed contact with older ones to develop their speech ability and to socialise as a whole. The next step therefore was the formation of family units by keeping together as long as possible, brothers and sisters within the same house and entrusting the young to the older ones so as to develop caring relationships. This was a fascinating time of experimentation which demanded of the Sisters much creativity and imagination.

Thanks to the reconstruction of the houses which pro-

gressed in the course of over 10 years, life was full of expectations and the children co-operated well. The change of atmosphere was also felt in the consolidation of the family spirit
so characteristic of St. Dominic's, with birthday parties,
concerts, outings (a large bus was donated to the Children's
Home), Carnival frolics and competitions, sports and music
(St. Dominic's brass band prepared some of the best men for
both the Police and Regiment Bands). Obviously the two
schools gained from the change of education in the Children's
Home and the teaching of religion as well.

In 1958, when Sr. Catherine Dominique went to Guadeloupe to take up a new post there, she left St. Dominic's
filled to capacity: 656 children (383 boys and 273 girls)
from a few days old to 16 years of age. The senior boys were
able to learn other trades such as cabinet-making besides
printing, tailoring and shoemaking. A modern bakery had
been installed thus making the work much easier for the
bakers. In those days, no less than four bags of flour had to
be used every day to make bread for so large a family!

By the considerable work she did, Sr. Catherine Dominique Viau left her imprint on St. Dominic's Home.

*Sr. Catherine Dominique Viau O.P. Manageress introduces
oldest girl of the Orphanage, Theresa Wells (86 years old) to
Archbishop Count Finbar Ryan O.P. in 1954.
At right, Fr. P. Keating O.P.*

The winning netball team of St. Dominic's Orphanage.

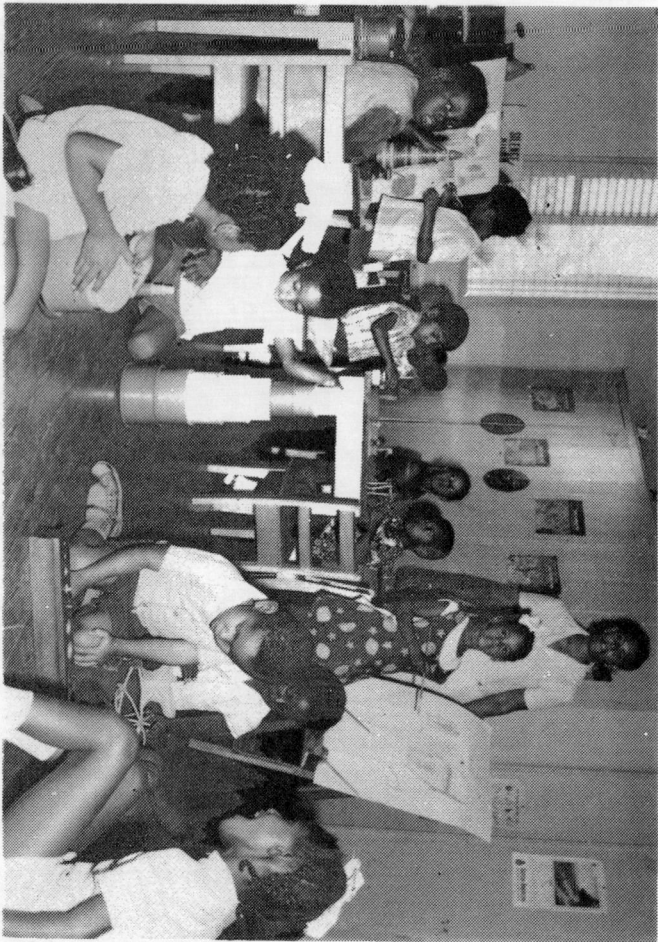

Children at work in the Montessori class (1970's)

Chapter

20.

Life on Chacachacare Island
by an ex-patient

*Matron Sister Hedwidge and Sr. Marie de Verteuil
with young patients.*

On October 10, 1926 an English physician, Dr. Welch arrived in Trinidad to take up residence at Chacachacare in the house at Rust's Bay. Dr. Welch was appointed Medical Superintendent of the Hansenian Settlement. At that time, patients numbered about 250 with more males than females.

In order to administer better medical treatment and to perform necessary surgery on patients, a hospital was built at Sander's Bay; it was inaugurated on February 22, 1928. Life at the settlement had been organised by the latter part of the 1920's. The male patients had their quarters at Coco Bay and the females at Sander's Bay. A road along the shore linked the two places.

The Dominican Sisters had their convent at Marine Bay, on the opposite side of the settlement. Every day a launch took them across the bay to take up their duties at the settlement. The Sisters would experience bouts of sea-sickness when the sea was rough. In the launch there was accommodation for eight sitting and four to five standing — one day a sister fell over-board! They also had to endure the discomfort of the scorching sun at noon when they returned to the convent for lunch. The crossing lasted about 15 minutes when the sea was calm.

At night, some of the Sisters took turns in keeping duty at the hospital. On July 7, 1928 a hurricane caused some damage at Chacachacare; among the main casualties was the roof of the Sisters' convent which had been blown off. The Sisters then had to seek temporary shelter at Sander's Bay; the launch had run aground and therefore they could not cross the bay.

Times were rough. In 10 years (1927-1937), eight Sisters had died at Chacachacare and were buried at Marine Bay. In 1919 it was discovered that one of the Sisters in Trinidad, Sr. Rose Vebert, had contracted the disease. Sr. Rose was born in France and volunteered to come to Trinidad where she arrived in 1893.

Her illness lasted 18 years which she spent at the Cocorite and Chacachacare leprosaria. She lived in isolation from her community and bore her trial with great courage and fortitude. The patients regarded her as a saint. Shortly after her death on June 17, 1937, the following appreciation appeared in the Port of Spain Gazette, penned by Dr. H.B. Morgan:

"A community of Catholic nuns have for decades performed invaluable work in the Trinidad Leper Settlement at a comparatively small cost to the Government, setting a noble example of self-sacrificing duty and religious devotion in a risky disease environment — in fact a saintly work. No praise can be too lavish for this single-mindedness. Grave risks are nobly faced, some nuns becoming lepers, uncomplaining in God's duty."

After the death of Sr. Rose it was found that another Sister, Sr. Ena, had also contracted leprosy. These were the only two victims among the Sisters which proves that the contagion — if any — is very limited: only two cases in 82 years of service to the patients and even these two Sisters were not in direct contact with patients.

One may wonder at the source of strength for the Sisters in relentlessly pursuing their life of dedication, cut off as they were from the rest of the world. The answer lies in their absolute faith in God and love for Him and for those whom the world had rejected; in them they saw the face of Jesus Christ.

It was my good fortune to meet the last Medical Superintendent of Chacachacare, Dr. Walter Van Crosson. He was assigned to the settlement at his own request shortly after returning from England as there were no volunteers in Trinidad. Dr. Van Crosson who lives in Port of Spain arranged an interview with his former assistant, Sultan Khan, and the last patient to leave Chacachacare, Arthur Ramsammy.

A teacher at the Woodbrook Canadian Mission, Arthur Ramsammy was told that he had leprosy when he was 18 years old. The physician's decision was irrevocable: he had to say goodbye to his family and the girl he wanted to marry and go to Chacachacare as a patient. Ramsammy spent 58 years at the settlement in constant struggle with the disease. Today, at the age of 76, he is still with us to recount his days at Chacachacare. The following is his account:

"The patients came from a cross-section of Trinidad society. We were divided between the Indian Friendly Society and the Christian and Catholic Friendly Societies. I used to write to addresses found in the newspapers of Trinidad offering a cure for the disease. Some medicine was sent to me from Germany; that did me well because I am still alive today.

Life at Chacachacare was not easy. One of the many hardships, besides the isolation, was the lack of water. It is a waterless island with only two salt ponds, so we had to depend on rain during the wet season and water tankers in the dry months. Water was always rationed: four gallons per day for eight persons and only for drinking purposes. All the water reservoirs had a lock on the tap.

Every morning the valid patients came with their containers to collect water; an attendant distributed it and kept records. Bathing had to be done either in the rain or in the sea and it was the same thing for the washing of wares. All the patients' clothes were washed in a common laundry. Meals were taken in the common refectories. The invalid patients were taken care of either in the infirmary or at the hospital.

Recreational facilities were then non-existent. Patients were not allowed to swim in the sea. All that was authorised was to get into the water no further than chest high; if caught disobeying the law, we were given two days in jail (located at La Tinta Bay). We were not allowed to fish (though sometimes we did fish in hiding and enjoyed cooking our catch as well!). Also, we were not permitted to come to the main land to visit our relatives and bury the dead of our families.

Every day we did maintenance chores at the settlement for which we were paid 25 cents a day. When Dr. Urich announced in 1934 that our pay was going to be reduced to 12 cents, we went on strike and I was chosen as the leader. The strike lasted two months. The authorities sent a commission of enquiry. At the end, we won and got back our 25 cents a day. We also received sport equipment and we began building a sports ground. I was put in charge of sports.

Men did gardening — tomatoes grow well in Chacachacare as well as watermelons and pumpkins. We reared fowls and sold their eggs to the management; we also reared pigs in the unoccupied bays of the island. The women did some sewing, crochet and handicraft.

In the 1940's, an English medical expert, Dr. Ernest Muir,

came to Chacachacare as Medical Superintendent. We didn't like his approach because he used to scare us, and the population of Trinidad as well so as to prevent patients from absconding.

This doctor looked at Chacachacare as a prison where lepers came to live and die. But we wanted to live, not to die; we wanted to be cured and we wanted our living conditions improved. Dr. Muir did not stay very long. He returned to England in 1945. He was succeeded by Dr. George Campbell from Trinidad.

During the 1939-45 war, food was strictly rationed and of poor quality. The patients went on strike on account of this and it lasted almost three months. In the end we got a salary increase as well as an authorisation for male and female patients to visit each other on any day and up to 6 p.m.

The nuns were quite opposed to this new regulation. They were very strict in imposing a code of morality on us. Men and women had to live in separate quarters — except for married couples — and even in church we had to be separated! Patients, though we did appreciate very much the good care of the Sisters, could not accept their rigid rule and we were on the side of the Medical Superintendent who was much more lenient than the Sisters.

Of course, after applying this new rule, the birth-rate increased at the settlement; one of the nuns even had to go to the Colonial Hospital to be trained to handle deliveries of babies. It was hard for the parents because immediately after birth the babies were taken to Trinidad and placed in an orphanage; parents were not allowed to visit them.

It was only when Dr. Robert Archibald was appointed Medical Superintendent that we were issued passes to visit our families in Trinidad. We had to make a five-dollar deposit before getting the pass. If we returned only one day late we lost our deposit.

We had one more strike and it was directed against the American Sisters of Mercy who had come to Chacachacare in the 1940's to help the Dominican Sisters after the hard years of the war. Among the patients there was a communist who did not want the nuns at the Settlement and it was he who was agitating to have them leave the island. I was not in favour of the strike.''

*Tomb of Sr. Rose of Ste. Marie in the
patients' cemetery of Sander's Bay.*

Cemetery of the Dominican Sisters at Chacachacare.

Names of the Dominican Sisters buried in the little cemetery
at Chacachacare. The labour of love for engraving their names
was done by Petty Officer of the Trinidad & Tobago Coast Guard,
T. Frazer.

(SEE PLAQUE ON PREVIOUS PLATE)

DOMINICAN SISTERS BURIED IN
CHACACHACARE

Sr. Marie de la Purification Chatelain. Born in France
12-2-1883, died 22-1-1927 aged 44.

Sr. Joseph Agnes Rigamme.
Born in France 3-6-1873, died 3-7-1928 aged 55.

Sr. Jeanne de St. Dominique Escoffier. Born in France
29-8-1869, died 16-10-1932 aged 63.

Sr. Marie Elizabeth du Rosaire Hamard. Born in
France 8-11-1867, died 14-10-1933 aged 66.

Sr. Françoise du Rosaire Beauchateau. Born in France
30-9-1873, died 4-2-1934 aged 56.

Sr. Marie Henri Reverdy. Born in France
died in 1873 at Cocorite. Her remains were transferred to this cemetery.

Sr. Rose de Ste. Marie Vebert. Born in France
20-3-1866, died 17-6-1937 aged 71, victim of leprosy.
Her remains are buried in the patients' cemetery at
Sander's Bay.

Sr. Thomas des Saints Thomas. Born in Trinidad in
1854, died 13-12-1935 aged 81.

Sr. Stanislaus Diaz. Born in Madeira in 1871, died
16-4-1937 aged 66.

Sr. Stephanie Arnaud. Born in Trinidad 4-3-1859,
died 12-9-1942 aged 88.

* * * * * * * * * * *

Sr. Mary Luigi Sansoni R.S.M. Born 31-10-1918 in
USA, died 12-1-1946 aged 28.

Chapter 21.

War Years at Chacachacare

During the Second World War the Sisters and their patients on the island of Chacachacare had their share of suffering and anxiety. The Settlement, first of all, still lacked a proper lighting system (generators were provided only in 1946); launch men were very irregular in their attendance and the work of the sanitation staff was most unsatisfactory.

The situation became so bad that the Archbishop, Count Finbar Ryan, had to write to the director of the Medical Services at the Colonial Hospital, stating the following: "The Dominican Sisters are at the Settlement as nurses, not as scavengers and most certainly not as nurses and scavengers. If nothing can be done, and done without delay, to ameliorate the situation, I shall have to consider the withdrawal of the Sisters from the Settlement." (2-10-43).

The less handicapped patients employed by the government for sanitation work had gone on strike for nearly three months. At the end of it, they had their salaries increased while the Matron's own salary was decreased. Taking the Sisters' defence, Archbishop Ryan once more wrote the director of the Medical Services:

"The salaries paid heretofore to the Sisters have been meagre to niggardlyness, especially in view of the nature of their work and of the increasing demands made upon them by successive Medical Superintendents. It was with a shock, therefore, that I observed in the official Gazette list of altered salaries — one solitary explicit reference to the Leper Settlement — and that was a substantial decrease in the formal salary of the Matron. On enquiry I had been told that a paltry increase ($4.00) has been arranged for the staff Sisters amounting in all to a nett $30 a month."

In Europe, since 1939, Germany, France and England were once more at war and the country of Poland had been invaded by German troops. The Matron, Sr. Edwige, Polish by birth, was extremely worried about her family as well as the two other Polish Sisters, Sr. Marie Yolande and Sr. Stanislaus.

In 1943, there were 15 Dominican Sisters working at the Settlement. Since 1938, security had been threatened by the passage of warships and submarines through the Bocas, especially the Boca Grande between Chacachacare and Venezuela.

For security reasons, the lighthouse remained unlighted at night. An Italian ship struck Diamond Rock, near Chacachacare, and sank. In 1942, a German submarine sneakingly entered the Gulf of Paria and attacked two ships in the Port of Spain harbour. The war had come to Trinidad.

The British Royal Navy decided to reduce entry into the Gulf through the third Boca only and solely in daylight. (The Dragon's Mouth, west of the northern peninsula of Trinidad, has four "Bocas" or passages). However the U.S. Navy (occupying the northern peninsula of Trinidad by a lease agreement with the Government in 1942) disagreed with the British scheme and resorted to laying mines.

They laid 350 MK IV floating mines, recalled Gaylord T.M. Kelshall in an article published in the *Mariner*, 1985, despite the warning of the British that the Bocas are too deep and the currents too strong to allow proper moorings of the mines.

As forecast, mines drifted ashore and some of them exploded because the cables could not hold them. As a result, ships and schooners went down. In 1945, after the war, a dozen U.S. minesweepers moved in and began the dangerous job of sweeping the minefields. After four months of operations they had found only 35 mines. Some of them had reached the shores of Bonaire, Aruba and Curacao: others, the mangrove in Central America and Cuba.

On August 5, 1944, the "Island Queen" left Grenada with a wedding party on board and disappeared without a trace. It is almost certain that she was struck by a Boca mine.

Early in 1943, the island of Chacachacare became one of the Protected Places of the United States Forces. As a result, some 300 marines came to the island and built nine military barracks (three around the convent area in Marine Bay, one at Perruquier Bay, three on the heights by the lighthouse and two above Rust's Bay) and they also made a road to link their military strategic positions. The marines laid a fence-line to mark the boundaries around the Leprosarium and the convent at Marine Bay. All in all, the lease comprised four parcels of land at Chacachacare representing an area of 961.94 acres.

In the Lands and Surveys Division of Trinidad and Tobago there is an interesting map — drawn by a corps of U.S. Army engineers in July 1943 — which clearly shows the position of the military barracks in Chacachacare. These leased lands were re-acquired by the Government of Trinidad and Tobago on December 11, 1947.

Another effect of the war was the impossibility of the Sisters to receive help from France; no new Sisters could come to Chacachacare and meantime the present numbers were aging with less strength to carry out the work. Nonetheless, the Sisters held on valiantly placing all their reliance on God.

MAP OF THE ISLAND OF CHACACHACARE

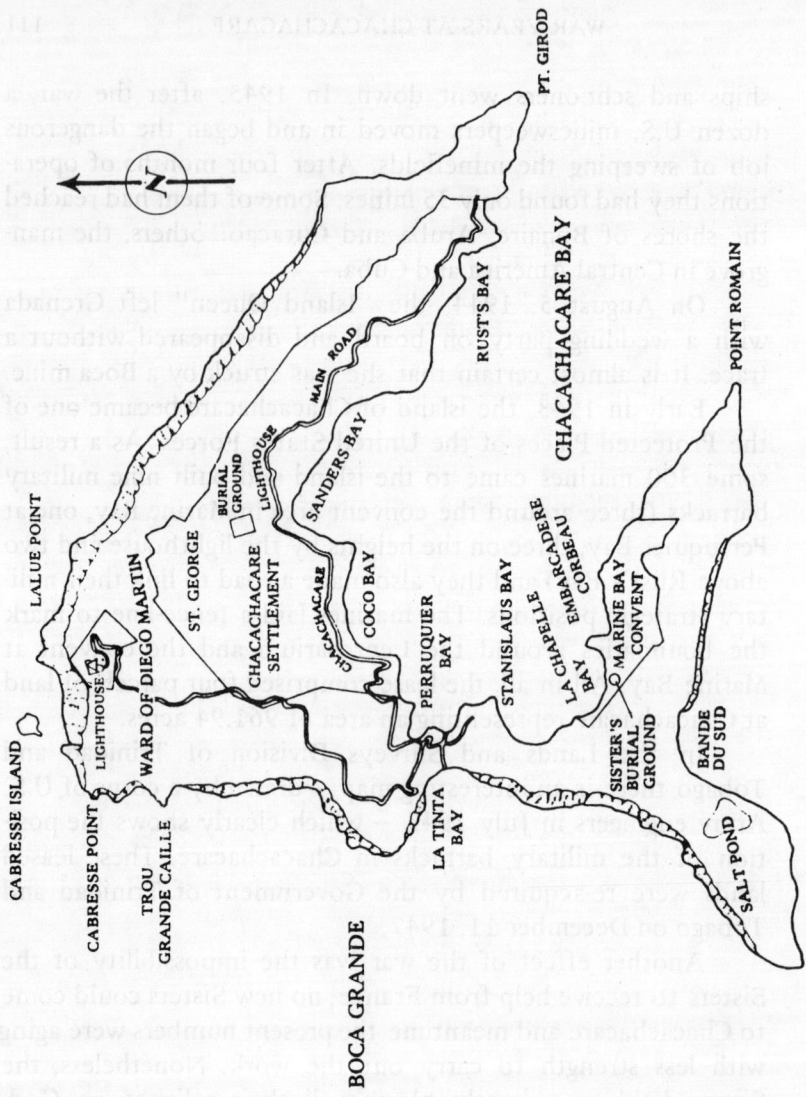

CABRESSE ISLAND

LALUE POINT

CABRESSE POINT

LIGHTHOUSE

WARD OF DIEGO MARTIN

ST. GEORGE

TROU GRANDE CAILLE

CHACACHACARE SETTLEMENT

BURIAL GROUND

LIGHTHOUSE

CHACACHACARE

MAIN ROAD

RUST'S BAY

SANDERS BAY

COCO BAY

CHACACHACARE BAY

POINT ROMAIN

PERRUQUIER BAY

STANISLAUS BAY

LA CHAPELLE BAY

EMBARCADERE CORBEAU

MARINE BAY CONVENT

SISTER'S BURIAL GROUND

LA TINTA BAY

BANDE DU SUD

SALT POND

BOCA GRANDE

PT. GIROD

N

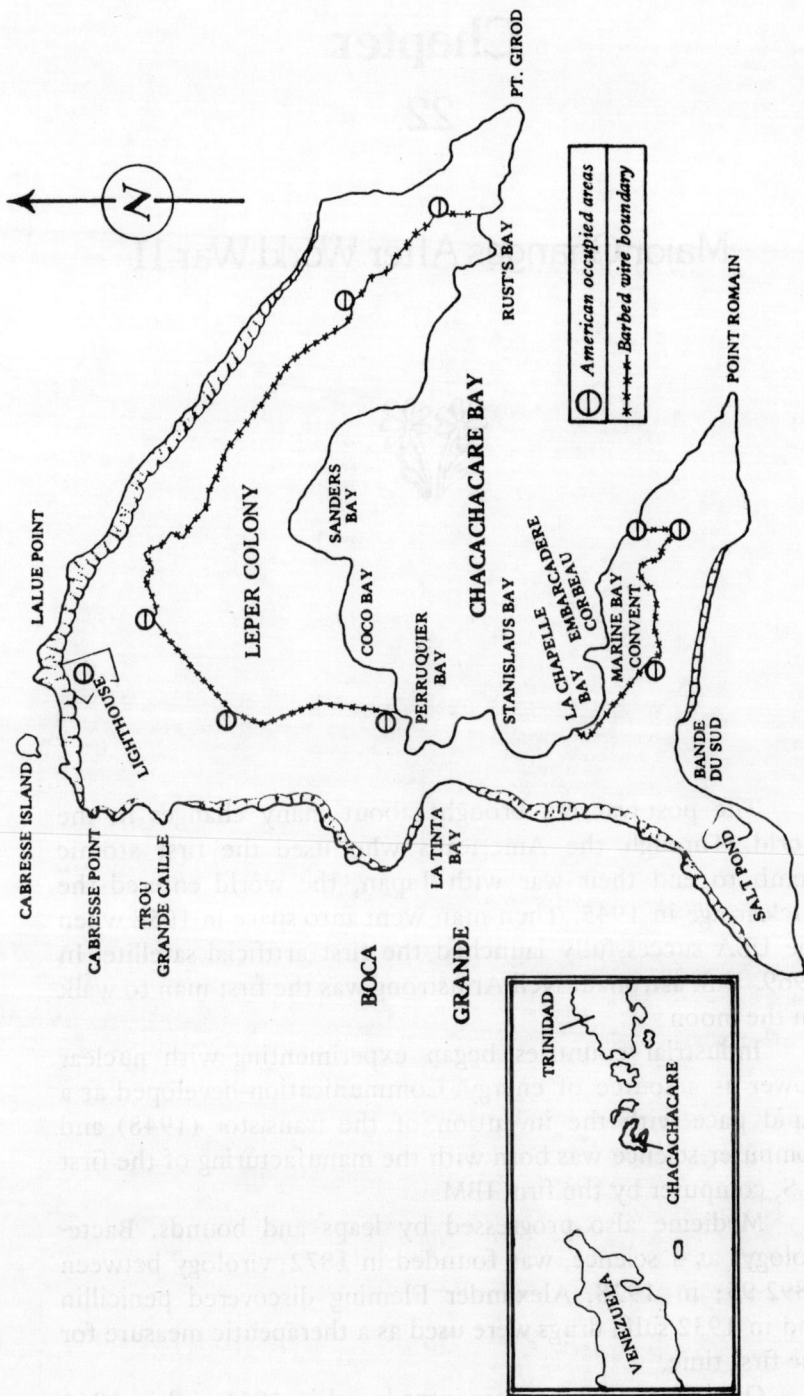

MAP OF CHACACHACARE SHOWING THE PARTS OF LAND LEASED AND OCCUPIED BY THE U.S. ARMY DURING WORLD WAR II U.S. CORPS OF ENGINEERS (20-7-1943).

⊕ American occupied areas
✕✕✕ Barbed wire boundary

N

PT. GIROD

RUST'S BAY

LALUE POINT

LEPER COLONY

SANDERS BAY

COCO BAY

PERRUQUIER BAY

CHACACHACARE BAY

STANISLAUS BAY

LA CHAPELLE BAY

EMBARCADERE CORBEAU

MARINE BAY

CONVENT

POINT ROMAIN

LIGHTHOUSE

CABRESSE ISLAND

CABRESSE POINT

TROU GRANDE CAILLE

BOCA GRANDE

LA TINTA BAY

SALT POND

BANDE DU SUD

TRINIDAD

CHACACHACARE

VENEZUELA

Chapter
22.

Major Changes After World War 11

The post-war era brought about many changes in the world. Through the Americans who used the first atomic bomb to end their war with Japan, the world entered the nuclear age in 1945. Then man went into space in 1958 when the USA successfully launched the first artificial satellite. In 1969, U.S. astronaut Neil Armstrong was the first man to walk on the moon.

Industrial countries began experimenting with nuclear power as a source of energy. Communication developed at a rapid pace with the invention of the transistor (1948) and computer science was born with the manufacturing of the first U.S. computer by the firm IBM.

Medicine also progressed by leaps and bounds. Bacteriology, as a science, was founded in 1872; virology between 1892-95; in 1928, Alexander Fleming discovered penicillin and in 1932 sulfa drugs were used as a therapeutic measure for the first time.

Open heart surgery was introduced in 1954 and in 1963 an artificial heart was made to circulate blood during heart surgery. 1967 saw the first surgical transplant of a human heart: since then, techniques for transplanting human organs have been developed and more and more drugs have appeared on the market.

Drastic changes in the world necessarily brought about drastic changes in the Church. An update in the Church became a necessity and this was done through the Ecumenical Council of Vatican II (1961-65). One of its 16 decrees promulgated in 1965 concerns the religious life and demanded nothing else than a reform.

Religious life was then a total institution with one theology, a unified practice of the vows, a fairly authoritarian system, a definite and unquestioned apostolate and finally a community bound by dress, place, meals, rules and regulations. At the beginning of these revolutionary times, how were the Dominican Sisters going to react in their isolation on the island of Chacachacare?

Archbishop Ryan, O.P. began by giving them a warning when he wrote them: "The Sisters must be on their guard against a danger common to all who have been doing good work, and doing it well, along certain lines, viz. of thinking that what is good cannot grow to better and that methods cannot be improved.

"In the particular matter of leprosy, all medical scientists are agreed that enormous advances in knowledge about the disease and about the methods of dealing with it have been made in recent years."

Then the Archbishop proceeded to advise the Sisters about respecting the role of the Government in the administration of the Settlement. To this effect he wrote in 1945: "All the works of the community are, and must be, under the general supervision of the Mother Superior; but the officials, once appointed, must be allowed to fulfil their duties without needless intervention, and those in a subordinate relation to these officials must recognise that their immediate duty is to co-operate.

"The Matron in the settlement must be considered the person directly in charge there, responsible as a religious to the Prioress and as an official to the Medical Superintendent, and in regard to the actual duties of the Settlement, the Prioress must not intervene without consultation with the Matron."

This duality of roles was a crucial issue and it had not always been properly understood by the Major Superiors in France: as a result, it caused great embarrassment to the parties concerned leading to unnecessary recriminations. In 1945, Archbishop Ryan had to intervene when the General Chapter of the Congregation in France appointed a new Matron for Chacachacare. He wrote to the Vicaress of the Prioress General in Trinidad, Mother Albert:

"You must, please, cable the Prioress General at once to suspend this nomination as it does not rest with the Chapter to name a Matron but with the Director of Medical Services in Trinidad. (23-11-45).

In the wind of change that was blowing after World War II, and in the circumstances prevalent in Trinidad and Tobago, particularly at Chacachacare, the authorities had made a volte-face as regards the Sisters at the Settlement. On December 3, 1945, the Archbishop wrote to the Vicaress of the Dominican Sisters in Trinidad, Mother Marie de la Compassion:

"Today I have been officially notified that Sr. Catherine (who was appointed by the Chapter in France) will not be accepted for the post of Matron, nor any other of the Sisters at present at Chacachacare. On my asking what qualifications are deemed necessary for the Sister holding this post I was informed that: (1) she must have full nursing qualifications and diplomas; (2) she must have actual experience of the administration of some large institution comparable to the Leprosarium and (3) she must, of course, be a fluent speaker of English.

"On my further enquiring what was to be done now, the resident Medical Superintendent suggested that Mother Hedwige should continue as Matron until such time as a Sister with required qualifications can come to replace and learn from her what has to be known about the Settlement."

Considering the urgency of a nursing update, it was decided that two Sisters would go to the Colonial Hospital in Port of Spain to take a nursing course. With their experience they managed to do two years of studies in one year and both qualified in nursing and midwifery. Two other Sisters took a course in dentistry in Port of Spain.

Meantime, a Sister was sent from France to England to study nursing. Afterwards she was to go to the Leprosarium of Carville in Louisiana, USA, to gain experience. But the situation at Chacachacare had deteriorated very fast due to a breakdown of discipline and morality as well as the pernicious influence of sects and ideologies antagonistic to the Sisters and the Church.

The government appointed Francis Mc Comie to Chacachacare as Chief Steward. As a member of the Royal Army Medical Corps, it was hoped that his military training would help him restore discipline and order in the place. He came with his family and spent six years in Chacachacare.

God certainly blessed him for his good work there and this was shown by the call of one of his daughters to join the religious life. She entered the Congregation of the Dominican Sisters and today Sr. Catherine Thérèse Mc Comie is the Novice Mistress of the Trinidad and Tobago Region.

Mr. Mc Comie admired the work and dedication of the Sisters but the age and the fatigue of most of them after years of labour were against them. Archbishop Ryan, most concerned about the continuation of the apostolate among the patients, made several attempts to find other religious Sisters to go to Chacachacare. He finally got the Mother Superior of the Sisters of Mercy of Baltimore, USA, to send six Sisters to Chacachacare.

His intention was that the Dominican and the Mercy Sisters would work together for the benefit of the patients. To this effect, he wrote to the Vicaress of the Dominican Sisters on August 7, 1945: "I am happy to think that the Dominican Sisters have a future before them that will surpass their most splendid and generous past."

The government had a small house built for the Mercy Sisters at Marine Bay. The first two arrived towards the end of 1944 and the others in 1945. The American Sisters of Mercy nursed the patients at Chacachacare for almost ten years when due to pressure from the patients themselves they chose to withdraw from the Settlement.

Sr. Hedwidge Dobrowolska, who was matron of the Leprosarium at Cocorite and Chacachacare up to 1950. She died in France in 1967.

Dominican Sisters who left their native land, Poland, and offered to come to Chacachacare. Left to right: Sr. Marie Stanislaus († 1952), Sr. Hedwidge († 1967), Sr. Marie Yolande (still in Trinidad), Sr. Stanislaus (in France).

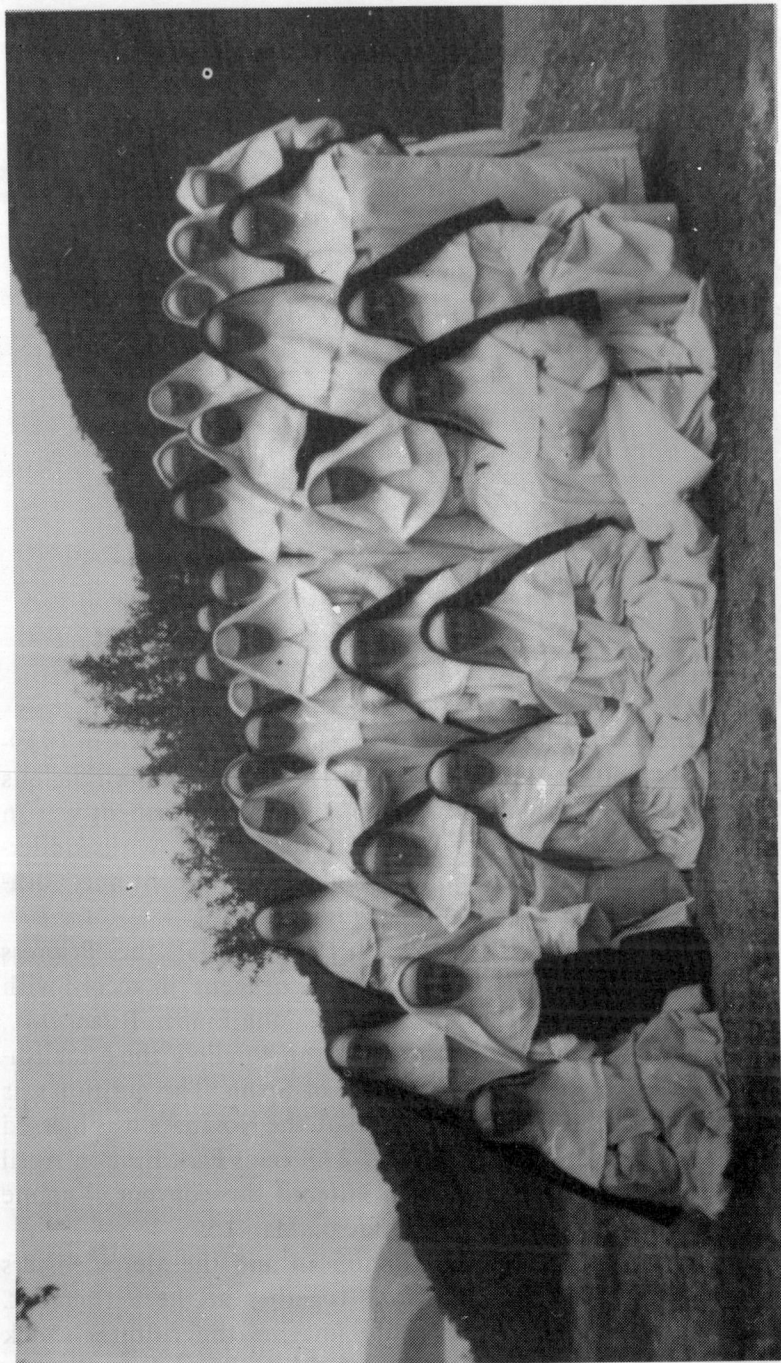

The two Communities: the Dominican and the Mercy Sisters (arrived in 1945).

Chapter
23.

Withdrawal From Chacachacare

One of the ill-effects of war in France between 1939-45 was a halt in the recruiting of vocations to the religious life. Sisters in activity were aging and no replacement was in view. It therefore became obvious that if the works undertaken by the Congregation in Trinidad were to continue, vocations would have to be found locally.

Consequently, on November 12, 1945, the Prioress General of the Sisters of St. Catherine of Siena, in accord with the Archbishop of Port of Spain, Count Finbar Ryan O.P., petitioned the Holy See in the Vatican to allow the establishment of a Novitiate House in Port of Spain. The petition was granted and the foundation-stone of the Novitiate was blessed and laid at Holy Name Convent, 2 Queen's Park East on April 14, 1946. Two young women entered the convent, Yvonne de Verteuil and Esme de la Bastide on May 16.

At Chacachacare, the Dominican and the Mercy Sisters were trying their best to work together at the Settlement. However, the reader can easily imagine the cultural shock experienced by representatives of the Old and New Worlds.

With the coming of the American Sisters, the civil authorities had seen hope of implementing their plan for a new administrative system with fully qualified staff. Dr. Peat, the director of Medical Services, assured Archbishop Ryan that he wanted to retain religious Sisters, preferably the Dominicans who had been associated with the Leprosarium for so many years. However, he made it clear to him that he had to comply with the demands of the government in finding fully qualified staff.

In a letter dated January 18, 1946, Archbishop Ryan pointed out to the Prioress General. "The public authorities have been very busy in trying to strengthen their grip and to lessen the influence of ours; and , of course, every defect in our organisation, and every refusal on our part to co-operate, provides them with an argument for getting rid of religious control altogether."

Faced with a number of defects which could not be remedied in the immediate, the Congregation chose to withdraw the Dominican Sisters from Chacachacare. To this effect, notification was sent to the government in Trinidad, giving it six months notice before the withdrawal of the Sisters.

When the news became known, patients sent petition upon petition to the Governor, Sir Hubert Rance, as they wanted to retain the Dominican Sisters. One of them declared: "The doctors seem to give us up at the time of death, the Sisters on the contrary care for us. The more miserable, pitiful, sinful we are, the more they show us love. They care for us until they have closed our eyes."

The Dominican Sisters received great suppport both from Archbishop Ryan and Fr. Reginald Barry, O.P. who had been the chaplain at Chacachacare for several years.

The withdrawal of the Dominican Sisters from Chacachacare took place at the beginning of October 1950; it was a painful experience for them and the patients. The departure brought an end to a period of 82 years of devoted care to patients — victims of Hansen's disease. However, for some of the Sisters, a similar task was awaiting them in the island of Desirade, a dependency of Guadeloupe in the French West Indies.

Several notes of appreciation about the Dominican Sisters appeared in the Press. Among them there was one signed "Voice of Experience" which read: "We refer to the Sisters of the Dominican Order to whom we owe our deepest gratitude and appreciation for the sacrifices they have made in the past. When we take into consideration the fact that these good souls were the pioneers in establishing a nursing system in our Leprosarium, they are, in our estimation, the unshakable foundation upon which the improvements that are now being made on our behalf rest."

In all fairness, mention must be made here of the Sisters' appreciation (which I found in the convent chronicles) for the Medical Superintendents under whom they worked during those 82 years. According to the Sisters' testimony, it was from those very physicians that they had learned most of their medical skills.

It was on January 1, 1951 that Governor Sir Hubert Rance made known to the population of Trinidad and Tobago that King George V of England had graciously approved the award of Member of the Most Excellent Order of the British Empire (Honorary) to Sister Slava Dobrowlska, religious Sister and ex-matron of the Leprosarium at Chacachacare. In religion, she was Sister Hedwige and she had been in the post of Matron for 28 years (1922-1950) in Cocorite and Chacachacare.

Even the United Kingdom had to bow to this heroic woman of God who had left her homeland, Poland, to devote herself to the care of the unfortunate victims of leprosy in Trinidad and Tobago. May Sr. Hedwige — who died in France in 1967 — and the 10 Sisters who are buried at Chacachacare rest in peace. Their memory remains an inspiration for those who endeavour to follow in their footsteps.

After the withdrawal of the Sisters from Chacachacare, the Government paid a pension to each nursing Sister. The Superiors of the Congregation decided to reserve the money of the pensioners as a fund to be drawn on for the needs of the Novitiate of the Trinidad and Tobago Region. A wonderful gesture of generosity for which we are most grateful.

Chapter
24.

Closing Down the Hansenian
Settlement in Chacachacare

In the Trinidad and Tobago Medical Journal (Volume 43 of 1982) Dr. Richard Keeler, an American specialist in Hansen's disease who came to Trinidad in 1971 at the invitation of the government, stated the following:

"Hansen's disease has shown a marked decline among children in Trinidad and Tobago over the past decade, from 65 cases in 1973 to only three in 1981. The decrease is attributed to the Ministry of Health's decision to stop admissions to the Leprosarium at Chacachacare and shift to an outpatient approach and the intensive case finding, treatment and follow-up of all Hansenian disease cases, not just of the children."

The important factor in the decrease of the number of cases came from the new drugs on the market, namely *Dapsone, Rifampin and Clofazimine* employed to combat the disease. The new drugs, the policy of the Ministry and the total support of Dr. Keeler led to the gradual closing down of the Leprosarium at Chacachacare.

Close collaboration was established between the last Medical Superintendent at the Settlement, Dr. Walter Van Crosson and Dr. Keeler; the former in discharging the patients from the Leprosarium and the latter in receiving them on the mainland of Trinidad and explaining the importance of attending clinics regularly.

Dr. Keeler was of great assistance with the rehabilitation programmes of patients and the opening of new clinics in Port of Spain and San Fernando. With the new medical treatment to combat the disease there is now no more reason for the isolation of Hansenian patients.

In Chacachacare, the cost of running the Leprosarium had skyrocketed. In 1979 it had reached the fabulous sum of $3 million a year; something had to be done. A consultation of patients was held in Chacachacare as regards a rehabilitation programme in Trinidad; the majority agreed to leave Chacachacare provided that each one — or each couple — be given a lodging and means to support themselves in one form or another.

The Leprosy Relief Association was of great assistance in the resettlement of patients. Of course, there were problems, many problems, but with time, patience and tact they were resolved little by little.

After the excitement of returning to normal life in Trinidad, the former patients of Chacachacare found out that they had lost their security as regards food, shelter, medical treatment and for those who were employed at the settlement, their salaries. Nonetheless, gradually they all adjusted to their new living conditions and the freedom they had acquired prevailed.

The last departure of patients from Chacachacare took place on July 23, 1984, Dr. Van Crosson left on September 11, 1984 and Arthur Ramsammy — who opted to stay at the Settlement and who organised his life to suit — finally left in 1985 and resettled in St. James, which he had left in 1927. How things had changed in 58 years!

After the closing down of the Leprosarium, vandals — or were they pirates? — started their work of destruction. In 1980 the Defence Force provided security for the former convent of the Dominican Sisters, who had left the island in 1950, and the quarters that had been occupied by the nurses who came to care for the patients on a shift system from the Port of Spain General Hospital.

In 1985 the Defence Force took complete control of the island of Chacachacare; it is now guarded round the clock by members of the Coast Guard.

The last medical superintendent of the Leprosarium at Chacachacare, Dr. Walter Ferdinand Van Crosson, and his assistant Sultan Khan who left the island on September 11, 1984.

Chapter
25.

Holy Name Convent After
World War II

The work of the Dominican Sisters at Holy Name Convent was to be given a totally different thrust in the post-World War II era. It became imperative to train young local women, called by God to the religious life, so as to ensure the continuation of the apostolic works in this country.

Prior to 1946, when the Novitiate was officially erected at Holy Name Convent, six young Trinidadians had joined the Sisters. Their formation to the religious life was done in France, in Etrépagny where the Mother-house of the Congregation is situated. Also, four Venezuelans and one Tobagonian were admitted into the Congregation as Extern Sisters. These were the first shoots from the implantation of the Congregation in the soil of Trinidad and Tobago.

The Sister destined to give a new impetus to the life of the Dominican Sisters in Trinidad was Sr. Bernadette Robert. She arrived from France on December 8, 1937 and was quickly enrolled to teach at the school. At that time the school was in a period of expansion. A two-wing building, designed by architect Maurice Acanne, was constructed in 1946/47 to accommodate more classrooms for the school as well as the Novitiate of the Dominican Sisters.

In 1948, after the death of a greatly admired Mother Albert, loved for her gracious personality and the remarkable works she had done, Sr. Bernadette was called to succeed her as Prioress of Holy Name Convent and Vicaress of the Prioress General over the convents of Trinidad and Tobago.

At the very beginning of her mandate, the two major tasks which confronted Mother Bernadette were, on one hand, the negotiations with the religious and civil authorities, both in Trinidad and in France, concerning the future of the Dominican Sisters at the Hansenian Settlement of Chacachacare; and on the other hand, the recruitment and formation of local vocations for the religious Dominican life.

With the growth of the Holy Name School, a Parent-Teacher Association was established on September 23, 1946 to assist in its development at all levels. Since 1938, the school was in the safe hands of Sr. Jeanne Emmanuel, the Principal. In June 1949, thanks to the high standard of education attained at the school, Sr. Jeanne Emmanuel obtained from the government the status of 'Approved Secondary School'. From then on, teachers' salaries were paid by the Ministry of Education, thus making it easier to pursue the improvement of school facilities. At that time the enrolment at the Holy Name School was 360 students. Starting in 1939 the school offered a range of subjects reaching the higher school certificate including commercial subjects.

The strong family spirit, which has been the hallmark of Holy Name Convent School, prompted some parents of the students to launch out two main fund raising ventures in order to help finance the running of the school. These were the Christmas Bazaar (which is still part of the life of the school today) and the Children's Carnival. These two events started in 1946/47 and in fact the financial assistance they brought saved the school. God bless those parents and teachers for their wonderful generosity.

On August 30, 1947 three more postulants were given the Dominican religious habit. The Novitiate too was growing and the young Sisters, not only had to be formed to the religious life, but also to be trained professionally to enable them to take their place in the works of the Congregation.

Studies are costly, therefore, to find additional funds, the Sisters opened a Boarding School for Venezuelan students. It lasted 12 years (1950-62).

Faithful to the wish of their benefactress, Mrs. Hannah Campbell, the Sisters engaged in the daily visitation of the patients at the General Hospital situated next door to the Convent. They were also giving of their time to the following organisations: the Past Pupils' Association (founded on June 29, 1936); the St. Luke' Association of medical practitioners and nurses (founded on October 16, 1942); the Sanctuary Guild to help poor parishes (founded in 1949); the Society of St. Cecilia; the Legion of Mary; the Dominican Tertiaries; the Amantes de Jesus and the Catholic Guides.

The year 1948 held a surprise for the Sisters. Due to the unexpected visit of a Canadian priest, Fr. Charles Martel, the Congregation was invited to go to Canada to examine the possibility of making a foundation there. Two Sisters were sent on this mission in March 1948. The Prioress General and her Council having been satisfied with the conditions for opening a home for children in need of care, the foundation started in Montreal in August 1948.

The convents in Trinidad were asked to contribute Sisters and seven of them went to Montreal at different intervals. Unfortunately, this foundation did not succeed but another one later on opened in Toronto as we shall see later.

With the closure of the convent at Marine Bay in Chacachacare (the Sisters' former holiday house) it became necessary to find a replacement. In 1950 a house was put up for sale at Toco/Mission on the north coast situated at a short distance from the church. The cost was very reasonable and the house was purchased by Mother Bernadette and her Council in 1951. Since then, much use has been made of it by the Sisters, their visitors and also groups of children.

The big plan of Mother Bernadette to mark the centenary of the Congregation was to construct a spacious hall on the site of the Pavillon Notre Dame (the former Devenish House). The idea was accepted by the Sisters, teachers and parents of students (at that time the enrolment was 376 with 50 pupils in the Kindergarten). The demolition of the old school began in 1953 to make place for the new structure. Contractors and builders worked hard and well and the 'Marian Hall' (named after the Virgin Mary since 1954 was a Marian Year) was well advanced for the week-long celebrations of the Centenary of the Congregation. Completion of the Hall took place afterwards.

At that time the Holy Name Community consisted of 22 Sisters; six novices and seven postulants were in the Novitiate. A big change had just taken place, namely, the removal of the grilles in the Sisters' chapels and parlours — vestiges of another age.

The joys of that year 1954 were accompanied by sorrows. It began by an epidemic of poliomyelitis which forced all the schools of the country to close down for a whole month. This was followed by an outbreak of the dreaded yellow fever epidemic which spread to some parts of the country. Next there was a fire at the school which was fortunately controlled in time thanks to the kind help of neighbours. Finally, on December 5, 1954 Port of Spain experienced no less than 35 strong earth tremors which caused much damage to buildings including the Holy Name chapel. It was a relief to see that year come to an end!

On December 19, 1958 Mother Bernadette Robert wrote the following letter to Archbishop Finbar Ryan O.P.: "Your Grace, one of the recommendations of the regular visitation of our convent last September, was to plan the transfer of the Novitiate from Holy Name Convent to some quieter place in the country. With this purpose in view, I have made enquiries and was offered two acres of land very well situated on Calvary Hill near Arima at a very reasonable price. The proximity of the college and Priory of the Dominican Fathers and other advantages of the location make it a good prospect. At present we are not in a position to open another convent but should it become feasible in a few years' time, will Your Grace approve of this plan?" The answer was prompt and concise: "Yes, it is a good move." Consequently, the land was acquired by the Dominican Sisters from A. Lazzari in 1959. However, the construction of a Novitiate House never started before the 1970's.

In 1958, the Holy Name student population had reached 653; the school was firmly established and the more than 50 years of experience in education made it fit and ready for giving birth to an off-spring.

The call came from Barataria, then a growing suburb of Port of Spain, through the parish priest Fr. Casimir O'Laughlin O.P. The proposal of establishing a Private Secondary School at Malick was accepted by the relevant authorities and Mother Bernadette worked assiduously to make it a reality. Sr. Jeanne Emmanuel with Sr. Marie Joseph were given the responsibility of starting the school. Classes began in January 1959 with 70 students on roll.

On September 9, 1955 an application was sent to the Government asking that the Holy Name Secondary School be accorded the status of 'Government Assisted'. The request was granted in 1957. As a result, the greater part of the school expenditure is covered by a government grant.

In 1962, with the introduction of free secondary education in the country, eighty percent of incoming students into Form I are admitted to the school as a result of their success at the Common Entrance Examination and twenty percent is left to the choice of the Principal from the Pass list of the examination.

Sr. Jeanne Emmanuel Barrière after her 23 years of fruitful principalship (1938-1961) continued as a member of staff until 1964 when she was assigned to the community of Barataria where she taught at the school for a couple of years.

At Holy Name Convent School, the new Principal, Sr. Bernadette de la Bastide, appointed from January 1, 1961, was educated at the school from a tender age and joined the Sisters in 1946. With her, Holy Name School was about to enter into a new phase of development.

Sr. Bernadette is best qualified to speak about Holy Name School. This is what she stated: "The foundations of Holy Name Convent as we know it today were laid by Sr. Jeanne Emmanuel and Sr. Bernadette Robert between 1938 and 1961. During these years the original buildings which comprised the beautiful Devenish dwelling house with servants' quarters, stables etc. were replaced by the Northern and

Southern Wings and the Marian Hall Block. Sr. Jeanne Emmanuel's unflinching determination to obtain the highest quality in work, discipline, moral and spiritual standards from her pupils has left an indelible mark. Despite her frail health, she worked untiringly to raise the academic standards of the school so that after 50 years as a Private School, it was finally recognised as an Assisted Government Secondary School in 1957.

Sr. Bernadette Robert (1937-1963) a great organiser, worked closely with Sr. Jeanne Emmanuel both as Prioress and Vicaress of the Prioress General. Together they started the Annual Christmas Bazaar in 1946 for, as a private school, the only source of income was the school fees of $16.00 per term. It is, therefore, to the credit of these Sisters, parents, teachers and pupils of the school to record that the proceeds of the Annual Bazaar have built the school.

The first government grant for the upkeep of the school was received in 1957 when it became 'Assisted' and the first building grant in 1969 amounted to $25,000 toward the Science Block which was constructed at a total cost of $172,000.

The tradition of Holy Name is therefore one of 'self-help' built up on the example, dedication and hard work of many French Sisters who are remembered with great affection by all who knew them. This is also the high price that Catholic schools have paid for being labelled 'prestigious' and for the right to preserve their own character."

Mother Bernadette Robert, Vicaress of the Prioress General,
who spent 26 years in Trinidad (1937-1963).

Group of students with school chaplain,
Fr. Casimir O'Loughlin O.P.

The community of the Dominican Sisters of
Holy Name Convent in 1956.

Venezuelan boarders at Holy Name with Sisters. Left to right:
Sr. Rosa Pia, Sr. Mary Assumpta, Mother Bernadette,
Sr. Jeanne Emmanuel and Sr. Bernadette de la Bastide.
The Boarding House was opened in 1947.

Legionaries with Sr. Jeanne Emmanuel (left) and Sr. Pierre Dominique in the late 1940's.

Class of students in 1947 with Sr. Jeanne Emmanuel and Sr. Rosa Pia.

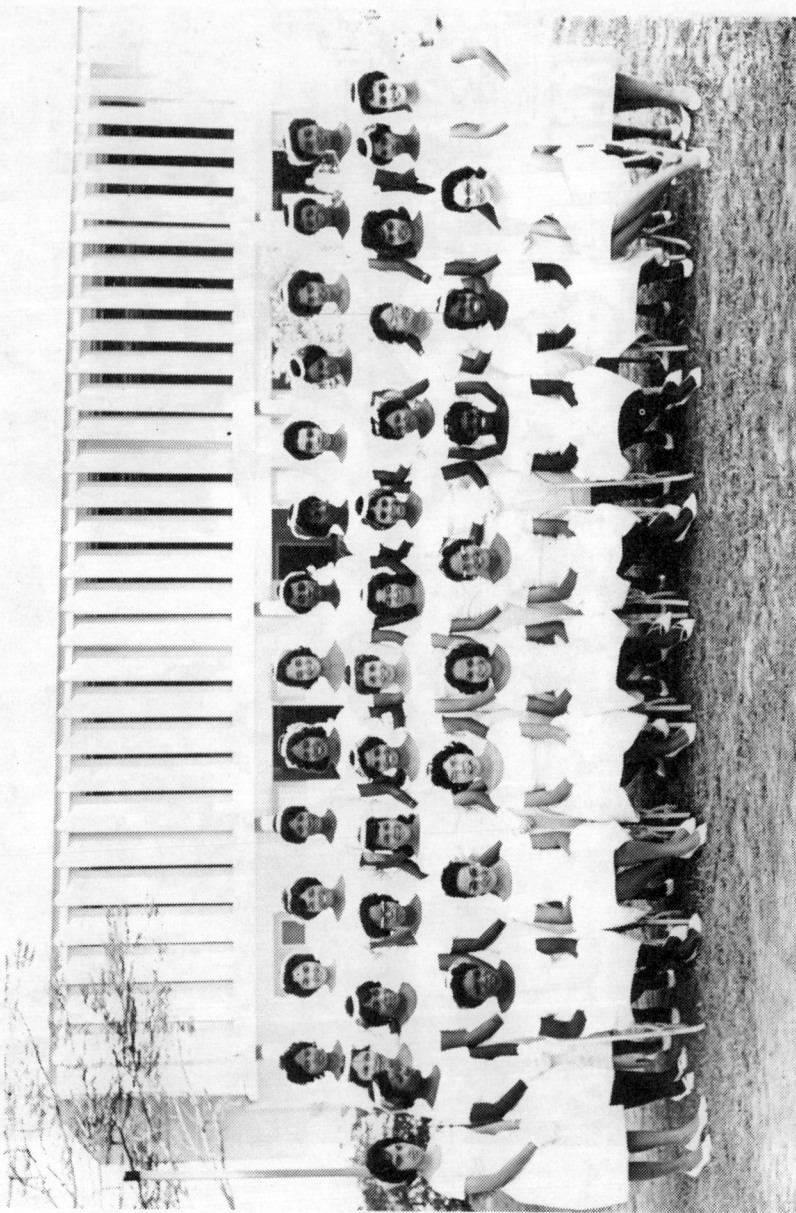

A graduation day at Holy Name Convent in the 1970's.

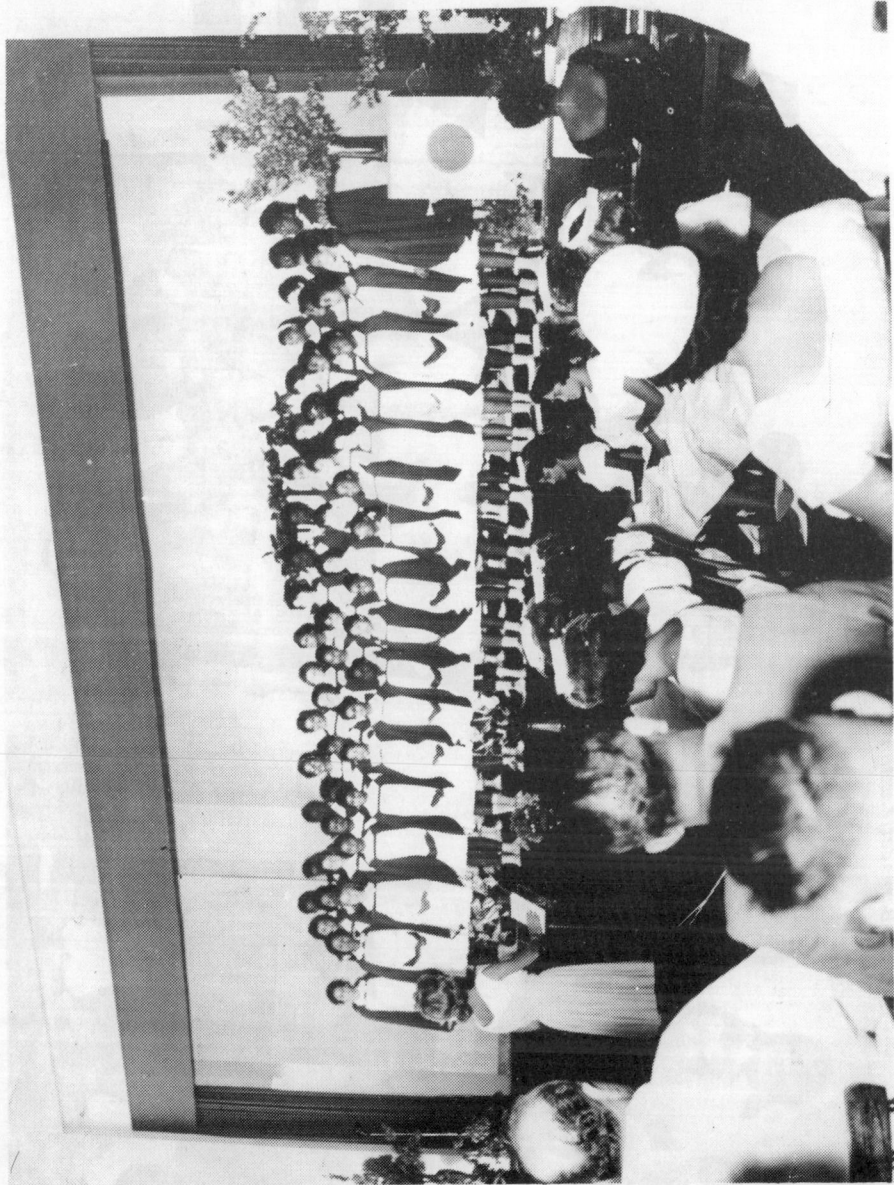

The Holy Name choir conducted by Juliet Littlepage.

Sr. Bernadette with Head Girl, Captains and Prefects.

Happy faces of Holy Name Convent girls in the 1980's.

(250 pupils) accelerated its expansion. With the full co-operation of the pupils' parents, the Sisters engaged in the construction of a building at the back of the school to provide more
classroom and an Assembly Hall. The Holy Name Preparato-y

Chapter
26.

Parents Welcome a New
Holy Name Preparatory School

The year 1962 was most eventful. It brought the beginning of a new era for our nation with the Proclamation of Independence on August 31.

With the introduction of the free education system in the country, it became imperative to remove the Kindergarten and the junior pupils below the age of 11 years to new premises. Consequently, a loan was taken for the purchase of a suitable house, the Y. de Lima family home situated at No. 10 Coblentz Avenue, Cascade. Transformations were made in the dwelling house and with the approval of the Ministry of Education, the Holy Name Preparatory School was opened in January 1962. The school was officially registered on August 20, 1963 (No. 41).

However, the continued growth of the Prep. School (250 pupils) necessitated an expansion. With the full co-operation of the pupils' parents, the Sisters engaged in the construction of a building at the back of the school to provide more classrooms and an Assembly Hall. The Holy Name Preparatory

School made a reputation for itself by the sound education its teachers imparted to the pupils under the able direction of Sr. Marina Cuthbert, the Principal.

Also, 1962 saw the complete renovation of the Holy Name chapel at No. 2 Queen's Park East, Port of Spain. It was spearheaded by Sr. Jeanne Emmanuel whose zeal for the beautification of God's house was only equalled by her indomitable will to succeed in the undertaking. Mother Jeanne's artistic talents then found a unique field of expression. She was most ably assisted in the renovation work by architect W.A. Ackelsberg. This was just another example of Sr. Jeanne Emmanuel's unstinting dedication to the Holy Name Convent to which she gave the best years of her life.

In 1985-86 the chapel was once more in need of repairs. The roof was leaking, and as a result, the exquiste gesso work on the ceiling and columns was fast deteriorating. The Congregation, the Secondary and Preparatory schools, and the Past Pupils Union, all pooled their resources to replace the roof and refurbish the interior. Mrs. Paula Craig, née Lanser, then President of the Past Pupils Union set the pace with great determination and generosity and we owe her a debt of deep gratitude for the restoration of our beautiful chapel which means so much to so many past pupils.

As for Mother Bernadette Robert, the last important work she did before leaving our shores was to organise and implement the transfer of the Novitiate from Holy Name Convent to Barataria in 1963. The same year, she was elected Prioress General of the Congregation and had therefore to return to France. In this capacity, during the 12 years of her generalate, Mother Bernadette regularly returned to Trinidad and Tobago for the visitation of our convents. Mother Bernadette possessed the faith and the foresight to come to grips with the reality of a newly independent people and to realise that the local Sisters would have to assume leadership roles and for which she prepared them.

It was during Mother Bernadette's generalate that the Congregation was re-organised into Regions and the convents established in Trinidad and Tobago became one of them.

A local Sister, Sr. Gloria Marie Laurie, was appointed Regional Prioress in 1969.

Through this new form of government, the Regions were given a greater autonomy in the administration of their affairs. In 1969 there were 47 Sisters in our Region and out of this number 38 were daughters of the soil of Trinidad and Tobago.

The 1970's caused a jolt both to our society and to the Church by revolutionary upheavals. Unrest in the Trinidad and Tobago army led to a mutiny and this stirred a social revolt. It was as though a new society wanted to be born but the birth was a violent one with shooting, looting and repression towards the end of the month of February 1970.

The Church, caught up in the turmoil, was forced to make new assessments of its institutions and outlook. At Holy Name, the Sisters felt that their convent was much too large for their reduced numbers; a re-organisation was obviously needed. Also the changes in the Church, as a result of Vatican II, had serious effects on the religious life.

After consulting with some businessmen, the decision was taken to build a smaller convent on a piece of the Holy Name property, on the left of the main entrance. In November 1947, a survery of the Holy Name property, including the chapel, was taken; it revealed that the property (Holy Name Incorporated Trustees) covers 155,065 superficial feet or a little more than three acres.

The late Bernard Broadbridge was retained as architect and designed the building. Construction went ahead and the new convent was blessed and inaugurated on December 4, 1972. Once the Sisters had moved into their new home, their old but spacious convent was then offered for accommodating the pupils of the Holy Name Preparatory School and No. 10 Coblentz Avenue was sold. With the consent and support of the pupils' parents, the necessary transformations were made in conformity with school requirements. The exchange was a good one and it has brought and continues to bring many benefits to the young pupils.

At the Secondary School, Sr. Bernadette de la Bastide, Principal, with the Board of Management and the full support of the students' parents, made remarkable improvements which consisted in the construction of language and science laboratories as well as the reorganisation of the library and the installation next to it of an audio-visual room equipped with modern apparatus. Sr. Bernadette's leadership was highly appreciated by all concerned. All in all, she had spent 34 years at Holy Name as a young pupil, student, teacher and Principal. The time had come for her to retire.

Great was her distress at being unable to pass on the torch of leadership to one of her religious Sisters. Several of the young Trinidadian Sisters who had acquired academic qualifications had left the convent during the critical years of adjustment to the changing times. The post was offered to Miss Lucia Roach who had spent two years in the Higher Certificate class at Holy Name. She was appointed Principal in January 1, 1982 with the approval of the Ministry of Education. Sr. Helen Gomes O.P. consented to take the post of vice-principal and Sr. Bernadette de la Bastide went into retirement. . . taking the post of Principal of Holy Name Preparatory School.

In 1986, Sr. Bernadette was elected Regional Prioress of the Dominican Sisters in Trinidad and Tobago. Fruitful years are continuing at the service of the Lord and of His people.

The Holy Name Preparatory School in the former convent of the Dominican Sisters.

The new convent of the Dominican Sisters, left of the main entrance of the school.

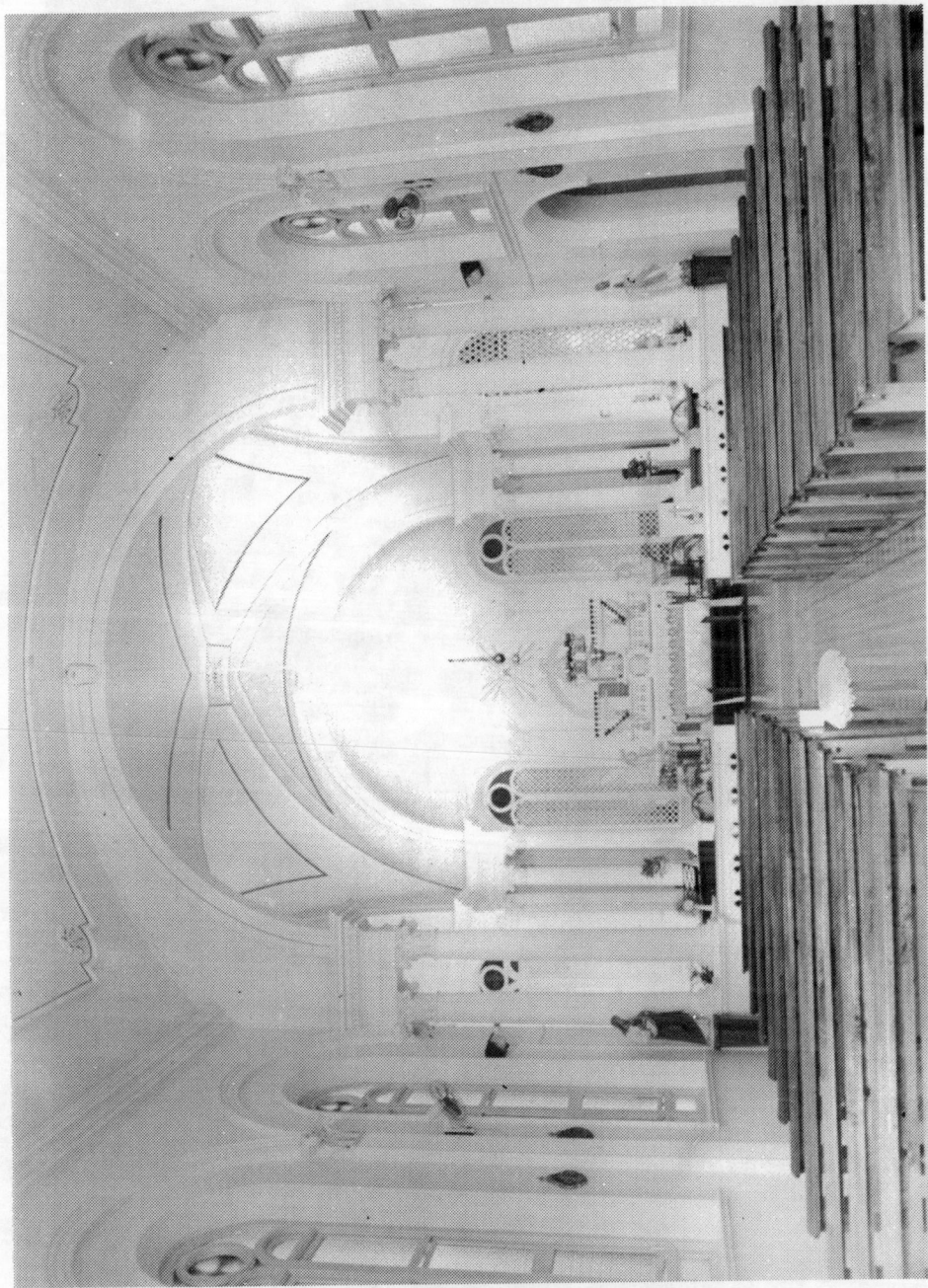

The Holy Name chapel after the 1962 and 1986 renovations. On May 3, 1920, three Benedictine monks from Mount St. Benedict were ordained priest in this chapel.

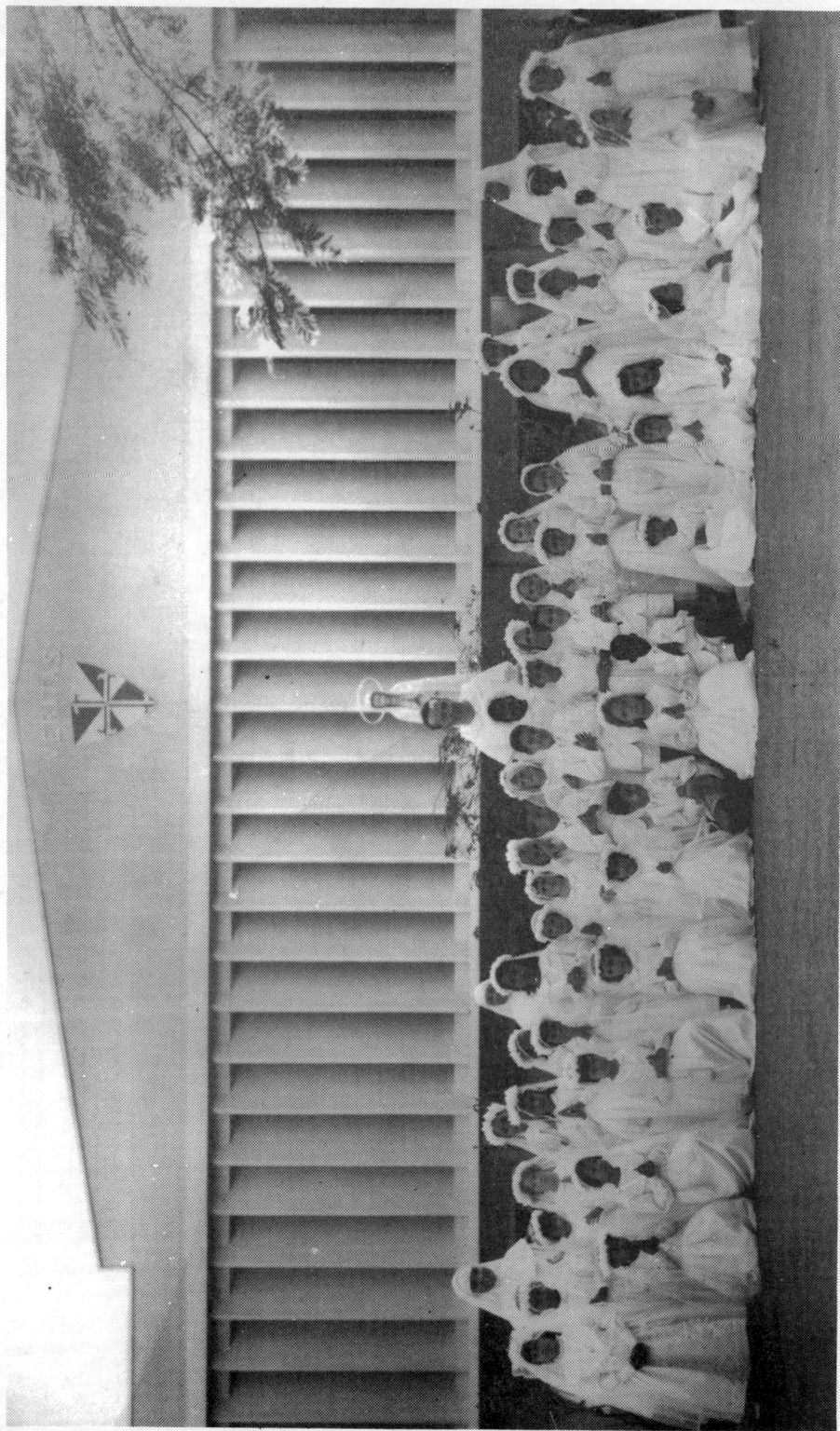

First Communion day with school chaplain, Fr. Aidan Mc Govern O.P.

Pupils of the Holy Name Prep. School with their teachers.

Chapter
27.

The Holy Name Training Centre

Sr. Rose Madeleine Clifton, Manageress of the Holy Name Training Centre with some of the trainees.

Let it be recalled that in 1890, at the request of Archbishop Patrick Vincent Flood O.P., the senior girls of the St. Dominic's Orphanage in Belmont, about 20 of them, were transferred to Holy Name Convent, 2, Queen's Park East, Port of Spain, where an 'ouvroir' as it was called in those days, meaning a charity workshop, was opened for them.

At first, the girls were initiated into printing works at the Catholic Printery, run by the Dominican Sisters and established on their grounds. On May 6, 1892 they printed the first issue of the Catholic News, a weekly which has a record of unbroken publication up to the present day.

The all-round training of the young working girls, under the direction of Sr. Ursula, who was in charge of them for 40 years, consisted in house-keeping, laundry work and embroidery. The latter craft was taught by the French Sisters who excelled in this art. The girls succeeded so well in it, that along with the Sisters they made a reputation for Holy Name as regards needle-work and painting.

A Dominican Tertiary, Miss Katie Yard, who had been assisting the Dominican Sisters at the Good Shepherd Reformatory in Belmont, left the work when the Reformatory was taken over by the Carmelite Sisters in 1923. From 1923 to 1983 when she died at Holy Name Convent, Miss Katie devoted herself unflinchingly to the care and training of the girls at Holy Name. Surely, those 60 years and more of utter dedication did win for her the crown of eternal reward.

In 1931 there were 49 girls at the 'ouvroir' (which now we are going to call the Holy Name Training Centre). A new source of income was provided through the construction of a laundry which enabled the Centre to accept work from private customers.

After the 1939-45 War, it became obvious that the Training Centre had to be reorganised in order to ensure its survival. As new girls aged 14-18, sought admission, assistance was obtained from the students of the Secondary School to give them private lessons in basic knowledge and also to train them in various sports.

As the country moved to Independence in 1962, new aspirations came to the fore for self-development. The girls were mostly primary school-leavers and secondary school drop-outs in great need of training to fit them for employment. Some of them came from rural areas where there was no hope of making a decent livelihood. Sr. Rose Madeleine Clifton, who is in charge of the Centre since 1946, managed to find avenues to expand the range of activities for the training of the young girls. In 1961-62 Sisters Rose Madeleine introduced classes in sewing/designing, hairdressing and cake icing; for those who had the aptitude, she had them attend commercial classes.

The old wooden house of the 'ouvroir' more than outlived its time and was in dire need of replacement. Times were changing in the 1970's and God pointed the way the Training Centre should go by sending two priests as advisers. The first was Fr. Kelvin Felix, a lecturer in Sociology at the Regional Seminary. He visited the Centre and made worthwhile recommendations in view of improving it.

Later in that year 1971 Fr. Pius Davy O.P., who was then deeply involved in the Credit Union movement, also came to visit and made a study for establishing the Centre on a more stable economic basis. The question of operating the Training Centre as a Junior Co-operative presented several difficulties in that the persons involved were teenagers and the group was often changing.

A decision was taken to accept the facilities offered by the Government in the form of evening classes held at Tranquillity Secondary School and at the John Donaldson Institute for technical training. Since the Holy Name Centre did not offer recognised certificates of proficiency, attending those classes was of great importance and benefit to the girls. The decision proved to be a success.

The Centre was moving in a new direction, therefore, the Dominican Sisters, headed by Sr. Rose de Verteuil, the Regional Prioress at that time, took a low-interest loan, thanks to the kind assistance of Messrs. Winston Dasent and Steve Solomon, to engage in the construction of a new building for the Training Centre.

The building was designed by the late Bernard Broadbridge; the work of demolition of the old one and the actual construction of the new started in 1973. Formal blessing of the new Holy Name Training Centre, situated at the back of the Holy Name Secondary School, was given by His Grace Archbishop Anthony Pantin on March 20, 1974.

That day was a milestone in the history of the Centre. Since then, what it offers to girls aged 14-18 is a four-year residential course in moral and religious education: sewing and dressmaking (the girls make all the uniforms for students of the Holy Name Schools); catering and home economics (they run the two school cafeterias); hairdressing (the Centre has its own salon) and handicraft.

Academic work is pursued through enrolment at the Tranquillity Secondary School for the GCE and CXC certificates, as well as at a Commercial school to learn book-keeping and typewriting.

The Training Centre has become self supporting thanks to the income provided by the sale of work produced during training in needlework and handicraft, school uniforms, household linen, baby layettes and the cafeterias.

In 1976-77 a section of the Sisters' old convent, on the side of the chapel (former parlours), was renovated and transformed into a boutique, the 'Keskidee', from which all the needle-work and handicraft are sold to customers.

Many friends of the Training Centre have taken a keen interest in the welfare of the girls over the years. There is no doubt that the seed planted 97 years ago has now produced a big tree despite the many hardships and difficulties; it now stands poised for its approaching centenary.

Six 'old' girls have manifested their attachment to the Centre by having their wedding receptions held there, a gesture which has certainly enhanced the family spirit of the Holy Name Training Centre.

One of the special blessings God has showered on this charitable institution has been the calling of five of the "old girls" to the religious life among the Dominican Sisters. The tree is still very much alive producing good fruit to the glory of God.

Past girls from Holy Name Training Centre with Sr. Francoise, Sr. Rose Madeleine and Miss Katie Yard, a Dominican Tertiary who lived and worked with the Sisters for 60 years.

Chapter
28.

St. Dominic's Children's Home

Sr. Mary Assumpta Brathwaite with some little girls of the Home.

The year 1958 marked a turning point in the history of St. Dominic's Orphanage which eventually took a name more appropriate to the condition of the children being cared for: The St. Dominic's Children Home. Nowadays the real orphans committed to the Home are few; most of them are children who are in need of care and protection.

In the 13 years she spent at St. Dominic's, Sr. Catherine Dominique Viau O.P., reconstructed the houses of the Home — a tremendous task which absorbed much of her unbounded energy. The pace of change was rapid. In 1958 Sr. Catherine Dominique was assigned to Guadeloupe to engage in a similar type of work in Pointe-a-Pitre. The loss to St. Dominic's was to be the gain of the Foyer Notre Dame de Grace in Guadeloupe.

After the departure of Sr. Catherine Dominique, who was Prioress and Manager at St. Dominic's, five more Sisters of the community were transferred to other convents — a real exodus! Sr. Françoise Arthus-Bertrand was appointed Prioress and Manager of the Home; she completed the work of renovation of the buildings undertaken by her predecessor.

The departure of the French Sisters had a profound effect on the staff members of the Home who had worked hand in hand with them for the welfare of the children for the past 82 years. Young Trinidadian Sisters were gradually filling the gap though they still had to gain experience in the work. Some of them were sent to England to qualify in the field of Child Care and Management of Residential Children's Homes.

In the late fifties, Trinidad and Tobago experienced labour unrest manifested in various protests and strikes. The Trade Union movement was very active. The day came when representatives of the staff of St. Dominic's Home announced to the Manager, Sr. Françoise, that most of the staff members had joined the Federated Workers' Trade Union and that this Union was going to be their bargaining power for negotiations with the management of the Home.

The Manager notified her Board of Management* about the decision. The Board Members, selected and appointed by the RC Archbiship, include a priest — the Archbishop's own representative — and the Sister Manager of the Home agreed to enter into negotiations with the Trade Union.

The aim of the staff was to attain the status of Public Servants. In 1969 they were represented by the Public Service Association which took the matter to the Industrial Court. An Agreement was signed on May 30, 1969 by the Chief Personnel Officer on behalf of the Government and a representative of the Board of Management on behalf of the Archbishop, whereby all the employees were to be classified and compensated as if they were Civil Servants. The payment of a pension was included.

Over the years, the demands made by the Union on behalf of the employees have been of great benefit to them: increase of salaries, reduction of working hours which have resulted in a major increase of staff, the provision of uniforms and meals while on duty.

*This Board, let it be recalled, was established in June 1935 by Archbishop John Pius Dowling O.P., to assist the Sister in charge of the Home Management. Ever since, the Board of Management has played a vital role in the affairs of St. Dominic's Home including the recruiting and monitoring of the staff.

The question can be asked, 'Have all these benefits to the staff resulted in better care for the children?' What is certain is that the eight-hour shift system has increased the insecurity of the children. Also, the number of Sisters working at the Home is now reduced to five out of a total of 101 employees.

In February 1980, without any advance warning, the St. Dominic's Home became a 'Statutory Authority' and was subject to the provisions of the Statutory Authorities Act. In accordance, therefore, appointments to vacancies on staff have to be made in keeping with the Act regulating these Statutory Authorities. In other words, this latest move in the administration of the Home has taken away from the Manager and the Board of Management the right to select members of the staff.

The religious character of the Home is very important and can only be maintained by the employment of persons of the same religious persuasion and those who can foster the ideals of the founders. The present administration of the St. Dominic's Children's Home, subject to the Statutory Authorities' Commission, defeats this purpose.

The situation is so very reminiscent of what Archbishop Count Finbar Ryan O.P., mentioned in a letter he wrote to the Prioress General of the Dominican Sisters on June 14, 1962: "The Orphanage presents quite a special problem because while, theoretically, it is Church property, in fact it is half a state institution."

Sr. Gloria Marie Laurie, the first Trinidadian Sister-Manager of the Home and Prioress of the community of Sisters, was appointed to both posts in July 1963. She was succeeded by Sr. Mary Margaret Griffith who went into retirement in 1985. At present, Sr. Martin Dominic Allum is Acting Manager. As regards the children themselves, they certainly enjoy much more comfort than in the olden days. Their numbers have been considerably reduced over the past 20 years which should facilitate the formation of family units within the Home. Children of secondary school age now attend public secondary schools in Port of Spain.

In 1971, to mark the centenary of the St. Dominic's Children's Home and in order to give a new thrust to this special work of education, the decision was taken by the Sisters to engage in the construction of a homestead to accommodate about 12 children from the Home. This was done on a piece of land belonging to the Dominican Sisters at Malick, Barataria where they have a school and a convent. On December 5, 1972 the 'Sunnyhill Homestead' was blessed and opened by Archbhishop Anthony Pantin C.S.Sp. This was a new venture in the field of Child Care in Trinidad and Tobago so as to enable deprived children to grow up in an atmosphere of trust and confidence as close as possible to that of a family. It is an annexe of the St. Dominic's Home. Sr. Marina Serrette was put in charge of Sunnyhill; she is at present in Canada on study-leave.

In 1979, the Sisters, supported by the Board of Management, engaged in another venture, namely, the opening of a Transient Home for boys on the grounds of St. Dominic's. This was to facilitate their adaptation to life outside of the Home after their discharge at the critical age of 16. The St. John Bosco's Home was entrusted to the care of Mrs. Jean Johnson, a dedicated house-mother at St. Dominic's, who shared her family life with the boys.*

In 1983, a similar move was made and another homestead was built on a portion of land of the Dominican Sisters at Calvary Hill, Arima, the site of their Novitiate House.

Sr. Mary Assumpta Brathwaite, with 29 years of service at St. Dominic's Home is in charge of 'Plainview Homestead' also built for 12 children. Brothers and sisters are preferably chosen so as to keep them together rather than having them separated in a large institution like St. Dominic's Home.

These three experiments, having given ample proof of the success of the new educational approach for deprived children, point to the way the Home should go in future. The hope of the Dominican Sisters lies in the new Government formed after the general elections of December 15, 1986. They look forward to its full co-operation in helping them to continue their work of Christian education among deprived children which will equip them to take their rightful place in society.

*   *The Transient Home for boys was a failure. The premises are now used for another family unit, named after St. Catherine, which was organised by the new acting Manager of St. Dominic's Home, Sr. Francine Scott O.P.*

Dominican Sisters and children of Mary (1966).

Boys lining up to go for an outing in their bus.

Some of the musicians of the renowned St. Dominic's Band.

St. Dominic's Children's Home seen from the western side (General Hospital).

"Plainview" homestead at Calvary Hill, Arima.

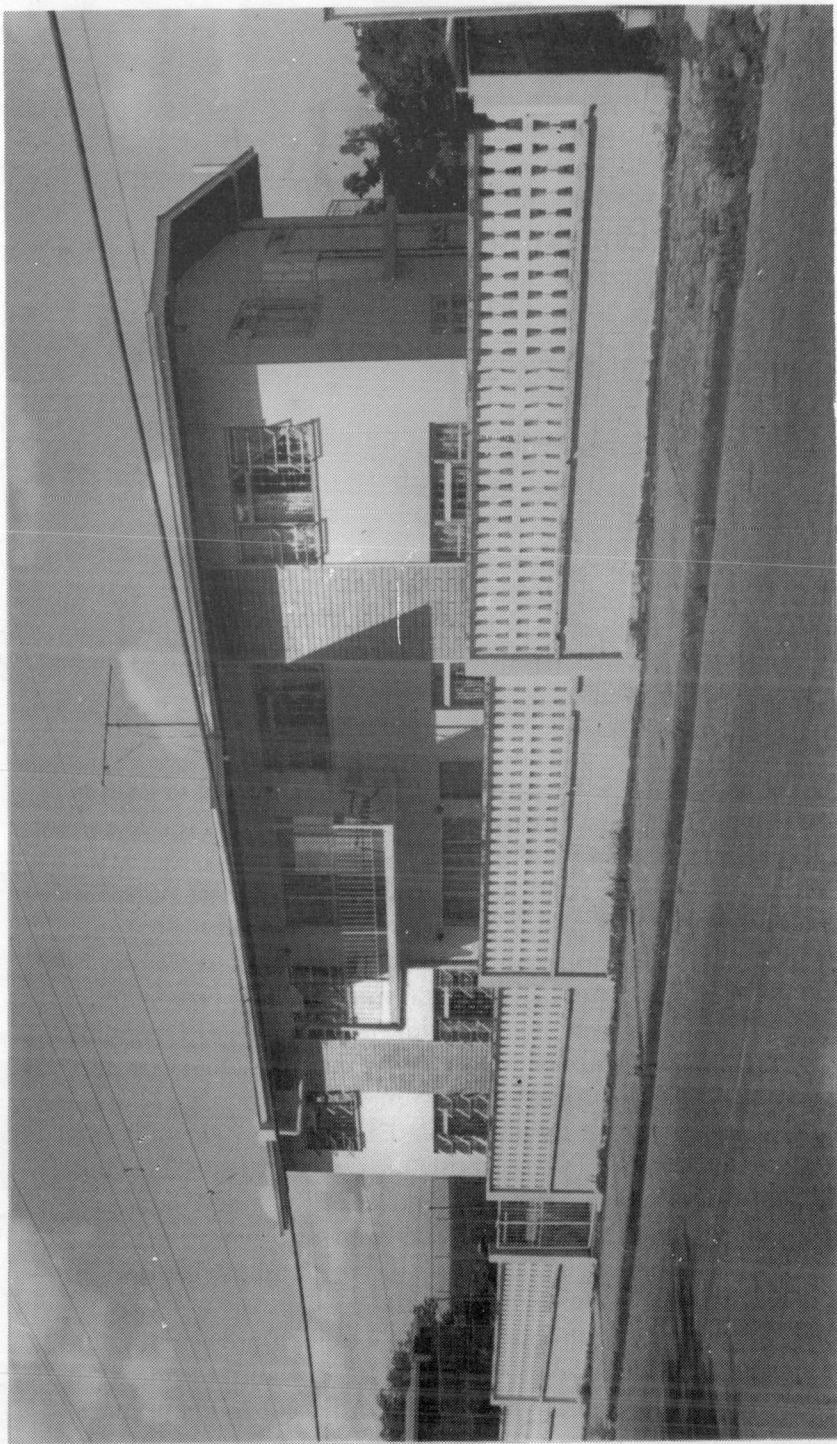

"Sunnyhill" homestead at Malick. Barataria.

Chapter
29.

Breaking New Ground:
Barataria

In the 1950's, the growth of the San Juan district was such that two new areas were developed — Barataria and Malick, the latter on the hillside, north of the Eastern Main Road. It was in 1956 that the Archdiocese of Port of Spain established the new parish of Barataria-Malick and Fr. Casimir O'Laughlin, O.P., was appointed its first parish priest.

The Catholic population was estimated at approximately 10,000 but there was no place for worship. Fr. O'Laughlin, undeterred, searched for ways and means to provide one and obtained from the American base in Chaguaramas a prefabricated building which he had mounted in Malick. The building was to serve a two-fold purpose: as a place of worship and as a primary school until the completion of a new building.

On August 30, 1956, Fr. O'Laughlin, whose greatest desire was to have religious Sisters in his parish, wrote to the Prioress General of the Dominican Sisters:

"The need of schools is evident and their provision is our major anxiety at present. We have already built a church, a presbytery and a primary school here. Adjacent to the primary school there is a piece of land, over one hectare in extent, which is very suitable for a secondary school and a future convent. The spot on a hill overlooking two valleys is a very healthy area. The whole district is being laid out under a new development plan and 650 new houses are to be built.

"His Grace the Archbishop is willing to hand over the lease of this land to your Congregation. (The deed of lease from Aranguez Estates Ltd. was dated December 28, 1955 in respect of two acres and 32 perches, situated at Malick, to build a secondary school and a convent. The lease was for a term of 99 years, renewable, from January 1, 1955 and the condition was that the land be used for educational or religious purposes).

"The Department of Education agrees to recognise the new school as a branch of the Holy Name Convent School but it will not contribute to the cost of the building.

"His Grace the Archbishop is willing that the necessary loan be made in his name on the understanding that the Dominican Sisters pay the interest and liquidate the capital debt little by little. In this way, the Sisters will own and control the school from the beginning. Later, it will be possible to have an independent convent on the site and, needless to say, we believe that the existence of a religious community in the district will have a tremendous influence for good."

The inviting appeal of Fr. O'Loughlin, supported by Mother Bernadette Robert, Vicaress, was heard by the Prioress General and her counsellor in Etrepagny, and the foundation was accepted. The responsibility for the implementation of this decision fell on Mother Bernadette who brought to this new call to service tremendous dedication and foresight.

On October 26, 1958 an entrance examination of candidates for secondary education was held in Malick. Out of the 170 who applied, only 70 could be retained as the scheme was to begin in a small way with two classes (aged 10 to 12 years) and to increase gradually from year to year.

St. Dominic's Secondary Private School, an offshoot of Holy Name Convent Secondary, opened its doors at Malick on January 29, 1959. The responsibility for its management was shared by Sr. Marie Joseph and Sr. Jeanne Emmanuel. Indeed

these two Principals, fully supported by Sr. Bernadette Robert
and Sr. Francoise Arthus-Bertrand, set the roots on which
was to flourish the modern day St. Dominic's Convent School.

Classes started on the side aisles of the prefabricated
church building with temporary partitions which had to be
removed every Friday and put up every Monday as the church
was used for divine worship on the weekend. Meanwhile, construction of the new secondary school was going ahead with
Mr. Deussen, architect and Mr. Norman Monsegue, building
contractor, as well as the determined effort and watchful care
of Sr. Bernadette Robert.

The blessing of the new St. Dominic's school took place
on January 29, 1960. At that time there were 115 pupils
enrolled. It became imperative that a community of Dominican Sisters should live next to the school, therefore, the decision was taken to build a convent as had been previously
planned.

For the construction and the furnishing of the convent,
which formed the northern wing of the school building, the
Sisters received generous help from the other convents of the
Congregation both here and in France.

On February 11, 1962, the little community of four: Sr.
Bernadette, Sr. Marie Joseph, Sr. Veronica and Sr. Mary
moved into their new convent; a few days later they were
joined by Sr. Catherine Lucy. The first Mass was celebrated in
the chapel on February 17, 1962.

The official blessing of the school and of the convent by
Archbishop Finbar Ryan O.P., was on March 12, 1962. In his
address, the Archbishop said that the opening of this school
continued the educational work of the Church which started
in Trinidad in 1850 when the first Archbishop, The Most Rev.
Patrick Smith, on being refused the necessary subsidies to
open schools to educate freed slaves, personally began to
gather children and to teach them basic rudiments of
knowledge in the Cathedral of the Immaculate Conception.

A few years later, long before the Government had taken
any initiative, there were Catholic schools in all important
centres of the country.

In October 1960 an application was sent to the Ministry

of Education and Culture to have the school recognised as an "assisted school" but this was refused and the status of "approved private secondary school" was maintained. The numbers of students kept increasing: in April 1962 the school had a roll of 240 students. In 1987 there are 380.

In 1963, after four years of dedicated service and hard work establishing the foundations of the school, Sr. Marie Joseph had to return to France to serve in other fields of the Congregation. Sr. Jeanne Emmanuel then took over fully the administration of the school. Past pupils still remember her with affection and gratitude: they also remember her as a strict disciplinarian who placed great emphasis on high standards of morality and striving after excellence.

Sr. Rose de Verteuil succeeded Sr. Jeanne Emmanuel as Principal in 1966 and continued to build on what had gone before. The financing of the school was and continues to be a strain. The problem was and still is today, how to cater, on the one hand, for students coming from the lower income bracket and, on the other, to allow for the employment of qualified staff. Sr. Rose concentrated on providing Library facilities and the furnishing of equipment so that the school could function adequately.

In 1971 the time had come for yet another change. It became evident that Sr. Rose de Verteuil, who had been assisting the Holy Name Preparatory School on a temporary basis, now had to assume full responsibility for its administration. On March 5, 1971, therefore, Sr. Moyra Ann Roach, a member of the school staff, was appointed Principal, a position she still holds 16 years later.

Sr. Moyra Ann is particularly gifted for understanding the students who come from very different milieux and with varying levels of academic ability. From its inception the school has been catering for the slow learner and has aimed at giving all students an all-round education.

This is a task that has always been challenging even more so in these times. Opportunities are provided for the students to participate in extra-curricular activities so that their personalities can be encouraged to develop.

In 1964 Fr. O'Loughlin asked the Sisters for the loan of

their assembly hall for the celebration of Mass on weekends as the time had come for him to build a new church and consequently the old prefabricated building had to be demolished to make way for the new place of worship. This arrangement lasted four years until a new octagonal church — the first of its kind in Trinidad — was completed and blessed on July 9, 1968.

Sr. Bernadette Robert who saw her dream become a reality when the Novitiate was established at Holy Name Convent in 1946, now saw the need for its removal to a more suitable place. The Convent at Malick was found to be appropriate. She, therefore, sought authorisation to do so and it was accepted both by the Congregation and the Church authorities. The transfer of the Novitiate to Malick took place on October 15, 1963 and Fr. Reginald Barry, O.P., blessed the new quarters of the Novitiate on November 15, 1963.

The first vocation for religious life to come out of St. Dominic's school was Kathleen Jackman. She was a member of the first class which began in 1958 and she graduated in 1963. Kathleen first entered the Dominican Congregation in 1964 but had to leave for a certain period only to return four years later to the Novitiate in Malick.

Sr. Kathleen served the Lord faithfully and with dedication in the fields of education and social work. In the last years of her short life she was deeply involved in the pastoral and social outreach to West Indians in Toronto, Canada. After a heroic struggle against cancer, she was called "Home" by God in January 1985. May she rest in peace.

From the very beginning of their presence in Malick, the Dominican Sisters helped in the parish, particularly in teaching catechetics. This they did in various schools. Today, their activity is centred more on the parish itself and they co-ordinate the baptism-first-communion-confirmation classes in Religious Education.

Students of St. Dominic's school in the early days with on the foreground Sr. Bernadette de la Bastide, Sr. Bernadette Robert and Sr. Marie Joseph.

First student of St. Dominic's Barataria Top right: Kathleen Jackman.

Sr. Rose de Verteuil O.P. and Mrs. Muriel Murray, teacher.

Sr. Moyra Ann Roach, Principal with a group of pupils in front of St. Dominic's school.

*Sr. Jeanne Emmanuel with a group of pupils of
St. Dominic's school on a visit at the Point Fortin oil refinery in 1965.*

The Hockey team of St. Dominic's school.

St. Dominic's school (main building) at Malick, Barataria.

Sr. Moyra Ann Roach with pupils (1987).

Chapter
30.

Dominican Sisters in the Oil Belt

On December 30, 1967, the front page of the Catholic News announced the following: "New Dominican Convent at Point Fortin — a gift from the Shell Oil Company. The blessing of the new convent, placed under the patronage of the Holy Name of Mary, which is being run by the Dominican Sisters of St. Catherine of Siena, situated at No. 67 Clifton Hill, is headed by Sr. Paul Dominic Clarke, O.P., Prioress and Novice Mistress.

"Officiating at the ceremony was Fr. Casimir O'Loughlin, O.P., who represented the Apostolic Administrator, Bishop William M. Fitzgerald, O.P. Assisting him were Fr. Norbert Grey, O.P., Administrator of the Cathedral and Fr. Michael Makhan, parish priest of Point Fortin.

"In their address, both Fr. O'Loughlin and Fr. Makhan thanked Shell Trinidad Limited for their generosity towards the Church."

For economic reasons, the Shell Company was ridding itself of all perquisites which were not directly connected with the production of oil. The Clifton Hill Preparatory school came under this heading.

The company's directors, therefore, desirous of handing over the management of the school to some reliable organisation, asked Mother Françoise Arthus-Bertrand, O.P., Vicaress of the Prioress General over the Dominican Sisters in Trinidad and Tobago, if the Sisters would be willing to take it over from them.

After some deliberation, a Deed of Gift was arranged between the Company and the Sisters, not only for the school but also for the house at No. 67 Clifton Hill situated on the camp, to be used as a convent for the Sisters.

The handing over took place in January 1968 and the Sisters have been there ever since. The Clifton Hill Dominican Convent occupies a picturesque site. It overlooks the sea on the western side and is surrounded by trees and hillocks. There is an aura of peace and harmony all around — a very conducive atmosphere for a convent. The Preparatory School, built on a knoll, is a short distance from the convent.

It was considered appropriate to accommodate the Novitiate of the Dominican Region of Trinidad and Tobago in the convent of Point Fortin. The plan was approved by the ecclesiastical and religious authorities and the transfer of the Novitiate took place at the beginning of 1968.

The General Manager of Shell Trinidad Company, who then occupied a handsome residence facing the sea, (bungalow No. 3 on the Camp), built in the midst of spacious grounds, offered it to the Dominican Sisters at a minimal cost for the purpose of establishing a second school there.

Though the price was low, the Sisters could not afford to buy the property. The purchase was eventually made by the Archdiocese and the Sisters undertook to open a secondary school in the house which they named after St. Bernadette. This was done on September 6, 1968 with 70 pupils as a start. Sr. Jeanne Emmanuel, the former Principal of Holy Name Convent School, was appointed Principal. She remained in the post until 1975 when she returned to France after having spent 47 years of utter dedication to the work of Christian education in Trinidad and Tobago.

In the early 1970's, Point Fortin and other areas around

in the deep south of Trinidad were very much deprived of facilities for secondary education. In those days, opening a private secondary school was a great risk on account of the uncertainty of the place of private schools in the overall educational plan for the future of the country.

Nevertheless, the Sisters took the risk and made an attempt with the view of helping families whose daughters had to travel long distances to attend school. In return, the parents were of great assistance to the Principal in raising funds for the administering of St. Bernadette's. Thanks to their combined efforts, more classrooms, a biology laboratory and a hall were constructed permitting an intake of 184 students.

Despite the progress made, once Sr. Jeanne Emmanuel had departed for a well-deserved retirement, the Dominican Sisters found themselves unable to carry out the responsibility of the school due to the lack of teaching Sisters. Archbishop Pantin then appointed a Board of Management for the school which continued to operate for a few more years, though with increased difficulties. Finally, it had to be closed down.

Today, St. Bernadette's has become an important centre for the Catholic Charismatic Renewal which serves the needs of its members in southern Trinidad.

After a few years it was found that if, on the one hand Clifton Hill was an ideal spot for a Novitiate, on account of its peaceful environment conducive to recollection and prayer; on the other hand, its position made it unsuitable for providing the intellectual training which is part of the religious formation of young Sisters.

To keep abreast, the novices and their Mistress had to travel to Port of Spain, or to the Regional Seminary, to attend lectures and classes; and this was onerous in many ways.

Consequently, in 1968, the decision was taken to temporarily accommodate the Novitiate at the R.C. Chaplaincy of the University of the West Indies at St. Augustine — also run by the Dominican Sisters — until the construction of the formal Novitiate House in Arima was completed.

A way of making use of the Clifton Hill convent was discovered in the demands from persons who, in search of God, were anxious to find a place for reflection and prayer. Sr.

Gloria Marie Laurie having the disposition for responding to this need, was asked to accept the challenge of transforming the convent into a Retreat-cum-Prayer House.

The convent was renamed *"Veritas" House of Prayer*. It was inaugurated on February 6, 1982. Groups of students, youths and adults have benefitted from this facility. However, with the present economic depression of the 80's, their numbers have drastically diminished.

Over the years, the Dominican Sisters at Clifton Hill, starting with Sr. Paul Dominic Clarke, have been very much involved in parish activities, namely, imparting religious education to children and adults, visiting the sick, and conducting religious services in out-stations of the parish. They have definitely taken their place in this pleasant town of Point Fortin — recently raised to the status of a Borough.

The Clifton Hill School is still administered by the Dominican Sisters, ably assisted by a lay Principal, Mrs. Grace Bradshaw, and a staff of dedicated teachers.

The school continues to enjoy some measure of success and offers a well-rounded education to its students, encouraging them to strive for excellence in and out of the classroom. Emphasis is placed not only on academic subjects, though the school enjoys a very good standing in this area, but also on extra-curricular activities which help to develop the whole potential of the students.

While school places are made available for the senior staff members of TRINTOC, (Trinidad and Tobago Oil Company), in keeping with the agreement at the time of the hand-over, students come from all walks of life. When the responsibility for the school was assumed by the Sisters, it was stressed that the school had to play an important role in bridging the exclusive area of Clifton Hill with the town of Point Fortin and its environs.

It is noteworthy that the presence of the Sisters on the Camp and their influence in the school have helped to bring about a change.

Sr. Gloria Marie Laurie welcomes retreatants

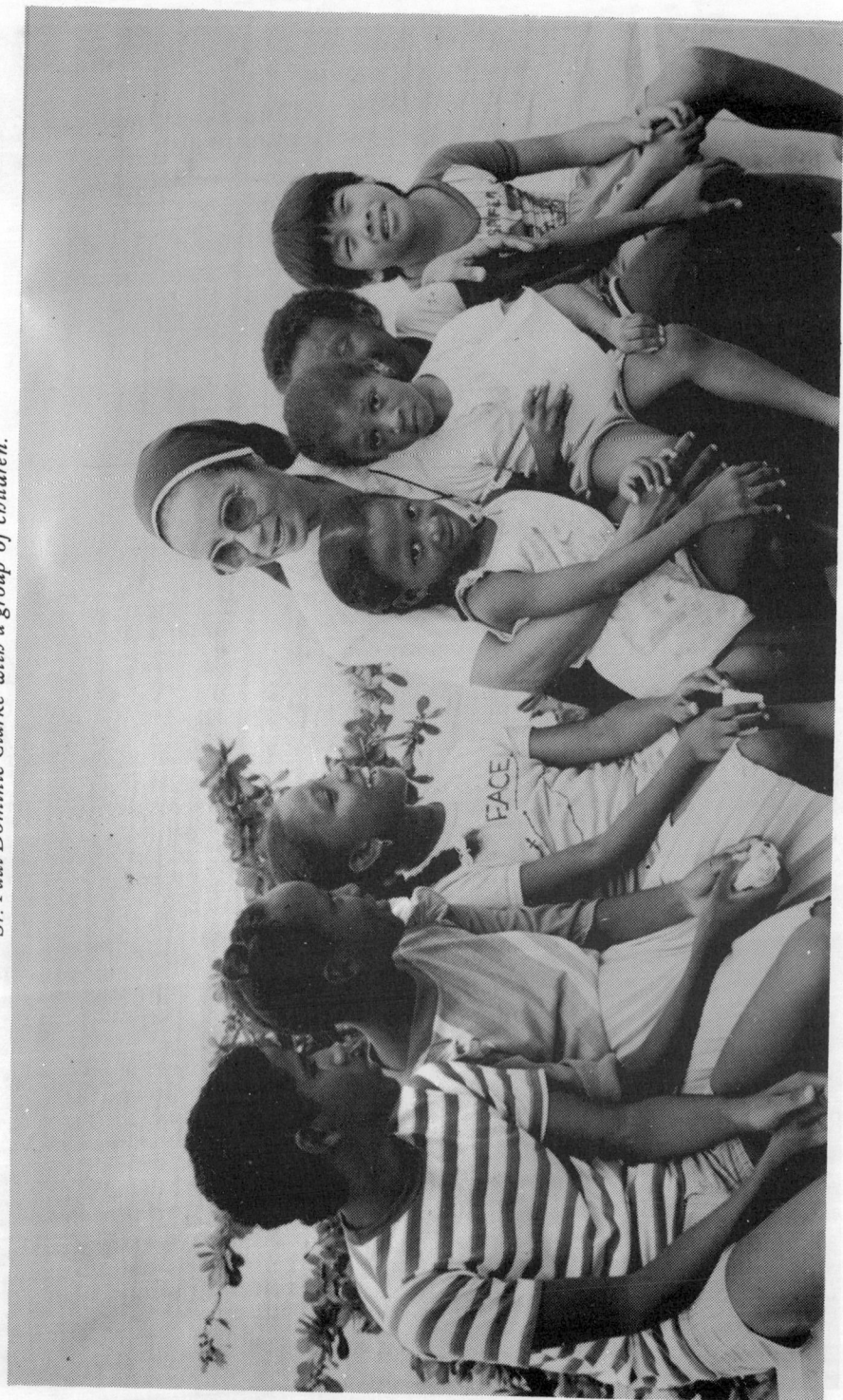

Sr. Paul Dominic Clarke with a group of children.

The 'VERITAS' House of Prayer of the Dominican Sisters at Clifton Hill, Point Fortin.

Pupils of Clifton Hill Preparatory school with teachers and Principal, Mrs. Grace Bradshaw.

Chapter
31.

Beacon on the University Campus:
The RC Chaplaincy

The presence of large numbers of ex-students of R.C. secondary schools in Trinidad and Tobago on the St. Augustine Campus of the University of the West Indies called for the establishment of an R.C. Chaplaincy as close as possible to the campus. Divine Providence facilitated its establishment.

In 1965, five years after the founding of the St. Augustine Campus, the Rostant's house situated at No. 2 Carmody Road on the border of the campus was put up for sale. The Archdiocese bought it along with the spacious grounds around it. Fr. Arthur Lai Fook, C.S.Sp., was appointed as its first Chaplain where he took up residence. Over the years, he was succeeded by several other priests.

In 1967, an appeal was made to religious Sisters to assist the Chaplain in his work; the Carmelite Sisters responded. An additional building was erected on the western side of the house to accommodate the community of Sisters on the upper floor and to provide a hall on the ground floor for the use of the ever-increasing number of students coming to the Chaplaincy.

In 1972, the Carmelite Sisters withdrew from the Chaplaincy.

Fr. Hildebrand Greene, OSB, was appointed chaplain for a year (1972-73). He was assisted by Sr. Caritas Lawrence of the Order of Mercy who came from Belize to Trinidad and Tobago for a sabbatical year.

Accommodation was provided at the Chaplaincy for religious Sisters who were students at the St. Augustine Campus of the University of the West Indies as well as some lay students.

In 1973, Fr. Jeff Belgrave succeeded Fr. Greene. The Dominican Sisters, who had accepted to take charge of the UWI Chaplaincy, sent Sr. Paul Dominic Clarke and she continued to run the Chaplaincy as an hostel.

The major part of the Rostant's house was then transformed into a chapel with a meeting room attached to it and a large gallery in front. The Chaplaincy thus became a place which could offer hospitality, worship, private prayer, quiet relaxation, study, discussion and counselling to all students who visited.

Students of other faiths, and even of no faith, are also welcome. As one of them remarked — and he was a foreigner — "I have changed my ideas about God since I came to the Chaplaincy and met such caring people who love one another so sincerely."

No matter how helpful the service of the hostel was to students, financially it was not viable and therefore had to be discontinued. The maintenance, of the old house particularly, and of the grounds had to come from fund-raising ventures which, with reduced personnel, proved to be extremely difficult.

In January 1975, Sr. Paul Dominic was elected Prioress of the Community at Point Fortin; her departure from the Chaplaincy was greatly felt by students. She was succeeded by Sr. Gloria Marie Laurie for a few months and then by Sr. Monique Moniquette in 1976 who is still in charge today (1987).

Once more, the Sisters' quarters were partly vacant but there was no question of re-opening the hostel. The decision was therefore taken, with the relevant authorities, to transfer the Novitiate from Point Fortin to the UWI Chaplaincy.

It was felt that the proximity of the Seminary would facilitate the novices' doctrinal studies.

The transfer of the Novitiate took place on September 19, 1975. In 1976, Sr. Monique had to shoulder the double responsibility of Assistant-Chaplain and Novice Mistress. Sister Rose and Diane formed the Community with Sr. Monique.

Once a week, Holy Mass is offered at noon in one of the large lecture rooms of the Campus; but the high point and central action of the Chaplaincy services to the University over the years has been and continues to be the regular Sunday evening Mass in the chapel which is well attended by students, former students, members of staff and their families. The singing is led by a group of students accompanied by guitarists.

The two main liturgical seasons, Christmas and Lent, are marked by special activities: Carol singing during the former and lectures followed by discussions in Lent for a better understanding of one's faith. Each year, the Chaplaincy prepares a play which is staged at the Campus theatre; it is usually based on the Gospel in a campus setting.

There are also days of reflection and prayer which take place either in the Dominican Sisters' Retreat House in Point Fortin or in that of the Holy Ghost Fathers on the island of Gasparee one of the five islands off western tip of Trinidad. Groups of students have engaged in visiting and helping people in deprived areas such as Matelot and they have been an inspiration to them.

In 1978-79, the ground floor of the Chaplaincy house underwent transformation to accommodate the Pastoral Centre of the Archdiocese and its eastern side was extended to provide living quarters for the Director, Fr. Michel de Verteuil, C.S.Sp. From that time on, the work of the Chaplaincy and that of the Pastoral Centre have been closely linked as both operate from the same premises.

The Chaplaincy-cum-Pastoral Centre has, over the years, become a hub of many activities. Continually, students visit the Chaplaincy especially as the time of examinations approaches; they appreciate being able to use the buildings and grounds for study.

Another activity which attracts hundreds of people to the Chaplaincy is the Charismatic Prayer Group founded in the 1970's by a student, Wayne Ganpat. Meetings take place every Thursday evening at the Chaplaincy Hall.

Once more, the UWI Chaplaincy, though existing in a lovely setting of greenery, proved not to be the place for a Novitiate. The time had come to build a proper Novitiate House as we shall see in another chapter.

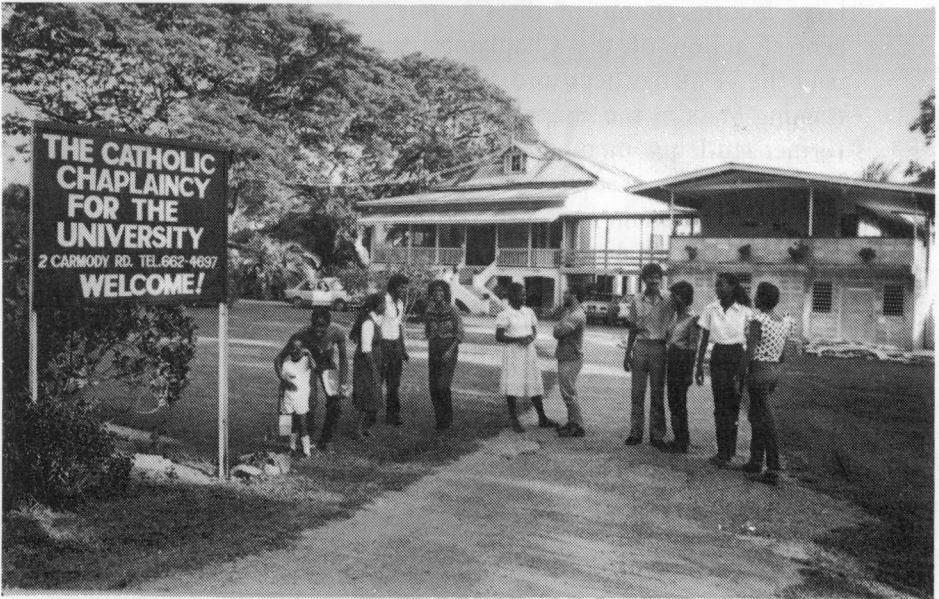

Sr. Monique Moniquette and students in front of the RC Chaplaincy, University of the West Indies at St. Augustine.

Chapter
32.

Overseas Thrust in Canada

In 1979, another opportunity was offered to the Domini-
can Sisters of Trinidad and Tobago to establish a foundation in
Canada. This time it was in Toronto, where, in 1979, the Holy
Ghost Fathers had opened a West Indian Centre.

The Chaplain, Fr. Philip Forde, C.S.Sp., in the course of
a visit to Trinidad expressed the wish to the Regional Prioress
of the Dominican Sisters, Sr. Moyra Ann Roach, that some
Sisters should come to Toronto to assist him in the running of
the Centre.

Sr. Moyra Ann asked Sr. Kathleen Jackman* if she would
be prepared to go there. She accepted the challenge and left
for Toronto. Later on, she was joined by Sr. Paul Dominic
Clarke and Sr. Barbara Clifton.

Sr. Kathleen did tremendous work during her short
lifetime. Striken by a fatal illness, she nevertheless continued
her work at the Centre with great courage until her failing
strength obliged her to give up.

In January 1985 she returned to Trinidad to die, aged 40.

* *See Ch. 29 p. 144.*

Her untimely death was deeply felt by her many friends in Canada and her family, religious Sisters and friends in Trinidad and Tobago.

Sr. Kathleen had, however, left her imprint at the Centre, and Sr. Cyrilla George, who had been with her since 1983, bravely continued her work. It is to the credit of Sr. Cyrilla that she built a vibrant choir which brings a true Caribbean note to the liturgies.

The years 1985 and 1986 were years of change. Fr. Forde was succeeded by Fr. Peter Wayow, C.S.Sp. Sr. Barbara, who for a year was of great assistance to the Mary Care Centre, (a home for unmarried pregnant teenagers founded by Archbishop Anthony Pantin in Port of Spain), returned to Toronto and two other Sisters were added to the growing community, namely, Sisters Elizabeth Blanc and Margaret Mary Griffith. The Sisters reside in an apartment situated a short distance from the Centre.

Caribbean liturgies are prepared with great care at the Centre and sometimes the attendance can reach 400 West Indians. Links are established with their families and some of them ask to have their children prepared for First Communion and Confirmation. Even adults want to be instructed in the Faith.

In response to these appeals, the Sisters have formed a catechetical team and Sr. Barbara makes herself available for counselling. These services are greatly appreciated by those who frequent the Centre.

Sr. Elizabeth pursues home visitation of West Indians which had been started by Sr. Kathleen; she is usually accompanied by a nurse. Sr. Margaret Mary visits those who are hospitalised and assists in many ways at the Centre.

A Soup Kitchen and the distribution of food parcels and articles of clothing are also part of the activities. Sr. Kathleen had succeeded in reaching out to a number of West Indian youths whom she helped greatly. This is being continued by her successors.

The Centre of Our Lady of Good Counsel of the Caribbean/Canadian Catholic Church in Toronto has been defined as a place of friendship, support and prayer for the Catholics of the West Indian community in this vast city of Canada.

Dominican Sisters at the West Indian Centre in Toronto. Left to right:
Sr. Barbara Clifton, Sr. Margaret Mary Griffith and Sr. Elizabeth Blanc with a
friend from Trinidad, Joan de la Bastide.

Two families of West Indians at the Centre with Sr. Barbara Clifton O.P.

Chapter
33.

A Dream Comes True

On the fifth day of August 1980, the house built on the heights of Calvary Hill in Arima was blessed by His Grace Archbishop Anthony Pantin, in the presence of the Sisters and officially declared a Dominican Community, known as the Convent of St. Catherine of Siena.

The document was signed by the Prioress General, Sr. Marie Christine Barré; the Regional Prioress, Sr. Moyra Ann Roach; Sr. Bernadette Robert and Sr. Rose de Verteuil.

To see a Novitiate House established on the land at Arima was a dream which had taken long to materialise. The construction of the building began in 1978 and was completed in 1980.

This project was financially possible because of the generous grants received from the charitable organisation of the R.C. Church in the Federal Republic of Germany, ADVENIAT, and the Congregation in France, as well as a contribution from our Sisters in Montreal, Canada, and a local benefactor.

Although intended as the Formation House, this community is also at present the centre for the Youth Co-ordinator of

the Archdiocese, Sr. Therese Dookeran O.P., and that of a
well-run sewing class for a small group of girls from the surrounding area under the direction of Sr. Patricia Goda O.P.

In addition, Sr. Mary Assumpta Brathwaite, who is cur-
rently the House-mother of the nearby Children's Home,
"Plainview", is attached to this Community.

Nevertheless, the atmosphere of this Novitiate House is
conducive to a life of prayer, reflection and study thus facili-
tating the integration of a life of contemplation and apostolate — a necessary preparation for a life of commitment as a
religious.

Formation is of utmost importance as it is like the building of a solid foundation on which the whole structure of life
rests.

The Sisters have used much ingenuity in transforming
the grounds around the house. They planted a lawn, fruit
trees, shrubs, vegetables and flowers, which, in this bounteous
land of ours, was prolific in record time.

St. Catherine of Siena, the patroness of our Congregation,
is obviously protecting her Community at Arima. Through
her intercession, may the Lord send many young women to
continue the work started 120 years ago.

St. Catherine's Novitiate House of the Dominican Sisters
at Calvary Hill, Arima.
Background: the Priory of the Dominican Fathers.

Chapter
34.

Missions Overseas and at Home

It is rather paradoxical that the Dominican Sisters in Trinidad and Tobago, who belong to a great missionary Order, have not made foundations in other parts of the Caribbean. Nonetheless, their missionary spirit is manifested in another form, namely, in the sending out of Sisters to other territories for particular missions.

In 1970, it all started with the implementation of Liturgical Renewal in the Church. In this Sr. Helen Gomes O.P., played a significant part in the late sixties and early seventies.

Between 1970 and 1973 Sr. Helen and a team visited most of the Trinidad parishes of the Archdiocese to introduce the singing of folk compositions. As a result of their efforts, a more indigenous type of divine worship was implanted. Soon invitations came for the team from Tobago (1971), St. Vincent (1971) and Barbados (1972).

In 1972 and again in 1973, Sr. Helen was part of a holiday project initiated by the Dominican Sisters at the request of the parish priest of Delaford, Tobago, Fr. Kevin De Loughry, O.P. A few lay persons joined them. The group did house-to-house visitation, brought Holy Communion to the sick, held prayer meetings, gave religious instruction to children and Bible classes for adults. There was a follow-up of the project in 1974.

In 1973 Sr. Paul Dominic Clarke, O.P., a teacher, spent some time in Grenada to give a Leadership Training course and also prepared a group of people for joining the Catholic Charismatic Renewal.

In 1974 another team formed by two Seminarians, two Dominican Sisters and seven lay men and women held a Holiday Camp in Dominica for the purpose of establishing some form of co-operation among Caribbean people at Church level.

A Sister joined the two Carmelite Sisters who were then living among the Amerindians of Aishalton in the Rupununi District, south of Guyana. She spent a month there but found the mission difficult due to the isolation of the place and the primitive living conditions of the people. A number of Amerindians are Catholics.

In 1986, another Dominican Sister joined a group of religious working among the people of Guyana in the northeast of the country.

In August 1974, Sr. Paul Dominic Clarke, Fr. Brendan Clifford, O.P., and two lay persons gave a testimony of Christian living in the parish of Couva. They visited the sick, prayed with people in the church, morning and evening, and were available for counselling. All their work was abruptly changed when hurricane "Alma" struck the district. The team members had to organise rescue work for the victims and used the presbytery as a centre for relief. Their stay lasted longer than expected.

In 1978 another Holiday Project took place in August 1978 with five Dominican Sisters and some lay persons in Kelly Village in Caroni. Various activities were organised for the children while a group carried out house-to-house visitation. Several liturgical services were held to the general satisfaction of the people of the village.

In 1978, and again in 1985 Sr. Monique Moniquette, O.P., spent some time in London working among West Indians in the parish of St. Mary of the Angels. These were very successful missions.

In 1979, at the request of Fr. Sebastian Madhosingh, parish priest of Delaford, a community made up of two religious, Sr. Gloria Marie Laurie, O.P., and Sr. Philip Geofroy, SJC, accompanied by a lay teacher, Miss Mary Lewis, settled in the presbytery for a two-year commitment to the parish.

Sr. Gloria Marie undertook parish ministry; Sr. Philip joined the staff of the Delaford R.C. School and Mary Lewis taught at the Roxborough Government Secondary School. Their presence was greatly appreciated by the priest and his parishioners.

A few months before they left, Sr. Catherine Bernard, O.P., joined the Community and remained in Delaford until the completion of the school year in 1982 as she too taught at Delaford R.C. School.

In 1984 the next mission was in the French West Indies where the Congregation made its first foundation in Guadeloupe in 1956. The Sisters from Guadeloupe were calling for help and it was Sr. Rose de Verteuil O.P., who was sent to them in 1984.

Besides being in charge of a community, Sr. Rose is engaged in campus ministry at the University of Pointe-a-Pitre as well as at the Catholic Communication Studio where she produces programmes in the English language.

In August 1987, two Trinidadian Sisters joined Sr. Rose for a project among English-speaking immigrants in Guadeloupe.

Most of these overseas projects are organised during the holidays of the Sisters and they have created new links with our Caribbean neighbours. These projects have been an excellent way of broadening one's horizon.

Chapter
35.

Dominican Sisters
Engaged in Special Missions

The new scientific developments of the 1960's and 70's brought about major changes in the world. To study the religious implications and to find ways and means to cope with them on a religious basis, the Roman Catholic Church convened an Ecumenical Council, Vatican II, which lasted from 1962 to 1965.

In one of its 16 decrees concerning the Religious Life, in paragraph nine, it is written that "the Council supports religious in their vocation and entreats them to adapt their life to modern need."

Sr. Rose de Verteuil who was then Regional Prioress initiated this adaptation. The Dominican Sisters in Trinidad and Tobago were then authorised by their Congregation to launch into new fields where special missions would be required.

In 1972 the first Dominican Sister in Trinidad and Tobago who was called to a special mission was Sr. Marie Thérèse Rétout, when in 1972, the then Editor of the Catholic News, Mr. Owen Baptiste, challenged her to write for this weekly of the Catholic Church in the country.

After overcoming the shock of such a call, with God's help she launched into the venture. As a freelance writer she developed journalistic skills with the training she received from the Editor.

In 1974, strengthened by the support of her Superiors, Sr. Marie Thérèse took up full-time employment as a journalist at the Catholic News. In 1987, she is still making her weekly contributions to this respected newspaper founded in 1892 and which has a remarkable record of unbroken publication.

Most of the contents of this book have been published in article-form in the Catholic News thus enabling the author to pursue historical research as part of her work as a journalist. The public interest in these articles has been a constant encouragement to her in the arduous work of research.

In 1974 Sister Diane Jagdeo of Port of Spain is a born teacher, especially in the field of religious education. To further her religious knowledge, she registered at the Regional Seminary in 1971 for a three-year course leading to the Bachelor of Arts degree in Theology which she obtained in 1974 from the University of the West Indies.

A major change occurred in her life when the then Rector of the Seminary, Fr. Michel de Verteuil, C.S.Sp., asked Sr. Diane to join the academic staff of the Seminary as a Lecturer in Theology. She accepted and taught this discipline for three years and even had to assume the duties of Dean of Studies for one year.

Responding to a need for further qualification in Theology, Sr. Diane enrolled at Yale University, USA, where she obtained her Masters in Sacred Theology in 1978 and then continued to study for her Doctorate.

Sr. Diane wrote her dissertation on the theme "Holiness and Reform of the Church" according to the writings of a great contemporary theologian, Fr. Yves Congar, O.P. After teaching once more at the Seminary for three years, she finally completed her dissertation at the Catholic University of Washington D.C., USA and in 1986 obtained her Ph.D.

On her return to Trinidad and Tobago, Sr. Diane resumed teaching at the Seminary and is often called upon to lecture at seminars and conferences here at home and in the Caribbean.

In September of 1980 yet another Dominican Sister was called to a special mission, namely, Sr. Thérèse Dookeran. At that time there was an urgent need for a National Catholic Youth Co-ordinator, and Sr. Thérèse, on account of her previous activities among the youth — especially in the field of music and the training of choir members — was chosen for the post by Archdiocesan authorities.

Her task was a vast one and demanded much travelling throughout the country in order to meet youths in their respective parishes. Gradually groups were formed by areas. Little by little Sr. Therese discovered how much our young people are in need of Christian education and moral guidance.

Fr. Ronald Mendes, C.S.Sp., introduced Sr. Thérèse to the COR (Christ in Others Retreat) Movement which he had seen at work in Canada. This movement involves the whole Christian community and more particularly the parents of young people.

The COR retreats have created such an impact on the Catholic youth of this country that Sr. Thérèse was called to other Caribbean territories to start a similar experience and in those places it has been well received.

The Spiritual Director of the R.C. youth in Trinidad and Tobago is Fr. John Theodore, C.S.Sp., who, with Sr. Therese, has a tremendous influence on them. Both have been able, with the help of the young leaders they have trained, to organise two National Catholic Youth Rallies in 1985 and 1987 both of which have been successful.

Sr. Paul Dominic Clarke's previous experience in pastoral work in Point Fortin prepared her, as it were, for what was to come. In 1983, when Archbishop Pantin made an appeal to religious communities for volunteers to work in the large parish of Toco/Matelot on the North Coast of Trinidad, Sr. Paul Dominic, Sr. Elizabeth Blanc and a Sister of the Holy Faith, Sr. Rosario Hackshaw responded to his call.

On November 3, 1983, the three of them settled in the Toco-Mission presbytery. They divided the nearly 50 km — long parish, which borders the coast, into three sections to facilitate the work.

Sr. Rosario, appointed to teach at the Matelot R.C. School, became co-ordinator of the Matelot/St. Helena/Grande Riviere section; Sr. Paul Dominic took charge of the Toco/ Sans Souci/Montevideo section and Sr. Elizabeth was responsible for the Cumana/Rampanalgas/Salybia area.

Initially, the presbytery at Toco-Mission was the base for the three Sisters. However, owing to strenous travelling on the Matelot road which is in a state of disrepair, Sr. Rosario settled in the Matelot presbytery.

Living and working in a parish without a resident priest is a great challenge. One has to endure the pain of a lack of sacramental life. Gradually, the Sisters became very involved in every aspect of life in the villages and this led them to establish contacts with the social and legal services and the schools — the Sisters are managers of five R.C. schools where they teach religion.

They also take part in extra-curricular activities of the Government Composite School in Toco and have established contacts with Village Councils and Community Development agencies. A major part of their involvement centres on protecting and defending the rights of the poor and helping the unemployed. Some regard them as an employment agency as the Sisters are on the side of both the unemployed and the employer.

The teams of fine lay ministers in the parishes are a great asset to the Sisters. Long before the latter came, these lay persons held meetings regularly during the prolonged absence of a residential priest. They conducted religious services and brought Holy Communion to the sick.

Training of youth was high on the priority list of work to be done by the Sisters and in this they have succeeded.

The Sisters have been accepted very lovingly by the people of the North Coast and there exists a harmonious co-operation in the evangelical simplicity of these people. A friendly attitude has developed with members of other faiths.

In December 1985, Sr. Elizabeth left her beloved people of the North Coast to go to Toronto where she was called to work at the West Indian Centre. Her presence had made a very deep and lasting impact on them and she is very much missed here.

In January 1986, Sr. Marie Anna Stelmack of the Sinsi-
nawa Dominican Congregation in the USA, who came to
Trinidad to give a two-year service to the Church, volunteered
to replace Sr. Elizabeth in Toco for one year. She was welcomed by the people and she too did a tremendous amount
of work during that year.

After her departure, Sr. Paul Dominic found herself
alone. Nevertheless, she continues the work as best she can.
She has even become engaged in the establishment and con-
struction of a St. David's Life Centre, next to the presbytery.
The Centre is run according to the principles of SERVOL.*
It is definitely a ray of hope for the youth of the district.

In this project Sr. Paul Dominic is helped by Sr. Paul
Sellier, SJC who, with Sr. Jacinta SJC, lives at Cumana on the
North Coast in the house of the Sisters of St. Joseph of Cluny
and both are looking after this section of the parish.

It is simply amazing to see how God provides for the
needs of His people. But, however good the work of the Sisters
may be, it is firmly hoped that one day a priest will join their
team on a permanent basis.

In 1969, Sr. Maria Goretti Gay O.P., completed her general studies in Nursing in London, U.K. After working for two
years as a Registered Nurse at St. Dominic's Children's Home,
she joined the nursing staff of the Maternity Ward of the Port
of Spain General Hospital and qualified as a midwife in 1973.
In 1987, Sr. Maria Goretti is still a staff nurse there.

In 1982, Sr. Francine Scott O.P., qualified as a Registered
Nurse at the Port of Spain General Hospital and was there on
the staff until August 1987 when she was then seconded to act
as Sister Manager of St. Dominic's Children's Home.

* *Servol is an organisation founded by Fr. Gerry Pantin C.S.Sp. at
Beetham in the outskirts of Port of Spain in the aftermath of the
1970's social upheavals in the country. It is open to all youth in
search of a meaning for their lives. At SERVOL not only do they
find loving care and understanding but they are also given an all-
round training in self-knowledge to develop confidence in themselves, in human relations and family life education. At SERVOL
the youths learn a trade of their choice all of which equips them to
take their place in society and earn a livelihood.
SERVOL continues to expand in Trinidad and Tobago and in the
Caribbean.*

Chapter
36.

Mother Dominic of the Cross

Reverend Mother Dominic of the Cross
(Marie-Thérèse-Josephine Gand)
Foundress and First Mother General of the
French Congregation of Saint Catherine of Siena.
July 1819 — February 1907.

Mother Dominic of the Cross, as foundress of the French Congregation of St. Catherine of Siena, has a singular record. She spent 69 years of her life in the convent, was professed for 67 years, bore the responsibility of the leadership of the Congregation as Prioress General for 53 years and died at the age of 88 on February 2, 1907. She is buried in the chapel of the Mother-house at Etrepagny, France.

In 1904, Mother Dominic wrote the following: "Soon it will be 50 years that our little Congregation exists. During that time we have given the religious habit to approximately 300 Sisters and 25 externs; 98 have died and some have not persevered in the religious life."

At her death, although the Congregation had established 11 convents, including four in Trinidad, the Mother Foundress always envisaged a Congregation small in numbers.

Mother Dominic was regarded as an outstanding personality in the Church in the 19th century on account of her indomitable will to restore in France the Third Order of St. Dominic, (founded in the 13th century), which had been wiped out by the after-effects of the 1789 Revolution.

Mother Dominic excelled in her ability to balance both the contemplative and active aspects of Dominican life.

The Dominican motto — "To contemplate and to give to others the fruits of contemplation" — was one of her guiding principles. To this end, she stressed to the Sisters of her Congregation: "The *raison d'être* of a religious congregation lies much more in the spirit which animates it than in the many works its members may accomplish."

This eminently religious woman was endowed with a great power of love, a strong faith, a vivacious character with an understanding and compassionate heart; she was never afraid to make decisions and to apply them with firmness.

Mother Dominic was a loyal and sincere person, generous, magnanimous and intelligent. She was most attentive to the intellectual formation of her Sisters. She regarded study as a protective rampart for the religious life. Herself an avid reader, she recommended the constant companionship of a serious and instructive book. She used to say to the Sisters: "What is the love of God when it is not founded on knowledge? It produces a sentimental piety based on the moods and imagination of one's temperament."

The Foundress herself set out to produce books to nourish the spiritual life of her Sisters. A prolific writer when one considers the list of her works: *the Constitutions of the Congregation, books of Customs and Directories for Sisters and Superiors* representing in all, 36 years of assiduous work.

Mother Dominic also wrote the *Memoir of the Congregation* (1861-1904) and six other memoirs concerning various foundations; the *biography of Fr. Francois Balme, O.P.*, her Spiritual Director and counsellor for many years, particularly, during the great trials of the foundation; *Meditations on the lives of the Saints and Blessed of the Dominican Order; Lives of the Sisters of the Congregation* in five volumes covering a period of 45 years; *a Day in the Dominican Way of Life;* over 200 *circulars* which she wrote to the convents, and finally, her voluminous correspondence.

In the course of her long life, and with the special mission God had entrusted to her, Mother Dominic went through many trials. At one time she confided, "Wherever I turn, I find only difficulties, but for all that, I do not lose confidence because I know that life is in the Cross. The more my heart is rent, the more it opens itself to Jesus' love."

This she experienced so deeply that she gave this motto to her Congregation: *In Cruce Vita* — In the Cross is Life —.

Her strong faith helped her to overcome the many trials she had to endure. The virtue of magnanimity, which she possessed to a remarkable degree, caused her to exclaim one day, "Let our hearts be big, not as the world — that is too small — but like unto infinity!"

Mother Dominic sought perfection in all that she did and urged her Sisters to do likewise. One day she said to them: "You must become saints in order to be God's instruments. Remove obstacles, deny yourselves in every way because a soul filled with self can never make room for Jesus and what will it give to others? It can only give self, not Jesus."

She lived a life of great austerity, very exacting for herself; she was, nonetheless, full of compassion for others.

Shortly before her death, she declared once more her boundless love for the Church: "I am the daughter of the Church. Oh! what happiness: I am dying a daughter of the Catholic and Apostolic Church. O Saint Peter! May our Congregation ever be riveted and sealed to you by faith and love!"

What is touching for us, Dominican Sisters in Trinidad and Tobago, is the fact that the last work Mother Dominic did on earth was for our benefit. In the last days of January 1907 (she died on February 2 at 6.00 a.m., at the sound of the Angelus) while waiting for death, Mother Dominic asked a Sister to read an appeal she had written in favour of our Trinidad convents. She suggested a few corrections and that was all. She had thus cast a last glance at the affairs of this world.

Her final recommendation was for the novices. To them she said: "My dear children, practise silence, obedience and charity — above all charity."

There is no better way to close this chapter on our Mother Foundress than by reproducing here her last testament:

I implore you my dear daughters, preserve the spirit which we had endeavoured to impart to you, that is, the spirit of St. Dominic.

Have a deep and loving attachment to your Congregation and its works. Esteem all the means given to us by our Rule and Constitutions to work towards perfection and at the same time respect those in use in other institutes.

Continue to live in peace and unity which constitute the happiness of our small family.

Be souls of duty knowing how to sacrifice everything in order to remain faithful.

Be attentive to the needs of each other; try to make life bearable and to edify others by your gentle manners.

Assume full responsibility in your works, whether in teaching or nursing. Above all things, be humble — the virtue which eases hardships. Sophie Barat used to say, "Humility is a needle which mends many tears." As much as pride is the principle of all evil, humility is the principle of every virtue. We must love to be hidden, leaving God all the space.

Mother Dominic of the Cross is indeed a mother and example to emulate.

Note: In French, the official name of our Foundress is Révérende Mère St. Dominique de la Croix. In translating it into English, we felt that we would be much closer to her if we were to call her simply 'MOTHER DOMINIC OF THE CROSS'.

Epilogue

Who are the Dominicans?

VERITAS

The Dominican Order is the brainchild of a man of God, St. Dominic of Guzman, born in Caleruega, Spain in the 12th century. He received the charisma of blending the monastic tradition with principles of democracy inspired by the Gospel. At that time this innovation was nothing less than a revolution in the Church.

St. Dominic rooted his Order, composed of men and women, in contemplation through an assiduous study of sacred truths. Prayer, study, fraternal life and preaching, whether by word of mouth or writing, are the main components of the Dominican way of life.

To search for Truth "VERITAS" is their motto and to live by it constitutes the Dominicans' aim; their second motto is to "Contemplate and to give to others the fruits of contemplation."

"Devotion to the truth in the intellectual world produces a philosopher; in the social world it produces a gentleman; in the supernatural world it produces a saint." (Walter Farrell, O.P.).

Dominicans are engaged in various forms of apostolic life, namely preaching, teaching, social communications (press, radio and television) as well as works of mercy.

The Dominican Order is in a constant state of mission. It has adapted itself to ecclesial, social and cultural changes for the past 800 years without need for reform.

St. Dominic, when sending his first brethren all over Europe, kept repeating to those who found him too daring: "Sow good seed and it bears fruit; store it and it decays." The universality of the Order makes its members look to the world as a convent — as one of the brethren put it — and to the oceans as an enclosure.

To become a Dominican, one has to have courage, to be of cheerful disposition, to be able to adapt oneself and to be creative. This corresponds to this definition:

"A Dominican soul is not regimented; it is not disturbed by progress, nor does it find new techniques disconcerting; rather, it marshals them into service of the liberating truth which is love. Thus the Order, throughout centuries, has preserved its youth and its creative spirit, always ready to answer every appeal."

An enlightened mind through contemplation and study; bold and loyal actions in fidelity to Christ and to his Church — such is the hallmark of the Dominican spirit.

In 1983, the Dominican family consisted of some 7,000 *friars,* the great majority of whom are priests and about 45 of them bishops. They were present in 82 countries of the world engaged in varied apostolic activities:

— *teaching* (7 universities, 15 university faculties, 15 higher institutes, 17 university colleges, 40 secondary schools),

— *missions* 490 parishes and 203 out-stations, nine apostolic schools, 27 pastoral centres, 20 Rosary Apostolate centres,

— *social communications* 15 radio stations; 68 magazines and 23 journals of specialised research.

The women are divided into two branches: — *the Dominican nuns* who are cloistered. Almost 5,000 of them are distributed among 255 monasteries. The Rosary Monastery at St. Ann's, Port of Spain, is one of them.

— *the Dominican Sisters* numbering almost 41,000, belonging to 140 different congregations. The Dominican Sisters of St. Catherine of Siena in Trinidad and Tobago with their convents of Holy Name, St. Dominic's at Belmont and Barataria, St. Catherine's at Arima, Holy Name of Mary at Point Fortin and the UWI Chaplaincy at St. Augustine comprise and are linked with their Sisters in France one of these 140 congregation.

Attached also to the Dominican family are the *Secular Dominicans,* men and women — over 70,000 — organised into hundreds of fraternities throughout the world.

Mother Dominic of the Cross, after she had founded her religious family, placed it under the patronage of St. Catherine of Siena, an eminent Dominican Sister and a mystic of the 14th century.

St. Catherine had a tremendous influence on the Church which, at that time, was in the throes of the approaching Great Schism. She persuaded Pope Gregory XI, then in exile in Avignon, to return to Rome. This he did in 1377 thus bringing some temporary relief to the existing tensions within the Church. Her saintly death occurred in 1380 at the dawn of the Great Schism of the Western Church (1378-1433).

St. Catherine's strength of character, her zeal for spreading the Gospel, her love of Christ and of his Church as well as the soundness of her teaching and writings, determined Pope Paul VI in October 1970 to confer on her the title of Doctor of the Church. This was the second time in the history of the Church that a woman had received such an honour. (The first one was St. Teresa of Avila in September 1970).

This is the heritage of the saintly man, Dominic, of whom numerous men and women are, today, zealous followers.

Shield of the Dominican Order

"Sable. Party per Argent Chevron Proper."
Symbolising an arrowhead of light piercing the darkness.

The religious habit of the Dominican Sisters before and after
Vatican II (1962-65).
Left to right: Sr. Marie des Saints Innocents, Sr. Martin of St. Mary,
Sr. Mary Assumpta, Sr. Martin Dominic.

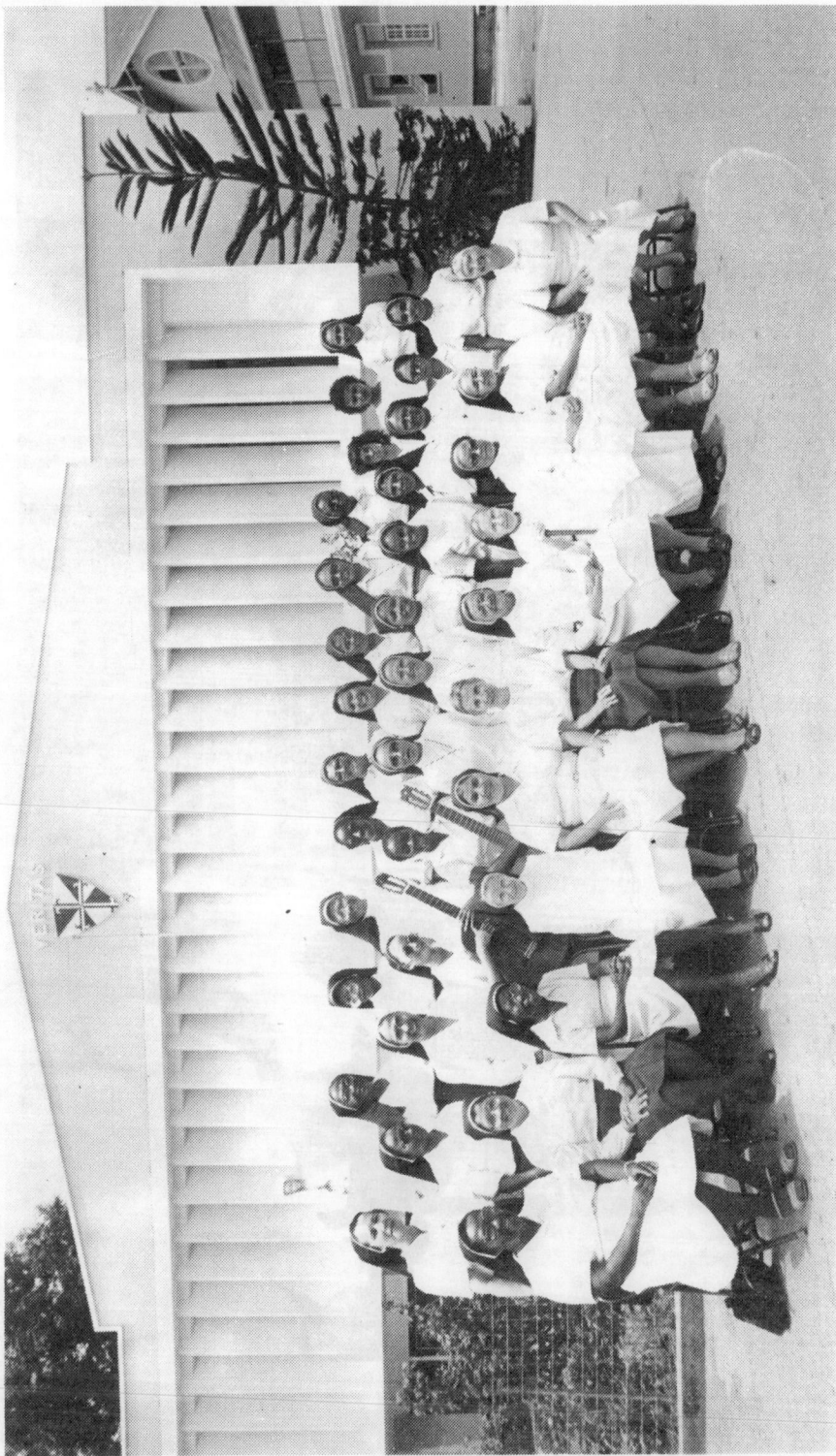

Group of the Dominican Sisters in Trinidad and Tobago (some are absent) in 1986.
Background: The Marian Hall of Holy Name Convent.

Most Reverend Anthony Pantin D.D. Archbishop of Port of Spain concelebrates the Eucharist in the Holy Name Chapel.

Chronology

MILESTONES IN THE HISTORY OF THE
DOMINICAN SISTERS IN TRINIDAD AND TOBAGO

1868: Arrival of the first five Sisters at the Cocorite Leprosarium.

1876: Sisters take charge of St. Dominic's Orphanage, Belmont.

1879: Construction of the chapel, convent and first house for children at St. Dominic's Orphanage.

1890: Establishment of Holy Name Convent in former Bolivar College, Port of Spain.

1892: Sisters and 'Ouvroir'* girls take charge of the Catholic News printery on the Holy Name grounds.

1903: Sisters take charge of the 'Good Shepherd' Industrial School, Belmont.

1906: Blessing of the new Holy Name Chapel.

1907: Installation of the Holy Name Private School in the former Devenish House, 3 Queen's Park East, Port of Spain.

1926: Sisters follow their patients to the island of Chacachacare. Cocorite Leprosarium closed down.

*Workroom

1927:   Sisters enter their new convent at Holy Name, 2 Queen's Park East.

1946:   Opening of the Novitiate at Holy Name Convent.

1950:   Opening of the Boarding School for Venezuelan students at Holy Name Convent (closed in 1962). Withdrawal of the Sisters from Chacachacare Hansenian Settlement.

1951:   Acquisition of a Rest House for the Sisters in Toco-Mission.

1954:   Inauguration of the new Marian Hall constructed on the site of the former Devenish House renamed 'Pavillon Notre Dame'.

1959:   Foundation of St. Dominic's Private Secondary School in Malick, Barataria.

1963:   Opening of the Holy Name Preparatory School at Coblentz Avenue, Cascade. Transfer of the Novitiate to the Convent in Malick, Barataria.

1967:   Foundation at Clifton Hill, Point Fortin.

1968:   Transfer of the Novitiate to Point Fortin.

1971:   Opening of the first Homestead 'Sunny Hill' at Malick, Barataria.

1972:   Opening of the new convent at Holy Name and transfer of the Holy Name Preparatory School to the old convent at 2 Queen's Park East, Port of Spain.

1973:   Sisters take charge of the R.C. Chaplaincy of The University of the West Indies.

1975:   Transfer of the Novitiate to the UWI Chaplaincy.

1979:   Foundation at the West Indian Centre in Toronto, Canada.

1980:   Opening of the formal Novitiate House at Calvary Hill, Arima.

1983:   Opening of the second Homestead 'Plainview' at Calvary Hill, Arima.

Note — No foundation has yet been made in Tobago; however, the Sisters have at one time or another engaged in various missions there.

Bibliography

La Réverende Mère Saint Dominique de la Croix, Fondatrice et Prieure Génèrale des Dominicaines de la Congrégation de Sainte Catherine de Sienne by Th. Mainage O.P., Paris 1929 Two volumes.

Diaries, circular letters, correspondence and annual reports of the convents of the Dominican Sisters in Trinidad and Tobago (1868-1986).

Fragments of the Past (1864-1914) by Fr. Marie Joseph Guillet O.P., Series of articles published in the Catholic News.

Anciens Couvents Chalonnais — Les Dominicaines by Marcel Lecroq Chalon-sur Saône 1971.

Short History of the West Indies by Parry & Sherlock Mac Millan 1956.

100 Years Together (1797-1897) by H.C. Pitts
The Trinidad Publishing Co. Ltd. Port of Spain 1948.

International Dominican Information. Rome. April-May 1983.

Historical Review of Social and Clinical Aspects of Leprosy by M. Elizabeth Duncan Leprosy Review June 1985.

The Trinidad and Tobago Medical Journal (1982) ABC of Hansen's by Dr. Richard Keeler.

Index

A MAP OF THE CARIBBEAN

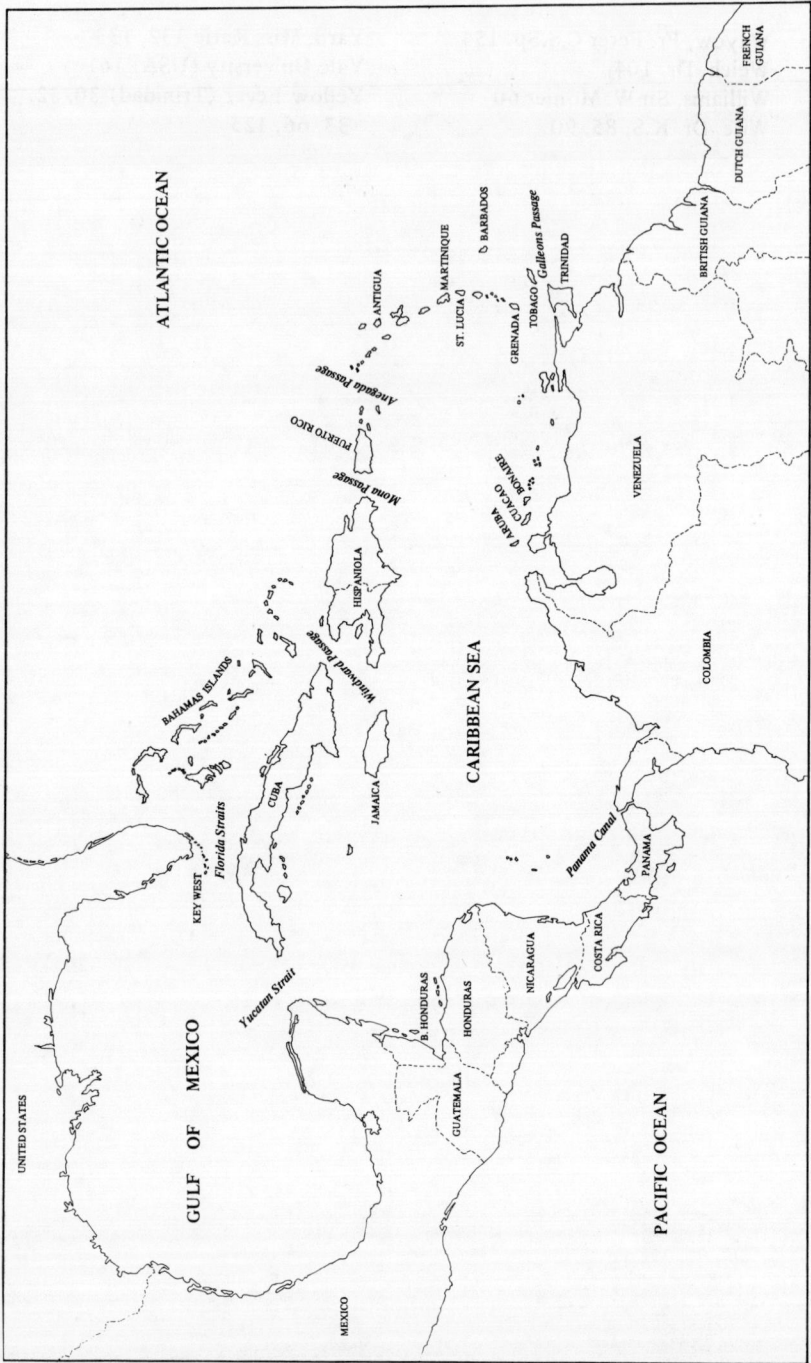

ATLANTIC OCEAN

UNITED STATES

GULF OF MEXICO

MEXICO

KEY WEST
Florida Straits

BAHAMAS ISLANDS

CUBA

Yucatan Strait

JAMAICA

Windward Passage

HISPANIOLA

Mona Passage

PUERTO RICO

Anegada Passage

ANTIGUA

MARTINIQUE
ST. LUCIA
BARBADOS

GRENADA
TOBAGO
Galleons Passage
TRINIDAD

CARIBBEAN SEA

ARUBA
CURAÇAO
BONAIRE

VENEZUELA

COLOMBIA

GUATEMALA
B. HONDURAS
HONDURAS

NICARAGUA

COSTA RICA

PANAMA
Panama Canal

PACIFIC OCEAN

BRITISH GUIANA
DUTCH GUIANA
FRENCH GUIANA

ACKNOWLEDGEMENTS.

Olga Penrose   }
Hospital saff — Past and Present   } for their help
Hospital committee members   } and information.
Morgan Hoskins   }
Joan Carr for typing the original manuscript.
And anyone not mentioned above who freely gave
their time and assistance helping me gather
information for this book.

PHOTOGRAPHS
Torrey Canyon: J. Bottrell.

Guillemots: Peter Glastonbury/ Pageant Photo Libray.

Pages: 20, 22, 54, 63, 64, Orchard Publications. Pages: 18, 60, Mobil Oil Company.

Other photos: Dorothy Yglesias reproduced with the kind permission of the
Mousehole Wild Bird Hospital & Sanctuary.

ISBN. 0 9519027 5 X

Will I Fly Again

First published 1993 by

ORCHARD
PUBLICATIONS

2, Orchard Close, Chudleigh, Newton Abbot, Devon TQ13 0LR.
Tel: (0626) 852714

Further copies of this book can be obtained
from Orchard Publications.

Typeset, Illustrated & Produced by WATERMARK,
(WATERMARK IS A TRADING NAME OF TOP DESIGN)
Teignmouth, Devon. Tel/Fax: (0626) 779499

INTRODUCTION

"Be careful, those rocks must be slippery", but the boy was far more concerned in trying to catch the sea bird floundering helplessly in the water, than heeding his mother's warning. Each wave dashed the bird against the rocks then snatched it back again on the ebb. Eventually the youngster was able to reach out and grasp the exhausted bird. It was a guillemot, another victim of oiling — the bird's feathers were clogged and matted with a treacly light brown sludge, and in a few more minutes would have surely given up its desperate fight for survival and, in all probability, drowned. Yes, sea birds can drown. The boy scrambled back across the rocks and rejoined his mother on the coastal path from where they had first noticed the bird's plight

Walking the coastal paths around the West Country afford the rambler superb scenery and unrivalled opportunities to observe wildlife, be it at sea or in the adjoining fields and woods. The walker possessing a feeling for the environment and appreciation of sighting wild birds and animals, often has an eye and instinct for noticing such creatures in distress. Many passers-by would have paid little attention to this particular bird, not realising anything was wrong, but the boy and his mother recognised at once the bird's floundering was unnatural.

Taking an old towel from their rucksack they carefully wrapped it around the bird, avoiding the token resistance of the odd stab from its beak. A peck from a healthy guillemot can easily draw blood but this pathetic creature presented little danger.With the youngster clutching the live parcel to his chest, oblivious to the oil stains appearing on his jacket, the couple turned and retraced their steps along the cliff path into Mousehole. Within the hour they were climbing the steps to the Wild Bird Hospital and Sanctuary and ringing the bell to summons help for an injured bird.

This guillemot was lucky; although looking to be in a sorrowful state, it had not been in the oil too long and being unable to reach the shore or rocks had been prevented from preening itself, thereby avoiding suffering further internal damage to add to its problems. With the expert care and attention it would now receive, a full recovery and release to the wild again was more than just a possibility.

The scarecrow standing with arms outstretched protecting his crops from the rooks and crows is a common enough sight as we pass by. A not so common sight, but one still practised by some farmers, is the scarecrow with a dead bird dangling from its arm, or even a single stake with a bird hanging from it as though on the gallows; the inference to other birds being "come near me and this is how you will finish up". Imagine then the pain and suffering of a young jackdaw, shot and then hung in such a fashion, whilst still alive. However, unbeknown to the farmer in this instance, his cruel act had been witnessed by a young boy. When the farmer had departed the boy left his hiding place and cut the jackdaw down. Wrapping his jumper around the bird the boy ran across the fields and took the unfortunate victim to Dorothy and Phyllis Yglesias at the birds' hospital. The jackdaw was still bleeding, suffering from shock, and had sustained leg injuries. Although never able to fly again, the bird was nursed back to health and lived in the hospital's sanctuary for seven years. For those seven years the jackdaw led a contented, stress free, happy life, receiving and giving much love.

Both these incidents happened many years ago but illustrate perfectly on the one hand man's disregard of nature, and on the other man's love and appreciation of the wildlife. It is interesting to note that in both cases it was a child's awareness of suffering that came to the fore.

Whilst writing this book I have met people who have voiced the opinion that of those birds found suffering injuries and illness, they are just nature's victims of culling, and that the hospital and sanctuary's work is somewhat frivolous. To these people and their suggestions I reply that sea birds subjected to oiling as a result of a tanker washing out its holding tanks whilst still at sea, land birds poisoned by pesticides and chemicals used on their natural feeding sources, so-called 'game' birds shot but only winged and left to die slowly and painfully, are the result of man's insensitivity and lack of caring for his environment and bear no relation to nature whatsoever. And all the while such examples occur then may the Mousehole Wild Bird Hospital and Sanctuary continue its work and long will I support it.

This book records the history of the hospital from its inception in 1928 to the present day, and relates some humorous, many loving, many moving, and, sadly, a few sorrowful, events during those years.

Dorothy Yglesias - one of the last pictures taken of her in her Love Lane cottage.

CHERRY ORCHARD

Dorothy and Phyllis (Pog) Yglesias were born in London during the late nineteenth century. The first time they visited Cornwall was in 1912 whilst on holiday with their mother and sister, Mary. Their father, an artist, died in 1911 and a change of holiday scene was decided upon, as previous holidays with him had been spent in Kent and Sussex. At this time Pog was an art student, Mary still at school, and Dorothy undecided as to where her future lay. They all immediately fell in love with the village of Mousehole and the surrounding countryside and coastline, an emotion with which I can easily identify, and subsequently spent several more holidays in the area. As their love affair with the village continued they became quite recognised and their affection for this part of Cornwall soon came to include the Mousehole community. In 1925 they said goodbye to London and moved to Mousehole, where they rented a cottage near the harbour whilst their new home was built on land off Raginnis Hill, land their mother had purchased several years earlier, having anticipated her daughters' wishes to become part of this community.

They named their new home "Cherry Orchard" for the land was rich with wild cherry trees. In one corner of the orchard garden Pog built a studio and here spent many hours drawing and wood carving.
She had become a proficient carver and was soon receiving many commissions. This studio, and subsequent ones were to figure prominently over the years as adjacent hospital premises. Mary stayed a while and then moved to Goldsithney, a village a mile or so East of Marazion, where she began a taxi service. She was probably the first female taxi driver in Cornwall. Dorothy's income was gained selling flowers and produce grown in Cherry Orchard's gardens, at local markets. The garden's position off Raginnis Hill, being sheltered from the prevailing South-Westerly weather, was ideal for early season flowers and vegetables. However, when the wind blows in across Mounts Bay from the East hang on to your hats! For two or three years life was reasonably uncomplicated, the sisters were making ends meet with their various

business ventures and were soon accepted by most of the locals as "one of us". But the routine of their life style was soon to change, to change forever — Jacko, the jackdaw, was about to arrive on the scene.

Jackdaw. The main patients in the hospital's early years. Their plumage is black except for the ash-grey sides of the neck, nape and back of the head. Has pale eyes. Jackdaws are widespread throughout the British Isles although not so common in NW Scotland.

1928 - JACKDAWS' HOSPITAL

Mary, the youngest Yglesias sister, found an injured jackdaw seeking refuge in the relative safety of an old disused drainpipe in her back garden in Goldsithney. The bird had been shot in the wing and would never fly again, but rather than have it put down Mary placed it in a box and settling this safely on the back seat of her taxi drove over to Mousehole hoping Dorothy and Pog would look after it. Pog housed Jacko in her studio, eventually building a smaller hut and enclosure for him. Jacko turned out to be a Jacqueline, but the original name was much preferred. She lived in her little sanctuary for four years - four happy years she would not have had but for Dorothy and Pog.

The second patient soon arrived, another jackdaw, again with an injured wing. It was brought to the sisters by a gentleman who had found the bird whilst out walking, and having heard about Jacko had no hesitation in taking it to Cherry Orchard. The sisters named the bird Muffin, and this time had sexed him correctly. When Muffin had responded sufficiently to treatment he was introduced to Jacko.
Romance blossomed and in the Spring five eggs appeared though none hatched. Towards the end of the Summer and the mating season, with both birds seeming independent of each other, the decision was taken to release Muffin. He was by now fully recovered and fit enough to return to the wild. When released he flew off perfectly and for some time returned daily to Cherry Orchard for titbits. Then after several weeks of freedom Dorothy and Pog noticed him nursing an injured foot; they opened the studio window and in he hopped to be re-united with Jacko who greeted him like an old friend. When Muffin's foot injury was healed the sisters offered him his freedom once again, but this time the bond he shared with Jacko was too strong, and he showed no desire to leave his mate. For two years they shared happy companionship before sadly dying within days of one another. Because their deaths were so sudden and unexpected the sisters asked their veterinary surgeon to perform an examination "Thorn headed worm - nearly always fatal" was diagnosed.

Muffin's return to Cherry Orchard when in need of help was the first of many examples of birds seeming to know where help could be found. News of the sisters' work with the birds spread, and they soon found many a stranger on the doorstep with various baskets and live parcels containing sick and injured birds. As in Muffin's case, sick birds arrived as though guided by a sixth sense, rather like a doctor's surgery apart from being asked to wait two or three days for an appointment. The number of patients increased and as Pog's studio was given over to the birds' welfare, a new concrete block studio was built for her.

In those early years jackdaws were the predominant patients, Cornwall's landscape offering perfect habitat to them. They feed on virtually anything and nest in caves, quarries, old chimney stacks, mine workings, etc. They are also very intelligent birds, often displaying little fear of man, with an impish habit of stealing bright objects. Jackdaw chicks were often taken from their nests by boys and reared as pets, the jackdaw using the boy as a substitute parent. Thankfully this stealing of the young birds seldom occurs nowadays. Around this time Pog made and erected a sign outside Cherry Orchard inscribed 'Jackdaws Hospital'. Baby jackdaws were hospitalised with injuries mainly sustained by falling from their nesting places, and after being deserted by their parent birds.

THE EARLY YEARS

The number of bird patients increased annually, admissions being meticulously recorded, and during the early 1930's the cost of treating, feeding and housing them was beginning to place considerable strain on the sisters — time-wise as well as financial. Their joint income from Pog's wood carving and Dorothy's produce growing was under pressure because the more birds they accepted subsequently meant the less time they were afforded to pursue their work, and yet they needed to earn more to feed and treat the growing number of inmates. However, they soldiered on and such was their devotion and commitment that the birds always came first. More runs and pens were constructed, and with Pog's ability to utilise any piece of odd wood some very peculiar looking buildings appeared. Larger pens for the gulls to fly in were added, and rock pools dug out for the sea birds. On several occasions when the gales blew across Mount's Bay straight into Mousehole all the enclosures were evacuated and the birds taken to alternative accommodation until the storm abated.

With time more species of birds arrived and Dorothy and Pog were constantly referring to bird books to verify the name of the latest arrival. They also learned what types of food best suited the birds and the best ways to feed them. As Dorothy said, "we improved with time, but always it was the birds themselves who showed us the way". For a while the Mousehole and Newlyn fishermen were quite generous with free supplies, but as times became a little harder and the required quantities grew larger, the fish so necessary for the sea birds had to be purchased.

Although restored to apparent full health, several birds were unable to return to the wild because of the nature of their original injuries; these birds were provided with alternative accommodation known as the sanctuary, and so the Jackdaws' Hospital now became the Jackdaws' Hospital and Sanctuary. The hospital and sanctuary began to attract much attention, and with this attention came also a large offering of affection, especially from the local children who became a veritable source of supply of sick and injured birds. Even sixty years ago the occasional sea bird was brought to the hospital suffering from oiling, a problem that has grown larger nearly every year since, climaxing with the terrible Torrey Canyon disaster in 1967. This disaster is covered in detail in a later chapter.

Razorbill. Distinguished from the guillemot by its bill shape and pattern. They are rather clumsy on land and lack manoeuvrability in the air despite being swift and strong fliers. However, they are extremely agile in the sea, where they dive for food and swim underwater. Half the world's population of razorbills breed in Britain and Ireland.

Puffin. Britain's most colourful seabird with a large brightly coloured bill, white face and red feet. Large colonies exist in Northern Scotland, particularly on St. Kilda, West of the Outer Hebrides. Numbers declined considerably earlier this century due to changes in the sea temperature, which affected the fish distribution. The decline has now been halted.

One of the first oiled patients was a razorbill who, while recovering in Pog's studio, proved to be a very inquisitive bird. The sisters named him Billie and his curiosity in everything Pog was doing eventually helped save his life. He had developed a bad cough for which the vet prescribed an inhalant, but Billie would not co-operate with the administering of treatment. Pog draped an old coat tent-style over her head with the jar of inhalant inside. Billie's curiosity won the day - he had to investigate what Pog was up to. He poked his head inside the tent and he and Pog sniffed away. Billie was soon cured but poor Pog emerged each night choking and coughing!

Another species of bird to be brought to the hospital during the early years was the puffin, a member of the auk family, remarkable for its red and yellow parrot-like beak. Sadly they no longer frequent the coastline of Devon and Cornwall but colonies are to be found around Lundy Isle off the North Devon coast and on the Isles of Scilly. One Winter three puffins were sent to the hospital by the R.S.P.C.A. in London. All three were found suffering from exhaustion and hunger having been blown up the River Thames by a severe Winter gale.

A month's care saw them fit and well again, and all three were successfully released off the Cornish coast. The R.S.P.C.A. continued to send birds to Mousehole and the sisters felt quite honoured to be obviously receiving the Society's approval. It was plainly clear to everyone knowing Dorothy and Pog and with knowledge of their work with the birds, that they possessed a gift — the gift, and that is surely what it must have been, to receive the love and trust of a wild bird.

The first gannet to be admitted to the hospital impressed Dorothy and Pog greatly. They named him Lohengrin, but there was not to be a happy ending to Lohengrin's story. Although showing some initial response to treatment he died after a few weeks from internal injuries. The sisters nicknamed gannets 'birds of the ice age' because of their glacial eyes and staring gaze. Another, of which the sisters became very fond, was one found badly oiled at Sennen Cove. They named him 'The Viking', de-oiled him and nursed him back to full health. After a month he seemed ready to be returned to the ocean, but although flying off splendidly when first released he then flew very low across the surface and soon alighted on the sea. A few hours later some local youngsters fishing just outside the harbour noticed The Viking swimming around their boat. They reached out for him and when no resistance was offered lifted him into the boat, and within an hour he was reunited with Dorothy and Pog. He was clearly not yet strong enough to return to the wild so the sisters kept him for another twelve months before deciding to release him once more. This time, accompanied by another gannet, his departure was permanent.

Gannet. *It takes four years for a gannet to attain its full adult plumage. The adult body is brilliant white with black outer wings and a rich buff head and nape. Having no external nostrils they are able to dive head-first into the sea from up to 100ft. and at speeds of 60 miles per hour. A large proportion of the 750.000 world population, including 275,000 breeding pairs, are located around Britain and Ireland. The gannet population is increasing at a rate of around three per cent per year.*

THE CZAR.

A bird that genuinely touched the hearts of Dorothy and Pog was a great northern diver they named 'The Czar'. Dorothy's description of this bird's stay at the hospital in her first book "The Cry of a Bird" is beautifully written and extremely moving. I doubt my version will have the same affect on my reader as her's did on me!

Great Northern Diver. Largest of the divers, has a very large bill capable of catching flat fish, and cracking the shells of small crabs before swallowing them. They are Winter visitors, from Iceland mainly, and the occasional bird can be spotted on inland waters where fish are plentiful.

The Czar arrived at the hostpital in a large wooden crate via St. Ive's Police in very poor condition, badley oiled and suffering a foot injury. Pog carried him to her studio and laid him on an old divan where he spent the first night emitting, as Dorothy described, banshee-like wails. The dictionary defines banshee as 'a female spirit whose wailing warns of impending death', but The Czar had a mission to fulfil before joining his great ocean in the sky. He accepted his morning ablutions administered by Dorothy and Pog with great patience - the rapport between bird and the sisters once again almost immediate. The Czar progressed well and after nine days another great northern diver was brought to the hospital, again rendering the awful wailing. Although as large as The Czar the sisters were sure this was a much younger bird for it still displayed some of its down feathers. No injury was apparent and it seemed he was simply a young, lost and confused bird. The wailing continued all through the first night and in an effort to calm him the sisters put him in with The Czar. The effect was magic; the young bird settled down at once and The Czar watched over him like a fussing parent. Dorothy and Pog named him 'The Midnight Son'.

The two birds progressed well with Son growing into his adult plumage, so come mid-Summer the decision was taken to release them. Pog and a friend watched from the rocks on the shore as Dorothy and the fisherman in whose boat they were took up a position a few hundred yards offshore. Both birds were taken from their box and placed gently on the calm sea. They swam perfectly — Son following and watching The Czar. Czar dived, followed by Son, they made short circular flights and everything The Czar did Son copied. It was obvious The Czar was putting Son through his paces. This performance went on for over an hour and then came the finale. With their swimming and flying both birds had come to within fifty yards of the shore, then The Czar suddenly uttered his heartrending wailing cry several times over. With this the Midnight Son rose high in the sky, turned and took one last look at The Czar and then flew strongly and magnificently towards the horizon. The Czar, exhausted by his exertions, struggled towards the shore where Pog was already in the sea up to her waist attempting to reach him. She had realised all was not well and when finally reaching The Czar he collapsed into her arms. The gift of love and trust of a wild bird. The Czar's work was complete — he had launched his Son. They returned to the hospital and The Czar, after regaining some of his strength, was put back into his run. For two weeks he continued to eat well and seemed contented, then one day he simply went off his food and passed peacefully away. No pain. Dorothy said at the time "his first cry in the studio was a call to his Son to join him, and his last on the rocks had been a final farewell".

Towards the end of the 1930's the R.S.P.C.A., who were becoming increasingly aware of the sisters' work in Mousehole, sent a representative down to discuss matters generally. As a result of this visit a grant of fifteen shillings (75 pence) a week was made, with the promise of more practical help at the hospital and sanctuary to follow. This was a very generous sum of money in those days and helped ease the sisters' financial worries considerably. However, with the coming of the Second World War the planned improvements for the hospital were shelved, and of course Dorothy and Pog were now faced with the problems of feeding the birds in the face of food shortages and rationing. More birds than ever were being admitted but somehow with the help of friends and not a little ingenuity, the hospital overcame those problems and survived. As the war years passed there was a notable decrease in the number of oiled birds admitted to the hospital, and for one period of twelve months not a single bird suffering this condition was treated, the theory being that ships were no longer discharging oil whilst at sea, therefore hopefully avoiding detection by enemy submarines.

RIDER AND HEDGER

Dorothy's special day of the year was February 14th - Valentine's Day. It was her theory that by this day the bird population had chosen their respective partners for the coming mating season. It was also her belief that many birds mated for life, and this was certainly true of Rider and Hedger, two herring gulls, both admitted to the hospital in 1943 with identical injuries. They had each suffered a severed wing, possibly caused by flying into the wire towing a target behind an aeroplane. Of course neither bird would ever fly again. It was obvious from their plumage that both were very young birds, not yet twelve months old, and when put in a pen with a number of other gulls became firm friends. After a few years together they mated and continued to do so for several years, but Dorothy and Pog, not wishing to encourage a greater number of dependants than really necessary, always removed the eggs before the birds became too attached to them. However, one year one egg 'got away' and Empiricus, as he was later named, was hatched. Empiricus grew big and strong and when six months old was successfully released along with a number of other young gulls.

Rider and Hedger ceased mating when sixteen years of age but continued to be devoted to each other, and remained in good health for a further twelve years, obviously perfectly content with life in their sanctuary. Then the sisters noticed Rider becoming rather lethargic and it wasn't long before he passed peacefully away during his sleep. He was twenty-eight years old. Hedger refused another companion and lived a further two years before passing away in 1973 aged thirty. Their parting was a great loss to Dorothy and Pog who had of course become very attached to them, but Rider and Hedgers' lives were a bonus, both birds being fortunate enough to have had the sanctuary of Mousehole.

1945-1954

Soon after the war ended the sisters moved from Cherry Orchard into Green Hedges, a smaller bungalow built on another piece of their land. Cherry Orchard was sold. At this time the hospital buildings and runs were showing definite signs of needy repair and although still receiving the weekly grant from the R.S.P.C.A., running expenses and overheads were rising and the future was looking anything but rosy. The sisters were now subsidising the hospital and sanctuary far more than they could really afford. Then one day, out of the blue, a letter arrived from the R.S.P.C.A.; they had not forgotten their promise made to Dorothy and Pog six years earlier and were sending an officer to Mousehole to discuss with them the hospital's immediate and long-term plans and requirements. Subsequently the grant was raised to £2 per week and guarantees made to pay for hospital improvements. These included the laying of concrete floors in the runs, and the provision of mains connected water tanks, and hosepipes up to the runs — making the need for carrying pails of water to and fro redundant. A new sign was erected outside the hospital.

THE MOUSEHOLE WILD BIRD HOSPITAL
AND SANCTUARY ASSISTED BY THE R.S.P.C.A.

Main hospital building - late 1960's

The Winter of 1947 was very hard, biting cold, severe gales and heavy snowfalls. The houses and runs in the birds' quarters were full to bursting point with starving and half-frozen birds, and to make matters worse the road from Mousehole to Penzance was frozen over, preventing the birds' fish supplies getting through. Pog's ingenuity saved the day; she hastily made a sledge and hauled it the three miles each way, the return journey seeing it loaded with boxes of fresh fish. Such was their devotion to the birds that Dorothy and Pog only thought of their own comforts when satisfied the birds were as comfortable as possible considering the prevailing conditions.

NEVEREST - ANOTHER VERY SPECIAL JACKDAW
(1953-1973)

On May 29th, 1953, Edmund Hilary and Tenzing Norkey reached the summit of Mount Everest. On the same day a baby jackdaw fell down a cottage chimney in Mousehole and was taken to the bird hospital. Dorothy and Pog promptly named him Neverest. Neverest was to make a big impression upon the sisters, particularly Pog; Dorothy dedicated her second book "In Answer To The Cry", published in 1978, to Pog and Neverest.

Having suffered no injury from his fall down the chimney, Neverest was soon ready for release. He was given his independence with another young jackdaw nicknamed Link (found injured on a nearby golf course, hence the name). The two birds were loathe to sever connections with the sisters and returned almost daily for a chat and some tit bits. They soon discovered Pog's studio where she now often slept, as well as worked when time permitted, and began using it as a second home. During their second Spring together they started to build a nest between the studio's beams and rafters which they promptly transferred to an old box which Pog fixed up a little further along the beam when she tired of odd bits of stick falling onto her studio work. A few weeks later Golf Ball arrived yelling for food and demanding service from his fussing parents. Within five weeks he was flying from beam to beam in the studio and a week later he was taken on his first local flight by Neverest and Link. All three birds returned daily for food but as Golf Ball grew older and stronger he found the call of the wild too great to resist and eventually went his own way.

The following Spring, with the two birds now three years old, Link was taken ill and despite Neverest paying her every attention and the sisters treating her for what was probably an internal injury, she sadly passed away. Neverest continued to visit Pog in her studio until one day during the following Winter he suffered a wing injury which required urgent attention and hospitalisation for several months. When restored to full health he was released and soon resumed his old routine visiting Pog and the studio daily. A further two years passed before another mate arrived on the scene. Buttons, another younger ex-patient jackdaw, caught his eye and Neverest's second loving relationship was formed. Neverest and Buttons still visited Pog and often spent the night sleeping on the beams until one morning in January 1965 Pog was awakened by Neverest's calls of distress. Pog found Buttons laying dead with poor Neverest crying and distraught over her little body. Buttons was nine years old and had been faithful to Neverest all her life. Dorothy and Pog buried her in a rosebed under the studio window.

Pog's Studio

Neverest overcame his loss and started life again as a widower for the second time around until one day a few months later he returned to Pog with a badly injured wing. The wing was permanently damaged and his days of flying in the wild were over. When he had recovered sufficiently to flutter about he was returned to Pog's studio where he settled down quite happily in retirement sharing the day with Pog and any winged visitor who happened to call. During 1972 Pog noticed Neverest's sight beginning to decline so she built him his own spacious house in which he was quite safe until one day in March 1973 she noticed he was very quiet and still, and spent the whole time with his head tucked in his wing apparently asleep. Pog called Dorothy over to the studio and no sooner had she arrived when Neverest lifted his head, opened his eyes and looked straight at the sisters. Then he was gone. Dorothy and Pog were used to death at the hospital, for so many of the birds brought in were beyond help and were quickly and peacefully put to sleep, but the loss of Neverest upset them greatly. He was twenty years old and had been part of their lives every day for all of those years. The sisters laid him beside his greatest love — little Buttons.

20

The R.S.P.C.A.

Having lived in Cornwall for over twenty-five years, Dorothy and Pog had come to live for the day and not think or worry too much for the morrow, an attitude so prevalent in this part of the world. This is in no way intended as a criticism — far too many people plan for the future and in so doing lose sight of the value of the present. However, as the years passed their thoughts turned to the hospital's future; they were not getting any younger and the time would surely come when they would physically find the hospital's needs too demanding.

In 1951 they decided to approach the R.S.P.C.A., with whom they now had a respected relationship, to discuss the future. As a result of their letter the Society's Chief Secretary visited Mousehole and listened to the sisters as they explained the hospital and sanctuary's needs in respect of staff requirements, finance, refurbishing and improvements. They offered the R.S.P.C.A. the land on which the hospital stood by means of a 'Deed of Gift', if the R.S.P.C.A. in turn agreed to their proposals and to the hospital being managed on the same basis as they themselves had always operated. One of their main concerns was for the resident birds in sanctuary — birds happy in their adopted lifestyle, yet unable to return to the wild because of their injuries and other problems. The R.S.P.C.A. agreed to all their requests and conditions. The number of birds kept in sanctuary at this time was in excess of three hundred, and Dorothy's policy of life at all cost, was to eventually put a severe strain on the relationship she had with the R.S.P.C.A.

One thing further was agreed, but only orally, the return of the land and nullification of the 'Deed of Gift' if the R.S.P.C.A. pulled out of Mousehole at any future date. The 'Deed of Gift' was signed during August 1953, planning permission for a new main hospital building and further permanent runs was granted, and when all work was completed in1954 the new hospital entrance sign read **"The R.S.P.C.A. Wild Birds' Hospital"**. Two years later all financial responsibility was handed over to the Society. For a further three years Dorothy and Pog ran the hospital, ensuring the hand-over went as smoothly as possible;

the most important problem to overcome was finding and appointing the right person to assume the managerial vacancy.

The vacancies of chief warden and four assistants were advertised in the national and regional press and brought many replies from all over the country, and from applicants from all walks of life. One person to spot the advertisement was Max Robertson of the B.B.C. television programme "Panorama", although his interest was not that of a prospective employee, but one of a programme producer — he thought the hospital and the sisters' work would make an ideal subject for Panorama. The recording was a great success and the following Summer brought many extra visitors to the hospital eager not only to see the birds but the celebrities in the form of Dorothy and Pog. These visitors were very welcome for they brought much appreciated extra income.

The appointed Warden and staff were duly trained for their roles and took charge towards the end of 1959. Hospital records at this time showed that since 1928 Dorothy and Pog had admitted 4,066 birds comprising 116 species. The percentage of birds cured and released back to the wild averaged between 25-35, with the number helped and retained in sanctuary because of the nature of their illnesses or injuries being around six per hundred. The remainder were sadly put down, but it must be remembered that wild birds will only allow themselves to be caught and handled when their condition is desperate, therefore the success rate for complete rehabilitation is bound to be relatively small and the death rate that much greater. But even those birds destined not to survive were granted a quick, painless death — far better than the agonising, lingering one that awaited before the sisters' intervention.

Green Hedges
- now privately owned

22

OH-HE LIKES YOU

One member of staff engaged in 1959 is Eileen Burgess. Born in Essex, she had acquired a love for animals during her early teenage years when her parents ran a smallholding. She noticed the hospital and sanctuary's vacancy for a Summer Helper advertised in 'The Lady' magazine. The position was for a duration of approximately six weeks. At the time Eileen was working as a receptionist in the University College Hospital in London, and rather fancied an outdoor job and change of scene. She had never been to Cornwall but admits to imagining it as being all sunshine and sand. Well—it is sometimes. No interview was conducted — applicants seemed to be employed or disregarded on the impression their written application made. Eileen was initially turned down but when the hospital's first choice failed to impress she was approached and offered the position.

When arriving at Penzance Railway Station she was met by an R.S.P.C.A. officer and taken to Mousehole. Lodgings had been arranged for her in the Society's staff hostel a few yards down Raginnis Hill from the hospital. That evening she was invited to tea with Dorothy and Pog at Green Hedges. Not being too sure what to expect she dressed smartly for the occasion and with a little apprehension presented herself to the sisters. She noticed the table was neatly laid with best china, and delicately cut sandwiches and dainty cakes on display. A glass of orange juice was poured for her which she sipped and placed to one side whilst taking a sandwich. Eileen takes up the story, "Suddenly a large black crow flew in through the open window, landed on the table beside me and promptly stuck its great beak into my orange juice. As I sat there open-mouthed, Dorothy looked across and quietly said "Oh - he likes you". I thought to myself - he may like me, but I'm not sure I like him. It was then I noticed all the twigs and branches nailed across the walls of the dining room to serve as perches. I honestly wondered what I had led myself into."

Next day Eileen started working in the hospital and sanctuary. She joined the staff at Mousehole towards the end of June 1959, and expected

to be laid off during the Autumn. But things did not turn out quite as expected! Come September she was asked to stay on full-time to which she agreed — she had no ties back in London.

When Dorothy's first book "The Cry of a Bird" was published in 1962, it brought many extra visitors to Mousehole. Eileen recalls how that Summer so many people visited the hospital that one member of staff spent their whole time showing people around. Another occasion she remembers well is having to take a honey buzzard and a common buzzard to Gerald Durrell's Jersey Zoo. She flew to Jersey from Exeter Airport so an early start and late return were the orders for the day. She enjoyed her day, and although not meeting Gerald Durrell, was impressed with the Zoo.

Whilst working at the hospital and sanctuary Eileen mixed socially with some of the locals. She met and later married Bill, a young man she had noticed passing the hospital on his way to and fro work. Her six week holiday job in Cornwall during 1959 shaped the rest of her life. Mr. and Mrs. Burgess now live in Penzance. Eileen left the hospital's employ in 1964. When asked what she remembers most about her five years at Mousehole she recalls the affinity Dorothy and Pog had with the birds. She has never met anyone before or since who had such love and rapport with a wild creature.

DRUNK AND DISORDERLY

Just before Eileen Burgess left Mousehole, Sheila Berriman joined the staff. Sheila stayed for eleven years and during that time witnessed many changes and events at the hospital and sanctuary, the Torrey Canyon disaster, and the withdrawal of the R.S.P.C.A. being uppermost in her memory.

Sheila, like Eileen, speaks of Dorothy's tremendous affinity with the birds, and remembers her as the most sincere person she has ever met. Of the Torrey Canyon period Sheila recalls how very tired she and the rest of the staff were, and how hopeless their cause seemed at times.

She remembers also how the children took the hospital to their hearts; how they would arrive with the injured birds and insist they were nursed back to health. Many a time Sheila had to put her arm around a child's shoulders and break the news as gently as was possible that their poor bird was suffering and it would be kinder 'to put it to sleep'.

But there were lighter moments, and many of them. One afternoon a telephone call from the police informed the hospital they had arrested three seagulls in Newlyn for being drunk and disorderly. The gulls had been drinking the fruity dregs from a leaking wine container behind an off-licence, and were positively the worse for wear. When arrested they were swaggering three abreast along the high street giving much amusement to the locals. They offered no resistance when arrested, and Sheila remembers them being held in custody at Mousehole for three or four days before they were sufficiently sober to be released. All three were given suspended sentences and warned as to their future behaviour! This was not an isolated incident concerning drunken seagulls — several have been admitted over the years suffering the effects of over indulgence!

MILDRED CARTER'S GATE
AND NEIL JAGER'S BELL

News of the hospital's work was reaching corners far and wide and several national and local publications featured articles on the sisters and their endeavours. These articles invariably brought much correspondence and donations over the following weeks. One lady with whom Dorothy and Pog corresponded regularly was Mildred Carter who lived in the Midlands. From her letters they learned she worked as a secretary in Wolverhampton and had a quiet, rather lonely private life. One of her few friends was a rock dove which she had eventually to give to another friend when through failing health she was admitted to a London hospital. Each Easter Dorothy and Pog sent her some posies of Cornish Spring flowers until one Easter no 'thank you' letter arrived. Several weeks expired before a letter arrived from a solicitor containing the sad news of Mildred Carter's death; she had bequeathed a sum of fifty pounds in her Will to the hospital to be spent on whatever the sisters felt best. Some of this legacy was spent on general improvements and with the balance a wrought-iron gate incorporating the symbol of a bird's wings in flight was purchased. The gate is still in use at the hospital today.

Visitors to the hospital were always welcomed and often Dorothy would spend what little free time she had showing them around. Although just as devoted to the birds as Dorothy, Pog often stayed out of the limelight and was quite happy to let her sister take the leading role, although it was always the birds who held centre stage. Donations from visitors were never requested but were gratefully accepted if offered. Many friendships were formed with the hospital and sanctuary visitors, especially with some of the holiday-makers who would call in year after year to see the birds. One such friendship was made with a family from Birmingham: the parents, three boys and a little girl. Their name was Jager. The four children were extremely interested in the birds and spent many hours watching the sisters at work. A few months later came the very sad news that the second boy, Neil, had tragically been killed in a road accident. A school collection to buy flowers for Neil's funeral had raised so much money that his parents sent the balance to the birds' hospital and sanctuary as a donation in Neil's memory. With the consent of Mr. and Mrs. Jager, Dorothy and Pog purchased a new ship's bell which was hung near the hospital's entrance for people to ring when arriving with a sick or injured bird. The bell was inscribed with Neil's name and dates of birth and death, and his parents paid for a canopy in memory of their son. Neil Jager's bell is still ringing loud and clear today to summons help for a bird in need. When Neil would have been twenty-one, his parents gave another donation to the hospital which was used to pay for a special bath in which to clean oiled birds.

The late Nancy Price, the actress, was another source of great encouragement to Dorothy and Pog. She offered financial assistance on several occasions, and was always publically praising the hospital's excellent work. As a result of one of her donations the sisters were able to build an enclosure for the larger land birds, and this they named the 'Nancy Price' run.

After handing over the management and day-to-day running of the hospital to the new staff now working under the direction of the R.S.P.C.A., Dorothy and Pog were afforded more time to concentrate on other pursuits. Pog continued with her art work and wood carving in her studio, and Dorothy completed her first book "The Cry of a Bird" which was published in 1962. The bond with the birds was not to be broken, for ex-patients and wild birds alike soon found the sisters in their new surroundings and continued to call daily for their tit bits.

Under its new management the hospital was soon accepting even greater numbers of sick and injured wild birds, and during 1966 1,865 casualties were admitted — the highest annual total up to that time. However, 1967 was the year in which sadly all records were to be broken, the year of the Torrey Canyon disaster, which had such a devastating effect on the sea birds and Cornwall's coastline.

Because of the enormity of the Torrey Canyon disaster and the subsequent effect on the wildlife and environment, I think it best to summarise this unfortunate piece of history in two chapters: the first devoted entirely to the tanker's wrecking and eventual destruction, which although bears no direct connection with the hospital and sanctuary's history, nevertheless caused it a tremendous amount of work and heartache. It is for the latter reason I feel the reader will appreciate the chapter detailing the cause of such distress and because of its significance will forgive the author if feeling perhaps too much print has been devoted to it. The second chapter relates the mammouth amount of work undertaken by the hospital and staff in treating the innocent victims of the disaster — the sea birds.

Torrey Canyon - The tanker broken in two, it was later to break up into three sections. The Pollard Rock, though not visible in this picture, lies just yards to the left.

SATURDAY, MARCH 18th, 1967.

At around 8.30 a.m. the giant American-owned, Liberian registered oil tanker, Torrey Canyon, struck the Pollard Rock of the Seven Stones reef off the Scilly Isles. The Scillies lay twenty miles or so West of Land's End so when the news of the shipwreck and nature of the tanker's cargo was broadcast over the air waves the people of Cornwall became seriously alarmed. Within a week their worst fears were becoming reality.

Built in the United States in 1959, the Torrey Canyon underwent a major refit in Japan during 1964/65. This refit increased her length by one hundred and sixty five feet, and beam by twenty one feet. She was named after a canyon near Los Angeles where crude oil was discovered by John Torrey.

The Torrey Canyon on charter to the British Petroleum Company Limited was carrying 120,000 tons of crude oil from the then Persian Gulf (now plainly The Gulf) to the South Wales refineries at Milford Haven. She had rounded the Cape, made her way up the Atlantic, and as she neared the Western Approaches her presumed route would have been West of the Scilly Isles, to Milford Haven. However, through what can only be described as navigational error she found herself considerably Eastward of her intended course. The bridge officer, realising the mistake, changed course intending to bring the tanker onto a direction West of the islands, but the captain when advised of this manoeuvre reverted to the original incorrect course intending to bring his ship between the islands and Land's End. What prompted this action was probably the time factor; to have passed the Scillies on the West side would have cost him nearly an hour even at full speed, and he knew that if he missed the tide at Milford Haven a delay of several days was very likely until another tide could accommodate the tanker's great depth in the water.

The stretch of water between Land's End and the Scilly Isles is often very busy with fishing boats working from Cornwall and the Scillies, as well as larger boats from further afield. As the Torrey Canyon rounded the Eastern Isles the captain attempted to steer a course between the Seven Stones reef and the islands, another error, for a course further Eastwards between the reef and the mainland would have probably proved trouble-free. His intended route although not blocked by the presence of fishing boats, restricted and prevented the quick change of direction required to avert disaster.

Despite weather conditions being nigh on perfect, it being broad daylight with clear visibility, the lightship that guards the Seven Stones reef firing warning rockets and signalling frantically with an aldis lamp, the Torrey Canyon tore into the reef at full speed. With the ship's wake pushing on from behind she became well and truly gutted. Within two hours of the Torrey Canyon impaling herself on the Seven Stones, rescue and salvage boats were on the scene. The tug Utrecht, which used Mount's Bay as its base, secured the salvaging contract. Four more tugs and the Scilly and Mousehole lifeboats attended, as did helicopters from the Royal Naval Air Station at Culdrose on the Lizard peninsula. That evening on full tide the tugs attempted to haul her clear of the rocks but their combined efforts failed and all the while the oil continued to pour into the sea. The Canyon's crew were also pumping oil out of its vast holding tanks in order to lighten the ship.

During the Saturday night and on Sunday weather conditions worsened, and the decision was made to take off the stricken tanker's crew — only the captain, three crew and two radio operators from the tug Utrecht stayed on board. A few days later they were also forced to leave.

Within thirty-six hours, seventy-two square miles of the English Channel were covered by an oil slick, which by the Wednesday had grown to over seven hundred square miles. With the winds varying, concern was growing for the West Country's beaches. It was obvious that a prevailing South-Westerly would drive the oil onto the Cornish coastline and a North-Easterly onto the Isles of Scilly. Cornwall drew the short straw.

One of the first people to see the wreck was Captain James Summerbee, pilot of the helicopter flying daily between Penzance and the Scillies. The escaping oil was already covering a large area and he remarked that even three miles down wind and flying at seven hundred feet "a nauseous smell was apparent". A week later the stench reached Exmoor and Dartmoor, both nearly one hundred miles away.

Naval boats and many large private vessels were chartered to monitor and spray detergents onto the slick but with one gallon of detergent required to disperse one gallon of oil the task was virtually impossible. The Torrey Canyon's cargo represented twenty-five million gallons of oil, and taking into account the detergent cost nine shillings (forty-five pence) per gallon, the cost of the operation would have also been colossal.

Mr. Harold Wilson (now Sir Harold) Prime Minister and leader of the governing Labour Party at the time, appointed Mr. Maurice Foley, Under-Secretary for Defence (Navy), to monitor the situation. He was in constant touch with the salvage experts, the Naval Authorities and local authorities, and reported daily to Parliament. The weekend following the wrecking was Easter and Harold Wilson, who owned a holiday bungalow on the Scillies, flew over the scene on the Good Friday. When arriving on the islands he assured pressmen he was "in constant touch with Mr. Foley and the Navy".

The salvage experts were still hoping they would be successful in pulling the tanker off the reef on Monday, March 27th, when the tide was the highest of the year at just over nineteen feet. They failed, and with the oil pollution assuming catastrophic proportions, the decision to fire the Torrey Canyon was taken by the Labour Cabinet on Tuesday morning (28th March). That afternoon soon after 4.00 p.m. a Buccaneer jet scored a direct hit with its third bomb. A sheet of flame tore across the sky followed by a pall of smoke reaching thousands of feet high. To keep the tanker and oil burning, twenty-six Hunter jets from R.A.F. Chivenor, North Devon, continued to deposit over five thousand gallons of aviation fuel over it. By 8.00 p.m. the bombing was completed and the rising tide doused the flames an hour later.

The Torrey Canyon was insured for £6,000,000. So now began the clean-up operation on Cornwall's beaches; the degree of pollution varied but the coastlines as far north as Hartland Point and all around the peninsula, into Mount's Bay and down the West coast of the Lizard, were affected. In many cases as soon as the first contamination was cleared another load of filthy black slime deposited itself. Local folk have told me the sands of the beautiful Sennen Cove held the oil for four years before holidaymakers were tempted to use them again. Thousands of troops and volunteers were engaged in operation clean-up.

The Liberian government held an inquiry into the loss of the Torrey Canyon. Their subsequent report found that the stranding was entirely due to human error. They blamed the master, Captain Pastrengo Rugiati, and recommended his licence be withdrawn. On Thursday 16th June, 1967, three months after the disaster, naval divers completed an underwater survey of the shipwreck, and declared it free of oil.

THE INNOCENT VICTIMS

Oiled Guillemots.

When news of the Torrey Canyon disaster reached the Mousehole Wild Birds' Hospital and Sanctuary the staff made immediate plans in preparation for the challenge to come, but their worst nightmares would not have prepared them for some of the pitiful cases about to be admitted. If ever there was a need to justify the existence of the hospital the next few weeks were about to supply it a thousand times over. Knowing space for the birds would be at a premium, Dorothy and Pog prepared the studio in order to accommodate as many birds as they themselves could attend to.

For nearly a week all was quiet, the wind continued to blow offshore keeping the oil slicks well out at sea. Then on the Thursday night/Friday morning the wind direction veered to South-Westerly. The tremendous task of cleaning thousands of pathetic, suffering sea birds began.

Members of the public patrolled the beaches and other accessible parts of the coastline and if unable to take the oiled birds to Mousehole arrangements were made for R.S.P.C.A. officers to'pick them up from collection points. The R.A.C. set up radio control centres directing bird patrols to the distress areas as they were discovered. Many local people offered their houses as extra reception and cleaning points when it was realised the hospital would not be able to cope with the vast numbers of birds arriving.

The Royal Society for the Protection of Birds warned of the potential loss of thousands of guillemots, razorbills and shearwaters which were gathering on the open sea preparatory to the nesting season. Their prediction was proved correct in so much as it was the guillemots and razorbills who suffered the most. The brown, treacle-like oil, penetrated the birds' feathers right through to the skin, breaking down nature's own waterproofing supplements. If the rescued bird was found on a beach often the sand grains had stuck to the oil causing further aggravation and sometimes blindness. Those birds still capable of preening themselves suffered burnt mouths and throats. Added to their oiling problems, the birds endured more stress by being handled and confronted with the strange environment of the well-meaning rescuers. Hundreds of the birds were put down straight away, their condition being beyond help. At least their suffering was quickly ended, although death was never dignified. The appalling suffering and screams of agony from the poor birds, along with the sacks full of lifeless bundles of oiled feathers caused many moist eyes among the volunteer helpers forced to witness such carnage. Several found the work overwhelming their emotions, and had to relinquish their posts and transfer to other useful tasks away from the visual suffering and distress.

Over the years several different methods have been suggested and tried as to the best way to clean and care for oiled birds. Although the overall procedure remains much the same, advancements have been made and the success rate nowadays is significantly greater. At the time of the Torrey Canyon disaster oiled birds were cleaned by massaging a lanolin-based, waterless hand cleaner into the bird's feathers for between five and ten minutes. The bird was then thoroughly rinsed, and left to dry and preen itself in front of fan heaters. Once the oil was removed the remaining brown stain gradually disappeared as the bird preened itself and new feathers formed. Sadly many of the cleaned birds succumbed to problems caused through internal oiling — the oil having been consumed by the bird's earlier attempts to clean itself.

When an oiled bird is admitted now its condition is quickly appraised. Those showing light oiling are cleaned virtually immediately. If not given prompt attention they will attempt to clean themselves and inevitably suffer the aforementioned fate. The inside of a sea bird's mouth and throat should be pink, but if the colour appears yellowish it is a sure sign the bird has consumed oil and the burning of the oil has caused this condition. Badly oiled birds are left in the warm for four or five days to regain their strength. Ironically they often have a better chance of survival, being far to weak and ill to make any attempts to preen themselves. They are fed sprats, forcibly if needed. A mild antibiotic is administered along with a small dose of milk of magnesia. Solitary birds can be reluctant feeders, but the hospital staff have noticed time and again that when in groups they nearly always seem to eat eagerly.

Shearwaters. The most common Western shearwater is the Manx. Can be observed skimming the waves displaying its black upperparts and white underparts. They feed out at sea taking mainly small fish. Shearwaters nest and breed in underground burrows on offshore islands, and the young and adult birds alike, move South to Winter off the Eastern South American coast.

When the time comes to clean them they are soaped gently with a mild detergent, rinsed, and dried under a lamp. Two days or so later the operation is repeated but instead of rinsing they are showered in the form of a fairly strong spray. Every particle of oil must be removed. The feathers should by now dry naturally. The birds are then introduced to the pond to ensure they have regained their natural waterproofing and are confident on the water. If all goes well they are returned to the sea several days later. A bird should be able to swim for prolonged periods without the feathers getting wet. The water should run over the feathers and appear as droplets, never having a soaked look about them.

The Torrey Canyon disaster made headlines in the daily newspapers for several weeks and at times the hospital was virtually besieged by pressmen and photographers clamouring for details of victims and more pictures. Sometimes their attentions almost brought work to a standstill and were a severe hindrance. However, the media's coverage encouraged sackloads of mail and donations. Over £4,000 was received in the few weeks after the disaster, a considerable sum in those days. Some of this money was spent on the construction of a substantial pond, deep enough for the diving birds to use in preparation for their release. A plaque was erected and inscribed:

Given in Memory of the Birds
who lost their Lives
in the Torrey Canyon Disaster
March 1967

Vanloads of towelling and rags arrived and an appeal went out asking the public not to send anymore. The hospital premises took on the appearance of a giant jumble sale.

Nearly two thousand birds were received at the hospital and sanctuary over the first five days with no sign of any let up. Washing and cleaning operations overspilled the hospital, Pog's studio, and several of the volunteer centres close by. Dorothy, Pog and the hospital staff worked night and day cleaning the birds — sleep could come later. Once again the birds always came first. Mousehole's community spirit was answering the birds' cries for help, ably assisted by volunteers from Penzance and surrounding villages.

Apart from the birds mentioned earlier, several more species, all suffering oiling, were received. Puffins, swans and gulls were added to the casualty list. Many of the victims brought in after a week or so were obviously in a far worse condition than the earlier ones and their survival rate was much less. Not only were they so very weak, but also badly blistered by the detergents used in trying to break down the oil slicks.

Recuperation and rehabilitation of the cleaned birds proved to be the hospital's next problem to overcome. All available space was being used to capacity and alternative accommodation had to be found. This was solved by moving many of the birds to the R.S.P.C.A. premises near Taunton, especially enlarged to cope with the extra numbers, and to other reserves and sanctuaries including Slimbridge.

Morgan Hoskings, the Newlyn gentleman mentioned again later in this book, believes the oiling of the beaches and the rocks encouraged many of the gulls and jackdaws to leave their nesting places on the cliffs and move onto the rooftops of nearby houses for future nesting.

Thankfully the number of oiled birds washed in on the tides slowly dwindled, and although the West Country beaches and coastal wildlife took many months, and in some instances many years, to recover, life at the hospital and sanctuary gradually returned to as normal a routine as was possible.

During one morning's cleaning operations Neil Jager's bell rang out — the signal for someone bringing an injured or sick bird. Olga Penrose went down to accept the new patient and was handed a large box by a gentleman who simply said "We thought you'd like something different for a change", before turning away and leaving. Olga carried the box carefully back up the steps and into the clinic where she called for assistance before removing the lid. Inside were dozens of golden daffodils. The gentleman was Derek Tangye.

Derek and his wife, Jeannie, lived a few miles further along the coast near La Morna, where they worked a small flower and vegetable farm. They and their farm have become known all over the world as the result of the Minack Chronicles: a series of the most wonderful books relating Derek and Jeannie's adventures and experiences over the years as written by Derek, starting with "A Gull on the Roof " in 1961. Derek and Jeannie knew Dorothy and Pog quite well, having taken several injured birds to the hospital. Derek gave Dorothy much encouragement and advice whilst she was writing her own books. He still lives at Minack, though having sadly lost Jeannie in 1986.

I regard it a privilege to have come to know him recently and his gesture with the daffodils is so in keeping with the warmth and goodwill of Minack. The daffodils helped to lift some of the gloom at the hospital and sanctuary and were so much appreciated.

Over eight thousand birds were received at the hospital, of which more than half were dealt with at Mousehole alone, the remainder being sent to other cleaning centres throughout the South-West. Sadly many of these birds were put down. But how many more thousands must have perished at sea? Oil pollution still remains a problem, and a new de-oiling unit was included in the alterations undertaken at the hospital and sanctuary during the Spring and Summer of 1992. The admittance of oiled birds averages around two hundred each year.

I suppose it's human nature, but it always annoys me that whenever a tragedy or disaster is reported by the media there are always people who see it as an opportunity to get rich quick — to take advantage of other people's suffering for their own ends. On the one hand there are the good samaritans helping the injured and afflicted, and on the other always a few parasites. They are in the minority, but their presence is guaranteed. The Torrey Canyon disaster drew its fair share of this breed.

Olga Penrose, joint head warden at the time, remembers how during the height of the birds' cleaning operations, with staff working all hours and the public's concern virtually tangible, one chemical company offered to supply free of charge a vast quantity of cleaning fluids. Their offer was of course gratefully accepted. On the day the chemicals arrived a sign-written delivery lorry pulled up outside the hospital accompanied by an advertising agency's full production team and photographers. Their product was subsequently advertised: "As supplied to the Mousehole Wild Birds' Hospital and Sanctuary". Needless to say, the product proved positively useless.

Another company's genuine offer of cleaning chemicals unfortunately had a tragic outcome. This particular product was spirit-based, as opposed to water or lanolin-based, and although very efficient as a bird de-oiling agent gave off fumes which sadly proved fatal to some birds, and caused severe headaches amongst the staff using it. This after-effect was soon realised and only a few birds were lost to it.

BILLY

The horror and tragedy of the Torrey Canyon disaster will never be forgotten. When one has witnessed or experienced such an event the finest form of therapy is often complete immersion into work or some other pursuit. The tragedy must be put to the back of one's mind to become a memory, albeit a bad one, and not a preoccupation. Some of the hospital and sanctuary's staff found their work dealing with the usual run of the mill injured and sick wild birds provided this therapy, and eventually their faith was restored.

For Dorothy and Phyllis Yglesias a baby jackdaw they named Billy helped them find peace of mind once again. Billy was named after the young boy who had found him deserted and hungry. He soon recovered and when able to fly proficiently was released with several others. When a number of birds are released together some fly away never to return, whilst others come back to sleep at night and then fly away again in the morning. This can sometimes continue for weeks before they find the confidence to fend for themselves completely. Billy was no exception; he flew off and after a few days was independent of the hospital. Then after a few weeks he appeared again.

Dorothy was certain it was Billy; his shining bright eyes and mannerisms had not changed. One can only liken Dorothy and Pog's ability to identify their birds with pet owners being able to pick out their own dogs and cats or whatever, when faced with more than one of the same breed and sex. Dogs yes, cats maybe, but one jackdaw looks much like any other jackdaw to me! Dorothy gave Billy a piece of cheese from the 'cheese box' she always carried and when she returned to her bungalow (Green Hedges) Billy followed. For nearly two years he called on Dorothy and Pog on a daily basis. He would fly indoors, perch on the back of a chair, and have his piece of cheese. During 1970 the sisters left Green Hedges and moved to Love Lane Cottage — a little property standing next to and slightly above the hospital and sanctuary grounds; Love Lane being the name of the little track running along the hillside at the rear of the properties North of Raginnis Hill. It took Billy just a few hours to find the sisters' new address and the daily routine continued. The following Spring he mated and soon two baby jackdaws accompanied him on his daily visits. Dorothy and Pog watched with great interest as over the coming weeks Billy taught his offspring how to fend for themselves. The two youngsters grew into fine adult birds and eventually went their own ways. Billy continued to visit the sisters every day for his cheese titbit and it was several years before old age caught up with him and the day arrived when the cheese remained in the tin. The sisters mourned the loss of another very special friend.

Not to scale

Cherry
Orchard

Shop

Store

To Coastal path

Entrance

Main
Hospital

Runs

Love Lane

Runs

Runs

Runs

Ragginis Hill

Pog's
Studio

Green
Hedges

Love Lane
Cottage

To Mousehole

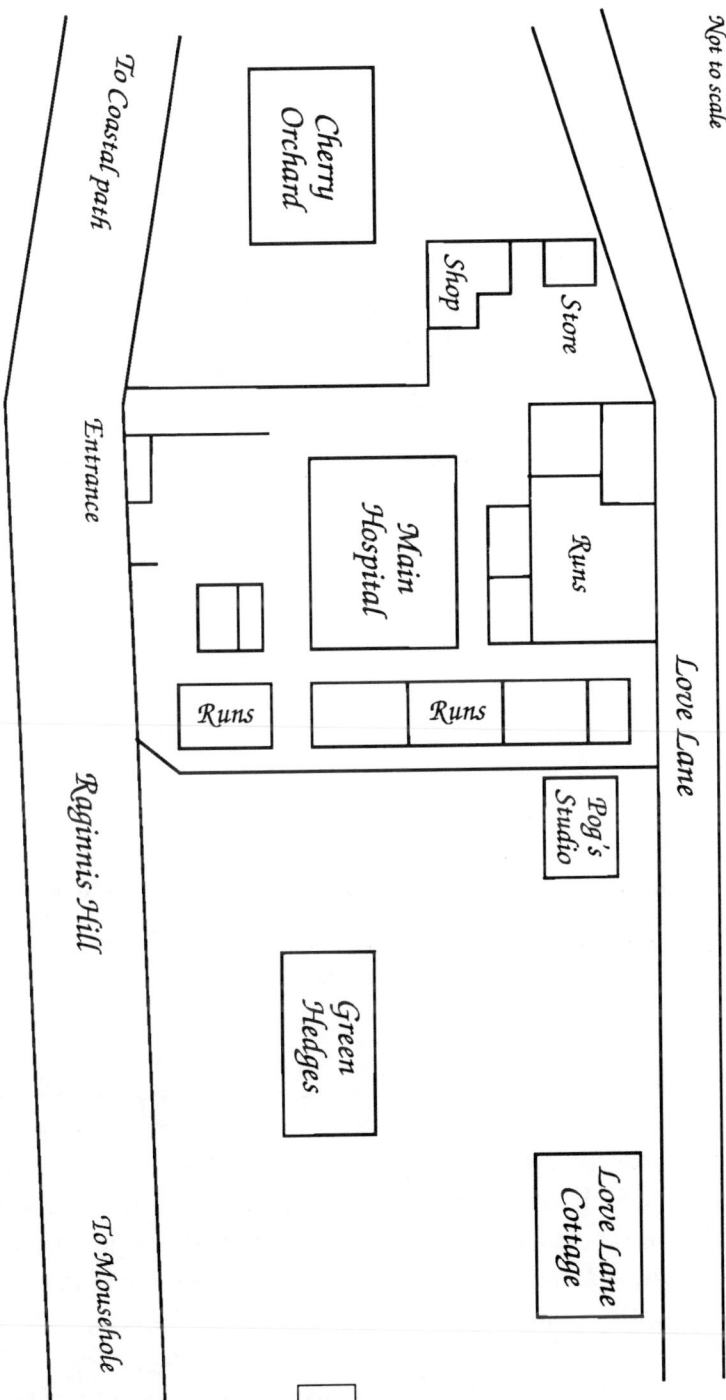

Cherry Orchard · Green Hedges · Love Lane Cottage & Pog's Studio now privately owned.

41

PEARDROP THE BLACKBIRD

Blackbird. A common and familiar bird found in gardens and the open countryside. The British breeding birds are resident and numbers increase in the Autumn with the arrival of migrant birds from Northern Europe, seeking milder wintering grounds. The adult male has jet-black plumage with a contrasting orange/yellow bill and eye-ring. Females are soot-brown with paler dark streaked throats and chest.

Whilst undertaking the research for this book I have met several people who share the view that if a wild bird cannot be restored to full health and subsequently released to the wild again, then it should be put down. Their line of thinking is obviously based on their belief that a wild bird kept in the sanctuary of a large cage or pen will be unable to find any form of contentment having once been able to fly free. A chapter later in this book mentions the work of a small bird hospital and sanctuary I know well in Devon which I believe disproves this theory, and the following story of Peardrop, the blackbird, is a perfect example of a wild bird coming to terms with its disability and finding fulfilment and contentment in sanctuary.

Peardrop, so named because of his love for pears, was brought to the hospital one Winter evening by some neighbours. He had been their friendly wild bird for three years, having adopted their garden as his home territory. When he first started calling they noticed he had only one foot, but managed to use the other leg as a stump. The disability was in appearance only for he was as quick and agile as any complete bird. Then one day the neighbours noticed his good leg had suffered a nasty looking injury. Examination confirmed he had broken the ankle and the bone was healing incorrectly. Destruction or sanctuary were the only options.

Peardrop displayed a tremendous will to live and showed no sign of being in pain from his injury. Dorothy and Pog prepared a home for him and laid foam rubber covered by a lawn of short moss as a flooring. His house was placed in one of Love Lane Cottage's sunny windows from where he was able to watch the world go by. He progressed well although it was obvious he would never be able to survive in the wild again. Winter passed and one early Spring like morning in March Dorothy was awakened by very gentle, soft, bird song. As Spring advanced Peardrop's singing grew louder and stronger and come May Day he was in full voice. Dorothy described his singing as a 'joyous sound'. The joyous sound continued splendidly until mid-July when it slowly became less forceful and gradually toned down until complete silence came during November. Come the following March Peardrop's singing commenced again and the previous year's routine was repeated. This pattern was followed for a further three years before Peardrop died peacefully in his sleep. The hospital, and Dorothy and Pog had the facilities and capabilities to offer Peardrop sanctuary. He accepted it. Who would have denied him those few extra happy years?

CLOSURE THREATENS

The hospital and sanctuary, under the management of the R.S.P.C.A., continued its fine work into the 1970s. Dorothy and Phyllis were enjoying their semi-retirement, although still visiting the hospital frequently in their roles of honorary wardens. The number of birds admitted increased annually and arrived from all over the country.

However, the problem of keeping so many birds in sanctuary continued to cause a certain amount of friction between the Society and the sisters. Morgan Hoskings, a Newlyn man and well-known throughout Cornwall for his work as a musician and later as conductor with the Penzance Orchestral Society between 1946-81, was also Chairman of the West Cornwall Branch of the R.S.P.C.A. between 1950-82. He had come to know Dorothy and Pog quite well over the years as they always attended his concerts and made a point afterwards of telling him how much they had enjoyed themselves. The R.S.P.C.A. appointed him Chairman of an Advisory Committee to liaise between the sisters and the Society. He recalls how he saw problems from the word go, and how the relationship cooled over the years due to the policy of having so many birds in sanctuary. The Society felt the number was excessive. The cost of keeping these birds was proving to be the hospital's main expenditure behind that of staff wages.

Olga Penrose, who joined the hospital staff in 1961 as a six months holiday relief, and subsequently stayed on as a full-time clinical assistant before becoming joint head warden in 1963, remembers a routine visit/inspection from an R.S.P.C.A. officer during the Autumn of 1974. His visit left her with an uneasy feeling. Her fears were not unfounded. During the early part of December the R.S.P.C.A. announced that owing to monetary problems they proposed closing the hospital and sanctuary. At the time the hospital was costing £8,000 per year to run and it was common knowledge that the Society was short of funds. The hospital's Advisory Committee asked them to reconsider their decision pointing out the wonderful work carried out over the previous forty-odd years, and the continuing need for such a care centre. Mousehole was the only hospital of its kind in the country.

The R.S.P.C.A. duly considered the request but on January 2nd, 1975 they confirmed closure would take place on February 28th as part of a nationwide half-a-million pound cutback. Several people close to the hospital hold the opinion that the cost of keeping so many birds in sanctuary swayed the verdict towards its closure. Not only were the hospital and sanctuary to close but it must be presumed a lot of the patients faced destruction. Their loss offered no threat to conservation, being of mainly common species, and because of their deformities they could not be released into the wild.

Dorothy was eighty-five and Pog eighty-three. They had run the hospital themselves for twenty-six years and been involved for a total of forty-seven years. Can you imagine how these elderly ladies must have felt upon receiving this news? Dorothy admitted at the time they were both completely stunned. But one thing was plainly clear — the hospital would not close. They were determined the hospital would continue and, if need be, they would take hold of the reins again.

THE HOSPITAL MUST BE SAVED

The sisters had £500 put aside in a bank account for a rainy day which they now made available to meet immediate needs, but plans had to be made urgently for long-term security. Upon hearing their plans the staff were delighted and pledged full support. When news of the Society's decision was made public it sent a shock wave throughout West Cornwall. The hospital and sanctuary at Mousehole had been part of its very life for so many years. Some local businessmen approached Dorothy and Pog and suggested calling a public meeting with a view to forming a committee and later applying for charity status. A local hall was used and on the night was full to bursting point with supporters united in their determination to ensure the hospital's survival. A committee was elected and asked Dorothy to become President. Local Justice of the Peace, Bill Young, was elected chairman. He has since passed away, but a garden seat presented to the hospital in his memory is still used in the hospital grounds.

Local and national newspapers carried the story and their articles brought many offers of help, some financial. Michael Moynihan of the Sunday Times and Donald Zec of the Daily Mirror both came to Mousehole to witness and report first-hand the strong local feelings and determination to keep the hospital and sanctuary alive. When their reports appeared in the press readers responded generously. Upon reading the Times article H.R.H. The Aga Khan wrote and enclosed a cheque for £1,000. H.R.H. Prince Bernhardt of the Netherlands donated £500. A greater accumulative sum was raised by local organisations: the Girl Guides, Brownies, Scouts, The Salvation Army, football clubs, Women's Institute and many more local bodies all rallied round with fund raising efforts.

The R.S.P.C.A. were informed of the sisters' intention to take full responsibility for the hospital after their withdrawal. A possible problem which had to be overcome was the regaining of the hospital from the Society. In 1954 when Dorothy and Pog handed the administration of the hospital to the R.S.P.C.A. they gave the hospital and grounds to the Society in a Deed of Gift. It was agreed at the time that if the R.S.P.C.A. pulled out for any reason in the future then this Deed of Gift would be rescinded and returned to the sisters. Although only agreed verbally, Dorothy said she accepted the word of a gentleman. The R.S.P.C.A. honoured this verbal agreement and the sisters regained ownership.

A few months later a gift of £1,000 arrived from the Staffordshire branch of the R.S.P.C.A. with a letter saying the donation was given with the consent of the Council of the R.S.P.C.A. who still 'feels warmly towards your work'. For two years at least the future was secure.

CHARITY STATUS IS GRANTED,
BUT A GREAT LOSS IS SUFFERED

Throughout the period of reorganisation the hospital and sanctuary continued its caring routine for the wild birds. Fortunately nature was reasonably kind and no disasters occurred which would have put the hospital under even more pressure.

During 1976 Rene Cutforth and Sandra Wainwright made a 'Look Stranger' television programme of the hospital's work which, after its broadcast during September, again resulted in more letters of support and donations. One such piece of correspondence came from an anonymous source in Luton, the postmark giving the only clue to its sender. Inside the envelope was a £1 note attached to a slip of paper saying simply 'Good Luck'. A £1 note and similar message arrived at the hospital every week for nearly four years.

Then came the day which was to shape the hospital and sanctuary's future. One October morning a letter arrived at the hospital informing them of its registration as a charity. This was tremendous news for now they could seek support from the large oil companies and other firms in the form of sponsorship from which such companies can gain tax relief. The future now looked much brighter.

When Dorothy and Pog resumed their roles as managers of the hospital and sanctuary upon the withdrawal of the R.S.P.C.A., they appointed Olga Penrose chief warden. When charity status was attained the committee decided to engage and maintain a full-time staffing system similar to the one used when under the auspices of the Society. Two clinical assistants were appointed along with some part-time help. Olga explained that it is so much more efficient to employ staff than to rely on volunteers. The work in the clinic requires comprehensive training and because of its nature staff reliability is paramount. A working shift system has also to be maintained. To rely on volunteers to fulfil these requirements would invariably lead to problems. At this time overheads, including staff wages and general running expenses, were between £9,000 and £10,000 per year.

By the close of 1977, in excess of twenty-eight thousand birds, comprising over one hundred and fifty species, had been admitted to the hospital, twenty four thousand of which had come in since 1960. Of course the Torrey Canyon disaster contributed significantly to this total. With the staff now handling the day-to-day running of the hospital and sanctuary, smoothly and competently, Dorothy and Pog were able to resume their posts as honorary wardens. Dorothy found time to complete her second book 'In Answer to the Cry' which was published in 1978. As with her first book 'The Cry of a Bird', it sold worldwide and entered the best sellers' list. Sadly, nearing completion of the book during April 1977 she suffered the great loss of her younger sister, Pog (Phyllis). For several months Pog's health had been fading and although strong in spirit, for the final two weeks she was unable to rise from her bed. Dorothy was with her when she died and recalls in her book how the room filled with peace and calm at her passing away. No pain. The hospital mourned her passing and Mousehole's community still remembers her with fondness. Pog's ashes lie below her studio window alongside Neverest's, the jackdaw with whom she had shared such special affection. Peardrop, the little blackbird, also lies beside her, having passed away just ten days later.

JUBILEE YEAR - 1978

1978 was the hospital and sanctuary's Golden Jubilee year. Fifty years had passed since Jacko was found injured in a drainpipe. From its very modest beginnings the hospital was now an impressive establishment. It was known throughout the world and attracted hundreds of visitors each year.

Despite all this acclaim the continual increase in running costs was causing the committee some anxiety. Although in no immediate danger, the long-term future prospects were rather daunting. Standards had to be maintained and it was becoming harder to see from where the finance could be raised to meet the required improvements. Then, as Dorothy described it, a miracle happened. On July 4th the Mobil Oil Company presented the hospital with a gift of £10,000: a year's expenses in one lump sum. Mobil also promised to donate £1 for every £2 raised by the hospital for a further twelve months. Now they had a sound base on which to work and build for the future. Another £5,000 was donated by Mobil during 1979 as a result of their £1 for every £2 promise.

DOROTHY YGLESIAS M.B.E.

Dorothy was awarded the M.B.E. in the 1980 New Year's Honours List. On hearing of her award she was absolutely delighted, not so much for herself, but for recognition of the work undertaken at her hospital and sanctuary. Olga Penrose recalls how determined she was to attend at Buckingham Palace and meet the Queen for her presentation. But, sadly, it was not to be. During the Summer of 1979 Dorothy suffered a heart attack. Upon leaving hospital in Redruth she spent two weeks convalescing in Lelant, near St.Ives, before returning to her Love Lane Cottage. She was soon back on her feet making her famous custard for the birds, and renewing acquaintances with her feathered friends. Then on February 14th, 1980. Olga found her collapsed on the floor in her little cottage. Dorothy had suffered a fatal heart attack.

Her funeral service took place on Wednesday, 20th February at St. Clement's Methodist Church, Mousehole, followed by private cremation at Truro. 'No flowers, donations to Mousehole Wild Birds' Hospital and Sanctuary', read the death column's notice. Who would have thought otherwise!

The Cornishman newspaper headlined Dorothy's passing: 'Dorothy Yglesias Dies in Village She Loved'. The people of Mousehole loved Dorothy in return and her death cast a shadow over the hospital and village community for several days. But soon the bird song returned. The hospital and sanctuary would continue its fine work and in so doing keep the memories of Dorothy and Pog alive.

The staff and regular visitors to the bird hospital and sanctuary missed Dorothy greatly. She had been its backbone for so long that her passing left a great void. But life goes on and injured and sick birds continued to arrive. Although not concerned anymore with the hospital's management, the R.S.P.C.A. still sent birds in need of help to Mousehole.

As stated previously, their withdrawal in 1975 came as a great shock, but no hard feelings were harboured on either side; commonsense prevailed and over the years a lasting and respected relationship has been sustained. In fact, whilst the hospital was undergoing extensive improvements during 1992 many of the oiled birds brought into Mousehole were forwarded to the R.S.P.C.A. quarters in Perranporth for treatment.

RECOLLECTIONS

Many local girls have worked at the hospital and sanctuary over the years under the direction of Olga Penrose. Some stayed for a few months, others for a few years, before leaving for a variety of reasons, but one thing they all have in common: they remember their time at Mousehole with warmth and affection. I have managed to meet several of the girls employed there over the past ten years or so, and will share with my readers some of the incidents they recall.

HERONS IN THE WHEELHOUSE

Janet Connors spent six years at the hospital commencing in 1982 and she remembers a telephone call one morning from Newlyn Fish Market. A Brixham trawler was in the harbour with two herons occupying the wheelhouse. By all accounts the trawler was rounding Land's End in very foggy, murky weather when two herons simply landed on board and made themselves at home in the pilot house. A full-grown heron stands between three and four feet tall and has a large dagger shaped bill.

Grey Herons. Having attained adult plumage the male and female birds are indistinguishable. A long-legged bird with dagger like bill found on fresh waters, lakes, ponds, marshes and the like. Thought to be around 7,000 pairs in the British Isles, so surprisingly not that common a bird. Their nests are made of large sticks and twigs and found in tree-tops mainly, although the occasional one is found in a bush and on the ground.

Yes, you've guessed it — no one on board felt disposed to removing them. With some difficulty the fishermen had managed to make it into Newlyn and ask for assistance. Janet arrived at the scene to find the trawlermen standing on the quayside observing captain heron and his first mate still in the wheelhouse. She introduced herself, put on her thick gloves for protection and boarded the trawler.

Readers are now probably seeing Janet as some sort of Amazon woman, showing no fear. You're wrong! Janet admits to have been very apprehensive at times, and is only slightly built. So can you imagine the scene? — four or five hefty trawlermen stand by whilst she enters the fray and in a few minutes emerges unscathed with the two pirates of Newlyn boxed snugly into proper bird containers.

It is usual for the birds to be secured in these purpose-built cardboard containers when rescued. Herons are concertinaed into these recepticals. Their legs are folded and the body lies flat upon them. Janet warns that when the box is opened they spring up like a jack-in the-box. These two herons had simply lost their bearings in the fog and were very hungry. By coincidence another younger heron had been admitted to the hospital two days earlier. The staff were convinced it was the offspring of the two pirates. After a week's rest and nourishment all three were released together at Marazion marshes.

Another amusing incident concerned a presenter from the local radio station. Radio Cornwall has broadcast several reports over the years on the hospital and its work. The hospital and sanctuary welcomes their attention for the publicity always creates interest often resulting in donations. This particular interview was going well until the presenter followed Janet into the gannets' pen. Gannets are also very large birds with wingspans up to six feet. The beak is an extremely dangerous weapon and can inflict serious injury. Not a bird to take liberties with! When one particular gannet started to show an interest in the presenter's microphone it was obvious this report was going to prove difficult. When the bird decided the head of the microphone was a fish and the reporter's fingers the side salad the interview was quickly concluded. Fortunately the presenter survived intact.

TWITCHERS

The night heron is a Summer visitor to Central and Southern Europe and although seen on the East and South-East coasts seldom reaches the West Country. They stand about two-thirds the height of the common grey heron.

One morning a night heron was brought to the hospital suffering a broken leg. It had been shot illegally by a local farmer. The leg was put in splints and the bird confined to a large pen inside the clinic. Word of its arrival soon spread and Mousehole witnessed a sudden influx of bird watchers or twitchers as they are also known. Janet remembers how disappointed they were when told the bird was being kept indoors and large numbers of visitors was out of the question. However, the fact that they could not actually 'sight' the bird did not deter some of them. Being shown the window of the premise in which the night heron was being nursed was good enough — a tick went into their book. Janet said for all the view they attained it might as well have been a stuffed parrot behind the glass!

The fishermen at Newlyn have always been very generous towards the hospital. Although the fish for the sea birds is purchased, there have been occasions when the market has rung the hospital offering a free handout. On one such occasion there was a glut of mackerel, and the hospital was invited to come and help themselves. Janet and Olga went down to the fish quay in the hospital van and filled it to the brim. When unloading the fish back at Mousehole the word soon spread amongst the seagull population. Janet remembers a black cloud flying overhead creating one heck of a din with their screeching, all the while the fish were taken from the van to the freezers. Since that day offers of free fish have been gratefully received but more discreetly unloaded.

ANOTHER ANGRY GANNET

Mousehole housewife, Jeanette Gillchrest, worked at the hospital and sanctuary for several years during the late 1980s. She remembers one day a call coming in from the life-guards at Sennen Cove. A gannet suffering light oiling had come ashore and decided to stay put. The life-guards' attempts to get near him only angered the bird. However, they eventually managed to pen him inside their beach hut by gently shoving him along at the end of several broomheads. Jeanette's husband, Paul, drove her over to Sennen and when arriving he was immediately approached by the life-guards informing him how they had bravely managed to secure the bird in their hut. When he explained he was only the chauffeur and his wife was the 'bird catcher' they were somewhat taken aback: "You can't go in there — he's in an awful mood" was the advice offered. Jeanette donned her protective clothing and heavy gloves and entered the hut. Within moments she was out again, with one hand over the gannet's beak and the bird tucked neatly under her arm. The life-guards broke into applause. She explained it was all down to experience and tricks of the trade.

On the drive back to Mousehole Paul asked her how she had managed to catch the bird so quickly and apparently so easily. "When I went into the hut he was fast asleep" came the reply. Butter wouldn't melt in her mouth! Mr. Angry was cleaned and successfully released a few weeks later.

Linda Penrose and Jane Bennett - cleaning operations, October '92.

NEVERMORE

Jeanette left the hospital's employ to start a family but continued to work there for several months into her pregnancy. One of her favourite birds was a crow the hospital staff had sexed as male and named Nevermore. He had been resident in the sanctuary for four or five years owing to a serious wing injury which ruled out any possible return to the wild. He had settled down well and enjoyed his new lifestyle, taking an interest in all the daily goings on. Whenever he saw Jeanette he always liked her to tickle the back of his neck. One lunch-time when she was on duty by herself she heard a lot of squawking and general mayhem coming from his pen. Upon investigating she found Nevermore very agitated. She opened the door, entered the pen and put her hand up to tickle his neck as usual. She got more than she had bargained for! Nevermore promptly turned around and laid an egg in the palm of her hand. Jeanette said the whole affair was conducted as if he was saying: 'I've noticed your condition — you're not the only one who can have babies'. Of course Nevermore was no more a 'he', and from that day on became a 'she'. Unfortunately the egg was not fertile so 'he/she' could not equal Jeanette's achievement after all.

Crow. 'A crow in a crowd is a rook - a rook on his own is a crow' - an old country saying, not always correct, though there is some substance in it. The most obvious distinguishing feature is the greyish patch of bare skin on the rook's face, whereas the crow is all black with a heavy black bill. The plumage of the all-black carrion crow often carries a blue/green sheen appearance. The hooded crow has grey back, breast and underside. Whereas the carrion crow is common throughout England and Wales, the hooded crow frequents Scotland and Ireland.

UNEXPLAINED HAPPENINGS

From the hospital and sanctuary's very beginning in 1928 Dorothy had always prepared a special custard for her sick and injured birds. Large birds were fed by spoon, but the smaller ones were fed from the hairy end of a little paint brush. The bristle tip was dipped into the custard and then pushed into the birds' open beaks. The custard consisted of milk, eggs, digestive biscuits and oat meal. The end product resembles porridge rather than runny custard, but all the birds seem to like it. When being cooked it gives off a distinct aroma.

When speaking to staff, past and present, I asked if any of them felt Dorothy's and Pog's presence around the hospital and the grounds. I was quite serious with my question and received some intriguing replies. By all accounts the custard aroma is often very noticeable and can last for several hours at times when nobody has cooked any custard for days. Pictures have fallen off the walls, lights turned on mysteriously. Very often these unexplained happenings precede an event which causes the hospital more work, such as the admittance of more than average numbers of oiled birds, or a storm resulting in many exhausted and bedraggled birds coming in. The staff now regard these happenings as Dorothy's and Pog's warning system.

Jeanette Gillchrest in particular recalls how she would be working in the vicinity of Pog's old studio and suddenly be aware of company. She was never frightened, quite the contrary; the presence she felt was warm and friendly. But she did admit to such occurrences making the hairs rise on the back of her neck!

Redwing. One of the smallest of the thrush family. Has distinctive streak lines on an almost white breast, although more easily identified by the prominent pale stripe above the eye. Redwings from Iceland Winter in the West and Redwings from Scandinavia Winter in the East.

Fieldfare. Another Winter visitor, although some arrive on our shores as early as September. A colourful bird, larger than the redwing, has a grey head, reddish-brown back, grey rump with black tail. The rich brown throat and breast are streaked with black. The mixed thrush flocks we see in Winter are usually dominated by fieldfare and redwings.

REDWINGS & FEILDFARES

Mrs. Pat Kay is the present secretary of the hospital and sanctuary's committee. She has been involved with the charity for nearly seven years, six now as secretary. Her main objective is to raise funds and correspond with the hospital members. However, living only a few doors away she invariably finds herself more actively involved — a role she greets with enthusiasm. She recalls a very sad period during the hard Winter of 1987. For a week Mousehole was virtually cut off, being held in the grip of snow and ice. Many redwings and fieldfare were brought into the hospital suffering hunger and exhaustion. These birds are Winter visitors often stopping off on their way to Southern Europe and North Africa. They usually feed on worms, insects and molluscs, but during severe weather conditions when the ground is very hard, seek out berries. A flock will strip a tree of its fruit in seconds. A hard Winter is often followed by a couple of years when these birds are noticeably scarce. Sadly Pat remembers that most of the redwings and fieldfare perished despite the warmth and comfort offered by the hospital. Readers will note in a later chapter that many more were lost during a very cold spell in February 1991.

57

FUR AND FUN

Pat Kay's commitment to the hospital also witnesses many amusing moments and events. The hospital was nursing a very reluctant young barn owl, efforts to make it feed proving almost futile. Owls feed on rats, mice, shrews, voles and small birds. It is a particular friend to the farmer in keeping vermin down. The fur and bones of these small creatures are essential to the owl's diet and digestive system. They are then regurgitated in the form of pellets — a common habit for birds of prey and insectivorous birds.

Barn Owl. Changes in agriculture, especially in arable farming, where hedgerows have been ripped up, and the destruction of many old farm buildings, are thought to be the main reasons for the decline in numbers of the barn owl. Certainly the loss of the rich prey sites and nesting places afforded by the hedgerows and old barns has contributed significantly to the decline.
The barn owl's remarkable sense of hearing is probably more important than its vision - prey located by ear can be caught in total darkness. Widely distributed though rare in North West Scotland, there are an estimated 10,000 pairs in Britain and Ireland.

One morning Pat's cat caught and killed a mouse, and before he could devour his victim Pat managed to snatch it away from him. Thinking of the hospital's Mr. Owl, Pat, carrying and swinging the mouse by its little tail, walked down the lane towards the hospital entrance. Halfway along she realised she was being followed and observed by another person out walking. The observer was an American tourist taking in the delightful view of Mousehole that Love Lane affords. Pat explained to him the reason for her behaviour, and assured him she was not practising an old 'swing the mouse by his tail' Cornish custom. Her purpose of mission proved successful, for the owl ate the mouse whilst still warm, and from then on discovered his appetite.

Occasionally the hospital and sanctuary act as a kind of animal hotel — not out of choice, but more by being the last resort.

A Penzance woman had to go into hospital for treatment which warranted a few weeks away from home. Having no family or close friends she asked the staff at Mousehole if they would look after her parrot. Somewhat reluctantly they agreed, looking upon it as just another beak to feed. However, this parrot was to provide plenty of humorous moments for them. The owner was a rather refined, well-spoken lady, and each morning the girls would be welcomed by the parrot saying "Hello, good morning" in a very posh imitation. Then it would really let itself and its owner down by following up with "Givus a fag, givus a fag".

Another parrot the hospital had as a guest for a while was an expert at imitating the 'glug, glug, glug' of spirits or the like being poured into a glass, and the wheezing and coughing of a heavy smoker. And they say it's children who always let you down!

JASON

Celia Falstead neé Foster worked at the hospital and sanctuary between 1980 - 1986. One morning a raven was brought in suffering a wing injury. It was a very friendly bird and had obviously been someone's pet. The girls named him Jason. When fit and well Jason's future needed careful planning. Because of his friendly nature he could not simply be set free and expected to fend for himself. His wing injury was probably

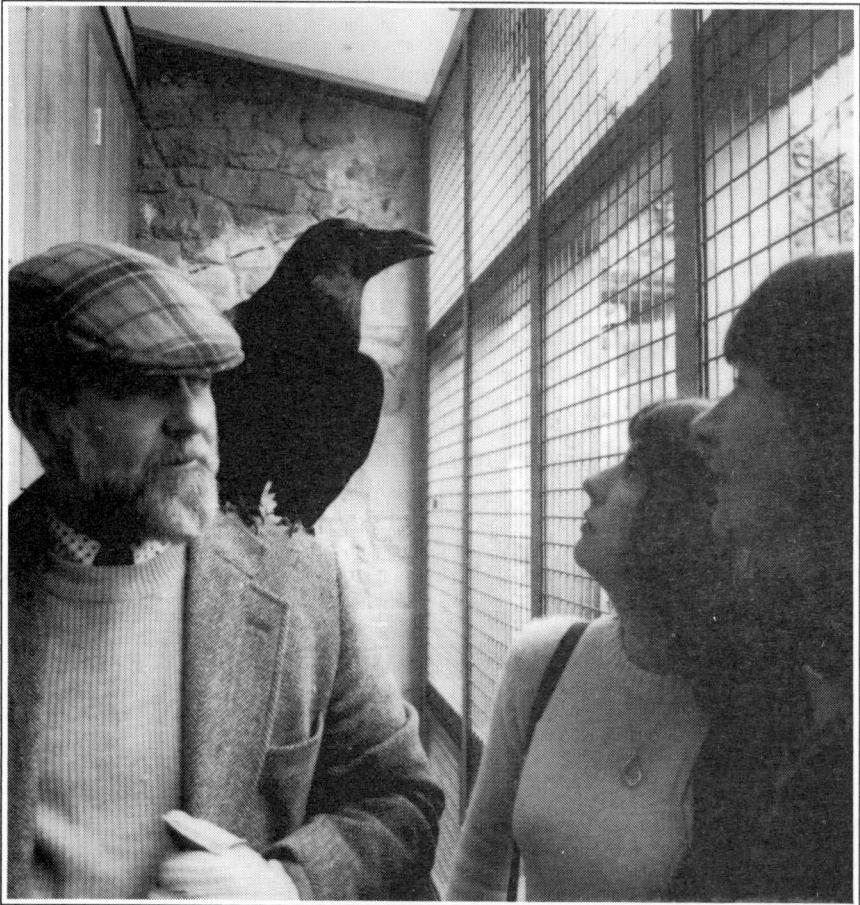

Jason at the Tower of London

the result of being attacked by other wild birds. The hospital staff contacted the authorities at the Tower of London to see if they would consider letting him join the ravens there. The Tower's management responded favourably, and British Rail offered to transport him free of charge. Celia and another staff member, June Watts, accompanied Jason on his journey. When his basket was placed in the guard's van Jason created such a fuss he had to be removed. He spent the remainder of the trip on the carriage seat between Celia and June. His behaviour improved considerably, and before journey's end he had become quite a celebrity amongst the other passengers. When arriving in London Jason and the girls were met by reporters and photographers from the London press. After his photo call he was duly taken to the Tower and released alongside the resident ravens. Celia and June were offered a free tour of the Tower of London and its grounds. Celebrity status was confirmed the following day when photos of Jason and his attendants appeared in the national press.

LONG TAILED TIT

Olga Penrose recalls a little story she wrote about in her Warden's Report for 1989/90. Late one Spring morning in 1989 a complete nest

Long Tailed Tit. Likened to a 'ball and stick' shape, both perched and in flight. The tail is longer than the body - overall length around 5.5 in. Adults are black, white and pale pink. Long tailed tits are rare visitors to the garden, and are found in the hedgerows, thickets and bushy areas where they live mostly on insects.

was brought into the hospital. It had been retrieved from the roof of a lorry when it pulled into its depot in St. Austell. The lorry had obviously brushed through some overhanging trees and dislodged the nest. Realising there were chicks inside, the finder jumped into his car and took the nest to Mousehole.

The nest was oval in shape and covered with moss and small pieces of tree bark. It was about eight inches long with a small hole at one end. Recognising it as being the nest of a long tailed tit, Olga thought there could be up to nine youngsters inside. Soon after its arrival the nest started shaking about and out popped a little head with beak wide open. It was fed some food on the end of a fine paintbrush. As soon as the chick had finished eating in went his head and out popped his rear end to deposit a sac of droppings. There was another shuffle of the nest and out popped another little head. This was repeated until all nine babies had been fed. Olga put her finger inside the nest to ensure the chicks were warm enough, as they didn't appear to have many feathers. She need not have worried for it was like a little oven inside and all the little bodies were warm and snuggled up together. Olga was reluctant to open up the nest in case the chicks caught a chill, and so carried on feeding them in the same way for a further two weeks. By this time the youngsters had started to emerge one by one until there were five on the outside. They were fully feathered but with only short tails. With no further signs of life from within the nest she decided to open it to see what had happened to the others. Sadly four of the chicks had died. Olga is sure it was by resisting the temptation to open the nest when it first arrived that the five babies survived by being left in nature's own little incubator.

The structure of the nest was incredible — handfuls of chickens' feathers and animal fur, tightly woven, with dried leaves and pieces of paper. This was then covered in moss, so that when built between the tree's branches would have been virtually undetectable. The five youngsters progressed well and when big enough were all released successfully.

A YEAR IN THE LIFE OF ....

The committee of the Wild Birds' Hospital and Sanctuary meet regularly and hold their Annual General Meetings in March. Like other A.G.M.'s the meeting follows an agenda. Two items from the agenda which I think are worth mentioning in detail are Olga Penrose's Warden's Report, and the Newsletter for the year. I am grateful to the hospital for allowing me to reproduce word for word the 1991/92 Newsletter, and extracts from the Warden's Report for the same period: The Newsletter is a lovely summary of the year's happenings, concluding with the species and numbers of fledgelings admitted during the Spring and early Summer months.

Olga's Warden's Report mentions the construction of a new oiled bird cleaning unit — the work to be completed by April 1992. Unfortunately many problems were encountered when this work was taking place. Some structural and under-laying faults were found which had to be remedied, and the final cost was more than double the original estimate. The best part of the year was taken to complete the work which meant the hospital and sanctuary had to be closed to the public for long periods for safety reasons. This in turn resulted in a considerable loss of public donations and revenue from shop sales for 1992.

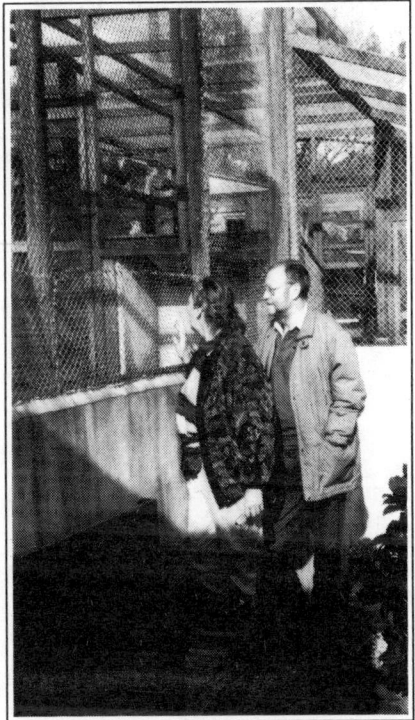

Visitors always welcome -
Bill Young's seat in foreground.

So when's this work going to be finished? - Summer '92.

MOUSEHOLE WILD BIRD HOSPITAL AND SANCTUARY ASSOCIATION LIMITED NEWSLETTER - JANUARY 1991 to JANUARY 1992

January started with a nip in the air, and the main admittances were seabirds, such as a blackheaded gull with a broken wing, and a couple of slightly rarer birds which were brought to us - two Little Auks - they were very exhausted and weather beaten.

A Black Necked Grebe arrived, who seemed very sleepy and had no sparkle in his usually glossy plumage. He seemed so weak, but after a preparation of glucose and vitamins, and a few days of good food, he was successfully released at Marazion Marshes - a few miles from here, and a haven for birds such as Coots, Water Rails, Moorhens, Herons, and every species of duck to name but a few.

64

Also, we had many oil-related casualties who were treated by the usual methods. We hadn't had the violent storms as in the previous year, and so we didn't have to devote ALL our time to the sad task of submitting these poor little creatures to days of washing, showering and drying their damaged bodies.

Towards the middle of February, the weather turned markedly colder and extremely icy. The days went by like this for a week, and as always we urged people to throw any scraps of food out, and to keep ponds free of ice for the birds. We had many weak and hungry birds brought in, and then someone brought in a Redwing - it's so sad to see a bird with barely enough strength to lift its head.

Redwings migrate through the Winter months, keeping ahead of the bitterly cold weather - this year they were unlucky, and they pushed on further and further South until they landed in the extreme South-West. Once they arrived here, not only starving and with no strength, they now had to compete with our country's resident birds, who also were in desperate need of food. Redwings and Fieldfares were admitted ; sadly the majority died. A Smew duck was also admitted. March and April saw a break in the weather, and during March we released 23 Guillemots, 1 Razorbill and the little Smew duck. Our first 'baby' arrived on the 20th April - a little Blackbird, who soon adopted us, and he was soon eating away and chirruping merrily.

For some reason we had an influx of woodpeckers - all kinds of different species, from the Greater Spotted to the Green Woodpecker - strange to have so many in a short period of time. Maybe their nesting trees had been blown down in storms, or I wonder if Man, in all his wisdom, upset the balance of Nature yet again? Let's see what happens next April.

The next few months kept us very busy, attending to our feathered friends' needs and demands. We had all types of birds in, from Jackdaws, Rooks and Crows, to smaller ones such as Sparrows and Tits; also a Raven who seemed to get better, but then went into a decline and died. Releasing our 'charges' into their natural environment is a wonderful experience; it compensates for the sadness when birds are beyond help.

May onwards saw many Herring Gull chicks arriving; they came in in varying stages of development: some as fluffy little bundles barely out of their shells, to big hungry flapping babies, who constantly called for food and who stared pitifully at the visitors who, if they didn't know, would think that "the poor little things..... were in need of food!!"

As well as the garden type and sea bird admittances, we had two little ducklings brought in - quite separate in species but who, over the next few months, were to become firm inseparable friends. One was a Shelduckling who was abandoned, and the other an Aylesbury, who had a broken leg. The leg was broken near the body, so we were unable to strap it. We confined him to a small cage for a week or so, where he was able to rest and allow the break to mend. After resting, we massaged the leg each day, and he soon regained the use of it. He and the Shelduck were then moved to an outside pen with a pond. They spent a long time there, and moved about in unison, almost as if they were tied together. When they were fit and strong, they were taken by the Aylesbury's 'rescuer' to Land's End, to a farm where they have a natural environment to live in, and they are very happy.

By September all the fit and able birds had been released, and we were left with our residents and a few Herring Gulls who were not yet strong enough to cope with the elements. We had glorious weather which carried on into October.

One Sunday a lady arrived carrying a box, and said she had a baby Blackbird that her cat had caught. On opening the box, a little Bantam chick popped his head out chirruping away happily. I found that her top beak was missing. So we found some deep bowls, and gave her corn, bread, cheese, glucose and water. Soon she was eating happily.

'Banty' soon had us eating out of her 'hand', she was a real 'star' and followed us everywhere. A few weeks later another lady came with her daughter - they had found another chick wandering down their road. This was a pure white Bantam chick who, unlike 'Banty', was very nervous and jumpy. We introduced him to 'Banty', who seemed unruffled by her new companion; but the white one wasn't so sure and kept his distance. As the weeks went by their friendship developed and they were both growing into fine young birds. 'Whitey's' plumage was turning a steel grey colour and he acquired a fine red comb; he was now a proud cock bird.

The two terrors have the run of the office and every morning when we let them out, so we can clean out their cage, they run to the fire and stretch out, just like two little kittens. 'Banty', the little hen, is very gentle and pecks about daintily, quietly chuckling to herself, whilst 'Whitey' is just finding his vocal chords and rejoices in the fact that he can nearly, just nearly, greet us with a 'cock-a-doodle-do' — in fact at the moment he can only 'cock-a-doodle' which, first thing in the morning after he's had many practices, is enough!

Now we are nearly at the end of the year. It's starting to turn colder, and still the injured birds arrive. It's lucky there is a place for them to recuperate in warmth and comfort with people who genuinely care for them.

Little Auk. Very small seabird, the size of a starling. Being birds of the high Arctic for most of the year, Britain and Ireland are at the Southern edge of the Little Auk's wintering range. They are only found in Britain during Winter, when the pack-ice of the Arctic drives them South for open water. They feed on the tiny plants and animals which comprise the plankton - often submerging for over thirty seconds.

SPECIES AND NUMBERS
OF FLEDGLINCS
ADMITTED DURING
SPRING/EARLY SUMMER

Bantam	2	Green Woodpecker	1	Rook	3
Blackbird	42	Guillemot	1	Shelduck	3
Blue Tit	7	Herring Gull	230	Sparrow	34
Bullfinch	1	House Martin	4	Starling	29
Collared Dove	9	Jackdaw	53	Swallow	3
Crow	21	Magpie	11	Swift	1
Goldfinch	4	Mallard Duck	8	Tawny Owl	1
Gr.Blackback Gull	1	Pigeon	4	Thrush	5
Great Tit	5	Pippit	1	Wood Pigeon	11
Greenfinch	1	Robin	23	Wren	1
Yellowhammer	2				

MOUSEHOLE WILD BIRD HOSPITAL AND
SANCTUARY ASSOCIATION LIMITED
WARDEN'S REPORT FOR
JANUARY 1991 TO JANUARY 1992

Our fund raising is down on last year due mainly to the fact that people do not seem to be spending so much. I suppose the recession has something to do with this. Also the lady I mentioned in my last Report, Patsy Allenby, has been ill and was unable to carry on with the wonderful work she did for us.

We are finding it so hard to find people to help with fund raising, as do lots of charities, I'm sure. Our own Council do what they can and did a marvellous job with the Bazaar which, despite the fact that there were another four large functions going on the same day in Penzance, raised £800. The Land's End collecting box brought in a wonderful amount over the year - just over £1,500. We are so grateful to Mr. Paul Johnson for allowing us to keep the box there.

The shop takings were well down due to the reasons I have already mentioned and that also we had fewer visitors. The raffle likewise did badly. The prize, a lovely pottery ornament, "Blue Tit on an Apple", was won by Mrs. Bottrall of Penzance, the first time a local person has won our raffle.

I should like to pass on a big "thank you" to those of our subscribers who sent extra donations this year to help with the new oiled bird cleaning unit. The work has now started and should, with luck, be finished in time for the baby birds in April. The cost is, as we expected, very high, £26,000 just for the building, but then we have to fit the unit out with tiles, sinks, heating system, ponds and new runs, etc. So we think it will be more than £30,000 by the time it is all finished.

We will be putting out an Appeal for money, materials such as paint, tiles, etc. The trouble is we are finding that things like water pipes, sewage pipes, and mains water all have to be remedied, as they have been there for at least fifty years and are in a very bad state. Also, as the Hospital is built into the hillside, everything has to be carried up or down by hand. But when it's all done I'm sure the Hospital will be run so much more efficiently and be better for both birds and staff.

The Council and Staff send all our Members good wishes for 1992, and grateful thanks for your continued support.

Memberships	£ 891.88
Shop Sales	2,441.67
Donations	3,766.77
Hospital Boxes	1,897.24
Outside Boxes	1,904.64
Fundraising	141.25
Bazaar	800.00
Raffle	19.00
	£11,862.45

Detailed below is a summary of the numbers of birds admitted to the hospital and sanctuary during 1991. Note the number of oiled birds admitted is down on the average mentioned earlier in the book — let's hope the trend continues.

When reading the chart for numbers of birds admitted, released and died, against each month, bear in mind the totals will not add up because many birds were already in care, i.e. a bird released or died in say February or March 1991 may have been in care since October or November 1990.

	Admitted	Released	Died
JANUARY	52	9	38
FEBRUARY	148	13	108
MARCH	51	32	31
APRIL	48	35	28
MAY	143	17	99
JUNE	284	24	173
JULY	226	45	166
AUGUST	114	108	64
SEPTEMBER	53	30	40
OCTOBER	62	48	40
NOVEMBER	37	43	25
DECEMBER	31	13	20

Birds that died within 24 hours - 502

	Admitted	Released	Died
Oiled Birds	82	42	40

SPECIES OF BIRD ADMITTED TO THE HOSPITAL DURING 1991.

Bantam	Fieldfare	Kittiwake
Skylark	Barn Owl	Fulmar
Lapwing	Snipe	Blackbird
Gannet	L/B/back Gull	Sparrow
Black Headed Gull	G/B/back Gull	Little Auk
Sparrowhawk	Black Necked Grebe	G/Crested Tit
Long Eared Owl	Starling	Blue Tit
Great Skua	Magpie	Storm Petrel
Brambling	Great Tit	Manx Shearwater
Swallow	Bullfinch	Greenfinch
Meadow Pippit	Swift	Buzzard
Grey Plover	Moorhen	Tawny Owl
Chaffinch	Goldcrest	Oyster Catcher
Thrush	Coal Tit	Goldfinch
Pheasant	Tree Pippit	Collared Dove
Guillemot	Pigeon	Turnstone
Common Gull	Heron	Puffin
Wagtail	Cormorant	Herring Gull
Razorbill	Warbler	Crow
House Martin	Redstart	Water Rail
Dunlin	Jackdaw	Redwing
Whimbrel	Duck	Kestrel
Robin	Woodcock	Dunnock
Kingfisher	Rook	Woodpecker
Shag	Wood Pigeon	Wren

The future of the Mousehole Wild Bird Hospital and Sanctuary looks secure. The Association now has a sound financial footing. It has benefited over the past few years from several substantial legacies. However, with running costs of nearly £40,000 per year efforts to raise funds must always be paramount. Apart from advertising in the appropriate publications, which hopefully will bring further bequeathals, the hospital depends upon its shop sales, fund-raising events, collecting boxes, public donations and membership dues.

If any reader wishes to make a donation then please forward it to The Mousehole Wild Bird Hospital, Mousehole, Penzance, Cornwall TR19 6SR. Alternatively, if you would like to become a member then apply to the same address for the necessary form.

THE GROWTH OF BIRD HOSPITALS AND SANCTUARYS

Many of the wild bird and indeed wild animal casualties are due to man's interference with the environment. Much of this interference is unintentional and to a degree unavoidable, as we strive to progress. Victims of road traffic accidents, flying into high tension wires, and some chemical poisoning often fall into this category. Then there are of course, victims of man's disregard and lack of caring as mentioned earlier. However, there is now growing awareness, and growing interest, in the rescue and treatment of wild animals and wild bird casualties.

The majority of us have always felt compassion for wounded and sick animals, and most readers probably know of someone in their neighbourhood or town who will accept such creatures, or offer advice on how to treat them. Dorothy and Phyllis Yglesias started their hospital in just such a way. Recognising this awareness and the existence of so many good samaritans running their own small hospitals and caring units, a number of the same formed a committee and started the British Wildlife Rehabilitation Council. It has the support of many national bodies including the British Veterinary Society, the R.S.P.C.A., and the Zoological Society of London. Its aim is to promote the care and rehabilitation of wildlife casualties through the exchange of information between people such as rehabilitators, zoologists and veterinary surgeons who are active in this field. It does this by holding seminars, distributing newsletters and publications, and recording a list of nation-wide rehabilitators.

Throughout the country there are hundreds of such units and many of them are now listed with the B.W.R.C. Earlier this year (1992) a European Wildlife Rehabilitation Association was formed. Although recognised by other wildlife national bodies the B.W.R.C. and its supporters wish to remain an independent body working to a respected Code of Practice.

Just recently via a Parliamentary Question, Mr. Tony Baldry, the Junior Environment Minister, was asked if he would "make it his policy to establish a register of wildlife sanctuaries, hospital and rescue services, with a requirement that before registration such bodies have suitably qualified members of staff or qualified veterinary consultants, who must visit the sanctuaries at least fortnightly" and "if he will introduce legislation to ensure that wildlife sanctuaries, hospitals and rescue services are subject to regular spot checks by local authority environmental health inspectors or other appropriately qualified inspectors".

Mr. Baldry's reply — "The Government recognise the excellent practical work already undertaken on a voluntary basis by the growing number of wildlife sanctuaries, hospitals and rescue centres. Existing legislation already protects captive animals against ill-treatment. The Government are not persuaded on the case for further statutory measures either for registration or inspection. In this field, it would be preferable for the bodies themselves to develop and agree voluntary codes of practice and thereby avoid incurring unnecessary cost and bureaucracy".

The existing legislation he referred to includes the Wildlife and Countryside Act 1981, which states that it is an offence to take or kill or have in one's possession wild birds. There are exceptions to this which allow the shooting of wildfowl and game birds during season, and the control of some species which may damage crops (crows and pigeons for example). It is permitted to kill any wild bird which is so badly disabled that there is no reasonable likelihood of its recovery, and it is permitted to take a sick or injured bird solely for the purpose of tending it and returning it to the wild when it has recovered.

One such small, self financing, independent hospital and sanctuary unit is the one I mentioned earlier in this book (Peardrop the blackbird). I have taken several injured birds to Jean and Roger Bradford in Teignmouth, South Devon, and have come to appreciate the hard work and devotion they so willingly undertake and give to them. Jean is a member of the South Devon Rescue Group and in this capacity receives and treats oiled seabirds. She also accepts any injured or sick wild bird and after giving it the initial treatment required for its condition, transfers it to another unit specialising in land birds. I recently took her a seagull which had been shot in one wing. She restored him to full health and released him to the wild.

To the sceptics who doubt a wild bird being able to adapt to a life in sanctuary, Jean is extremely dismissive. "Anyone with any experience of handling and caring for wild birds would not level such a charge. Life is as precious to a bird as it is to us, and if there is the odd one not willing to accept sanctuary, then it will simply give up and die. The majority have a strong desire to survive and will come to terms with their disability and adapt to a new life style".

To emphasise Jean's point her back garden is home to a shag. Six years ago he was brought to Jean having lost an eye and suffering a severe wing injury. He had been pepper shot whilst in flight. Jean named him Michael after his rescuer. Michael overcame his injuries and though now blind in one eye and unable to fly competently, has adopted Jean and Roger's garden as his home. If this bird was unhappy, he would have died long ago.

Will I Fly Again ?

by Ann Brightmore-Armour

I am a bird, once wild and free.
My forebears knew no other world-
Just Earth and Sky and Sea-
Pure and clean, sweet and fresh
As when Creation first began,
Rivers and seas watered the land,
Full of fishes, unfouled and clear,
Their sparkling waters safe for Life-
But Mankind made them streams of Death-
All through greed and lack of care;
Once I was a joyous thing-
A Spirit of the soft sea air,
Diving, soaring, fleet of wing
I did not heed that thick black tide
Pouring from the stricken tankers bowels,
I only saw the shoal of silvery fish,
Whirling and weaving through the waves,
And dived to make a sudden snatch-
But O, what horror came to me!-
The foul black sludge engulfed my wings,
I could not move, I could not swim-
What had happened to my sea?
Struggled, desperate, just to keep afloat,
Gasping in the filth and stench,
My body seared and racked with pain,
Dying, I gave a sudden wrench-
And on the seashore, Flung me down,
Exhausted, all my strength poured out....
Will I fly again? Will I live again?
Will I ever know again the joy of life?
Warm days of sunshine, stormy days of rain,
I am only a bird, help me,-
give me back my swiftness.

JANUARY '93

Just as this book was going to print, news came in that another ecological disaster similar to that which followed the Torrey Canyon's wrecking, is unfolding off the coast of the Shetland Islands. The American Braer Corporation owned, and Liberian registered Tanker, Braer, has run aground on rocks as she passed through the twenty mile wide channel between the Islands and Fair Isle. Braer is carrying 85,000 tons of crude oil from Norway - her intended destination being Quebec. With her tanks already vomiting oil into the sea at an alarming rate, it looks as though a good part of her cargo will finish up on a coastline several thousands of miles short of her intended discharge point. First reports suggest she suffered engine failure due to sea water seeping into the ship's diesel fuel.

The very cliffs under which Braer has grounded are the nesting sites of thousands of sea birds. At great risk are long-tailed and eider ducks, little auks, shags, guillemots and great northern divers. Already dead seals and hundreds of dead oiled sea birds have been recovered from the shoreline. Puffins, gannets and razorbills will all return to this area over the next few weeks to prepare for their breeding season. The R.S.P.B. are monitoring the situation, but warn of a possible major wildlife disaster.

Two Westcountry animal experts have offered their services to the Shetland authorities. Colin Seddon, manager of the R.S.P.C.A. Centre at West Hatch, Taunton, has already flown to Scotland to advise the seabird rescuers. It is anticipated that many of the oiled birds will be sent to Taunton to recover after receiving initial treatment in Shetland. James Barnett, resident vet at the Cornish Seal Sanctuary near Helston on the Lizard peninsular, is also travelling up to assist in the rescue and treatment of oiled seals.

Questions are already being asked as to why the Braer was taking the channel between Shetland and the Fair Isle when the Met Office had been warning for days of severe gales around the Shetlands. Although realising a disaster might still have occurred, the deputy director of the

Met Office, Roger Hunt, is reported as saying "On the face of it, to go through an area like that with the forecast of winds of that strength, might not have been the best thing to do".

Marine experts are calling for a review of maritime policy. They are concerned that many of the large tanker's routes are too close to the coasts; the use of multi -national tanker crews lead to potential misunderstanding in crisis, and to the age and condition of some tankers. The practice of registering ships in foreign countries under the so-called flag of convenience needs much stricter regulation.

Something must be done to protect our wildlife from this contamination — perhaps the Braer wrecking and the subsequent threat to the Shetlanders' likelihoods might prompt stricter vigilance. But I doubt it — or am I being too pessimistic?

Other Orchard Publications Titles:

Along The Lemon	(reprint)	(Flexi)	Judy Chard.
A Verse or Two on Dartmoor		(Flexi)	Garth Grose.
Churches, Characters & Country Walks		(Flexi)	Liz Jones.
Diary of a Country Lane		(Flexi)	Sue Kadow.
Bodmin Gaol - Cornwall		(Flexi)	Alan Brunton.
A Verse or Two on Dartmoor		(Hardback)	Garth Grose.